Jeff,

Great to fish
with you! Hurry
Back — Hope you like
the Book!

My best,

JRay

LEGENDS
& LEGACIES

A History of the
Nisswa Guides' League

RAY GILDOW

First published in the United States by Evergreen Press of Brainerd, LLC., P.O. Box 465, 201 West Laurel Street, Brainerd, MN 56401. (218) 828-6424. www.evergreenpress.net.

Project Management: Chip Borkenhagen

Editor: Jodi Schwen

Book cover, interior design, and production: Bob Wallenius

Production management: Bryan Petersen

Cover photographs featuring Al Lindner, Virgil Ward, and Judy Koep. Courtesy of Nick Adams, and Marv and Judy Koep.

ISBN 0-9755252-0-4

Printed in the United States of America

First Edition

Dedication

THIS BOOK IS DEDICATED to my good friend Marv Koep. As a young boy, Marv started working in the bait business with his father and brothers in Urbank, Minnesota. He learned the business from the bottom of the minnow tanks and went on to receive the the top honor any angler can obtain—induction into both a state and national fishing hall of fame. Now, more than sixty years later, Marv is still in the fishing business. He continues to have the passion to get on the water every day, and he still takes time out of his busy schedule to fish with a priest or a nun who needs some soul-searching time on the water. May God grant him good health, long, sunny days, and many happy sunsets.

This book is also dedicated to my wife, Gwynne, who does not share my passion for fishing or being on the water, but who has always supported me as I chased my many wild dreams for nearly thirty years.

LEGENDS & LEGACIES

A History of the Nisswa Guides' League

RAY GILDOW

Acknowledgments

I WOULD LIKE TO THANK Marv Koep for helping me through this entire project. He guided me to key interviews and helped develop its framework. Al and Ron Lindner offered assistance in any way they could, but helped the most by being great mentors in writing and in producing significant, high-quality publications and television products that have served all of us well in the fishing industry.

I thank Gary Roach for his time, insights, and access to his treasure of old photos. I especially thank all the individuals that I interviewed for this book. They took the time to meet with me and be interviewed, and they also provided photos for the book. Nick Adams provided a large number of photos and unique stories (half of which I didn't dare tell!). Delores Morphew was wonderful in sharing invaluable information about her father, Max Slocum. Joy Potthoff provided me with unique historic photos and information about her husband, Fritz, and her father-in-law, Papa Potthoff. Special thanks to the following folks who gave me feedback about the book: Sue Bowman, Steve Pennaz, Ron Schara, Chris Niskanen, Karen Pennaz, and Mitch and Melissa Albers. A special thanks to Mike Blanch and Bill Erickson, the previous and current owners of Koep's Pro Shop, for letting me use the store as an interview studio, meeting place, and general work site for the development of the book.

I want to acknowledge one of my best friends, Mike Hager. Mike died of a massive heart attack on Easter morning in 1999, two days after purchasing a new boat, motor, and trailer. He was going to enter the Professional Walleye Trail tournament as a pro, but he never got his boat on the water. Mike always said I needed to write this book. When he died, I told myself I would do it for him. He is in my thoughts on every trip to the water and I miss him dearly.

Finally, thanks to the people who really made this project possible. Chip Borkenhagen, my friend and mentor, steered me from wild dreaming to reality. Without his support, this book would not exist. Editor Jodi Schwen held the project together with grace, competence, understanding, and a wonderful sense of humor—along with the entire great staff at Evergreen Press.

Foreword

STOP BY RAY GILDOW'S lake place sometime, and I guarantee the conversation will eventually turn to fishing. I am okay with that, being a fisherman myself.

It didn't surprise me when Ray announced his intention to write a book capturing the history and lore of the mighty Nisswa Guides' League. Frankly, someone should have done it years ago, before memories began to fade and lives ended.

The league's legacy is firmly and deeply imprinted into this area's history. To not acknowledge and record this bit of vital area history would have been a travesty.

What did surprise me was how hard Ray worked on this book. It took him more than five years of hard labor to compile and write what is in your hands.

The results make the wait worth it.

Legends & Legacies—A History of the Nisswa Guides' League is more than a fun read, although it is the perfect book to pull out on a lazy, rainy day. It's a glimpse back to a time when thousands of anglers that visited the Brainerd lakes area watched in awe as a small group of guides based from Marv Koep's struggling Nisswa bait shop displayed nearly mystical angling abilities.

In many ways, the league's original eight (known to some locals as the Black Hats)—Harry Van Doren, Max Slocum, Cully Swenson, Ron Lindner, Marv Koep, Al Lindner, Rod Romine, and Ed Jensen, represent a micro-view of the revolution in angling that took place nationwide in the late 1960s.

Six of the eight relied on knowledge gained over years on the water, while the other two, the Lindner brothers, used a newfangled device known as the depthfinder and a concept that was to become known as "structure fishing" to find and catch fish.

Word of the giant stringers of fish caught by Nisswa Guides' League members spread, often by word-of-mouth, but mostly through the press. Articles in newspapers and magazines, regionally and nationally, helped fuel Brainerd's already strong tourism industry. Anglers from around the country flocked to area lakes in search of walleye, bass, and pike.

They still do.

And the Nisswa Guides' League, with the accumulated knowledge of 41,000 guide trips under their belts, is still there to guide them.

Legends & Legacies—A History of the Nisswa Guides' League captures the stories of league members past and present, a number now totaling more than forty. For an area known for its abundance of water, it comes as no surprise that master anglers are celebrated and honored for their contributions.

Take this copy of *Legends & Legacies* with you and stash it near your favorite easy chair. Author Gildow does a masterful job of capturing the essence and accomplishments of a group of anglers that history will remember for generations.

Steve Pennaz
Executive Director
North American Fishing Club
February 2005

About the Author

RAY GILDOW

I BEGAN WORKING as a substitute guide at Marv Koep's Bait and Tackle shop in the spring of 1989—by then, Koep's had become famous and well-known all over the upper Midwest. A good friend, Mike Hager, convinced me to give guiding at Koep's a trial run, to see if I liked working there. I had guided on my own for a few years and was excited about working at such a legendary place. Marv Koep said he was looking for someone who could help out from time to time, so he agreed to set me up with a few trips. A fascinating place to work and meet new people, I have been working at Koep's ever since. It is an honor to guide out of the same shop that was the haunt for guys such as Harry Van Doren, Max Slocum, Cully Swenson, Al and Ron Lindner, Gary Roach, and Marv Koep—fishermen who would someday become true legends.

I marveled at the rich history that was associated with the bait shop. After working there for a number of years, I was convinced that someone should write a book about Koep's, including the legendary guides who worked there and the impact the guides had on the fishing industry. While talking with many of the former and current guides about the concept, they thought it was a great idea. The format for the book began to take form in January 2000, when Koep told me that he would help in any way he could. Around the same time, I had a conversation about the book with my good friend, Chip Borkenhagen—a publisher and student of the outdoors. He, too, thought it was a venture worth "tackling" and agreed to help me develop the book. (We even made a gentleman's agreement that if something happened to me before the book was finished, Chip would carry on the project!)

I had no idea how much work this book would be. Nor did I realize how many people were connected in some way to Marv Koep's Bait and Tackle Shop and the Nisswa Guides' League. The more research I performed, the more I found I needed to know. The project grew and became even more fascinating. I conducted hundreds of hours of interviews and spent countless hours at the Brainerd Public Library researching documents that contained historical information.

The sixties and seventies marked dramatic changes in how fish were caught as well as the absolute evolution of a new era of technology and marketing in the fishing industry. Many lives changed dramatically during this period and some people were in the right place at the right time to become a unique part of the changes in the fishing industry.

In making every effort to keep this book historically factual, I spent more than five years researching documents and interviewing the people associated with the guides' league. Much of the information was gathered through old photographs and the stories told by those involved, so there is also a little folklore found in the book. Occasionally, I heard the same story from three different people with three different versions. I guess that is to be expected coming from fishermen, but it also makes it a challenge to get the story accurate. Due to my lifelong interest in fishing, the act of writing this book became a labor of love. I hope you find the facts and stories as interesting as I do.

With the good fortune of being born about eighty yards from the river in Pine River, Minnesota, I have always loved to fish. I was also blessed with two sets of grandparents who lived only five blocks from each other. Grandfather Rounds was an exceptional angler, decoy carver, trapper, and hunter. I am told he seldom went fishing without dragging me along, even when I was as young as two years old. Grandfather Gildow was a deputy sheriff, town constable, and in his later years, a city maintenance worker until his retirement in the late sixties. He liked to fish whenever he had time.

Grandfather Rounds lived a block south of the Pine River Dam and Grandfather Gildow lived five blocks north of the dam. I spent countless hours fishing on the banks of the river south of the dam with Grandfather

Rounds or north of the river in Grandfather Gildow's sixteen-foot, wooden, cedar-strip boat. Although I didn't fish the river in the cedar-strip boat until I was about twelve years old, I remember those days as if they were yesterday. The boat had a one-horse Johnson motor with a wrap-around pulley rope. A lot of folks fished from rowboats in 1956 and 1957. Driving up the river with a motor was a big deal, even though it sometimes took twenty minutes to get the motor started.

Grandfather Rounds showed me the skills of fishing and modeled the patience needed to stay on the water whether the fish were biting or not. He was my constant fishing partner and mentor in my early childhood years. We fished the riverbanks with old-fashioned cane poles—using grasshoppers, angleworms, or frogs for bait. I remember catching a lot of fish, but not many big ones. I give him a lot of credit for helping to develop my lifelong interest in the sport.

When I was in the third grade, my family moved to Bertha, a small Minnesota community about seventy miles southwest of Pine River. The Bertha area, too, had a small river close by—the Wing River—and it was about a thirty-minute bike ride to fishing holes that were good for northern pike. My family moved to Brainerd, Minnesota, after my freshman year in high school.

In 1960, my sophomore year in high school, I met Percy Trott, a gentleman in my church. An Englishman, Percy was a widower and an avid fisherman. A Brainerd city employee, he was widely known as the local dogcatcher. Percy was a good fisherman and a wonderful mentor for a few of us young guys who loved to fish. He didn't own a boat, but he was kind enough to rent equipment so we could fish Gull Lake, Lake Edward, Pelican Lake, or the Gull River. Most people didn't own a boat during this era—one usually called a resort to see if a small boat was available for fishing by the hour or the half-day. I spent a lot of time on the water with Percy during my first few years in Brainerd, but the time I spent fishing diminished as I became more involved in work and school activities. When Percy died of cancer a few years later, fishing in the Brainerd area was never quite the same for me. He was a wonderful man who had a good influence on kids. He taught me a lot about having a positive attitude even when things are tough—a trait he possessed until his life ended.

My dad and mom, Clair and Lorene, both fished, however, my mother died at the young age of forty-four. My father died in May 2004, when he was seventy-eight. I remember when they took fishing trips to Canada and came home with monster-size northern pike. Dad and I fished together until the last summer of his life. He was a small-business owner during most of his working years and found it tough to get away to fish. However he enjoyed the sport and had interesting tales to tell, including the big northern that got away on South Long Lake, as well as monster walleyes that got away on Mille Lacs Lake. I was fourteen years old when I caught my first musky. Dad, my Uncle Everett Gildow, and I were fishing Man Trap Lake near Park Rapids. It was a sixteen-pound silver musky—at the time, it seemed like a whale. We ate it, which I would never consider doing today.

I was a lake and river rat until my late twenties, when college and jobs took me away from the world of fishing for a few years. I began teaching in the early seventies and didn't start fishing again until the late seventies, when a good friend, Norm Card, took me to his cabin on Leech Lake. I was again caught by the fishing spirit. Soon I had a sixteen-foot Lund boat with a thirty-five-horse Johnson motor. I began spending many hours on the water, fishing Leech Lake and Lake of the Woods.

Fishing became more than a hobby. By the mid-eighties, I started to guide independently on area lakes. As of this writing, I am still a guide as well as a part-time tournament fisherman.

I remember driving by Koep's Bait and Tackle shop in the sixties. It was called Nisswa Bait and Tackle at the time, but I didn't get there much because Nisswa seemed like a long way to go for bait when there were so many bait shops in Brainerd. I also remember seeing guide boats in the area with names printed on the sides of the boats. I didn't understand or appreciate the revolution that was taking place right under my nose in that bait shop. I don't think most people in the Brainerd area realized how famous the store would become or how some of the guides working there would become household names for anglers all over the country.

Five Minnesota Fishing Hall of Fame anglers worked for the Nisswa Guides' League: Marv Koep, Al Lindner, Ron Lindner, Gary Roach, and Jeff Zernov. Many other well-known fishermen have guided through the league and Marv Koep's Bait and Tackle store. This book tells a part of the history of the league and some of the people who have guided through the organization. The history of this business covers more than forty years. I did not try to write something about every person who worked at Koep's or who guided through the league. Some people only guided for a month or two and found they didn't like guiding. Others worked on and off for a period of time and went on to other ventures. I tried to highlight the individuals who made an impact as guides as well as those who made impacts on the fishing industry. I sincerely apologize to anyone I may have missed in my research.

Leech Lake

Walker

Longville

Hackensack

Backus

Pine River

Whitefish Chain
of Lakes

Jenkins

Crosslake

Pequot
Lakes

Pelican
L.

Nisswa

Gull
L.

Long L.

East Gull Lake

Brainerd

Garrison

Mille Lacs

Minnesota

Moorhead

Duluth

Lake
Country

Minneapolis
St. Paul

Chapter One
The Early Years

THERE WERE MANY RESORTS in the Brainerd lakes area in the early sixties. It is difficult to say exactly how many, but most were small family operations and many have been sold over the years. A likely estimate is that less than half of the area's small resorts that were in operation during the sixties are still in business. In 1998, there were 1,155 resorts in Minnesota. They are now part of a $9 billion tourism industry in the state. Most resorts are family businesses operating in rural areas. The seasons for the Minnesota resort business have gradually increased to include spring and fall, often called the "shoulder seasons." (Source: *Explore Minnesota*, Minnesota Office of Tourism.)

There were fewer privately owned cabins in the early sixties. For many people, going to a small resort was the real "up north" experience. Some of the larger resorts in the area today have six hundred to eight hundred beds. In the early sixties, none of the resorts were that large. Many of the resort owners were also seasonal visitors to the area. They opened their resorts in the early spring and closed them after Labor Day—moving back home for the winter months, just like their customers. Some stayed open until cold weather set in and then closed before pipes would freeze. Staying open year around wasn't worth the investment. The few that stayed open all year catered to winter customers, but they were the minority. It was common for families in the Brainerd and Nisswa areas to rent cabins at area resorts for family gatherings and to hire local guides to go fishing. Many resorts have the same families visiting them that first began coming forty years ago.

Tourists from all over America visited the lakes area in the sixties, with a major portion coming from the upper Midwest. As some of the area resorts grew in size, expanded their seasons, and began catering to conventions, more tourists began to visit the area from other parts of the world.

Making money in the resort business was challenging. Profit margins at resorts were tight. One resort owner reported that his profit for 1961 was $2,500—equal to the amount of money he received for cleaning fish. The rest of the resort business paid for itself or lost money that year.

Few people owned boats. Those who did, usually had smaller boats and smaller motors. The average boat was twelve- to fourteen-feet long with oars or a small one- to five-horse motor. Public boat landings were also uncommon during the early sixties. Most access to area lakes was through resorts, privately owned property, or isolated public landings. Public landings were seldom paved, which made it difficult to land boats without a good towing truck. It was standard practice to rent boats and motors from resorts or fish from shore whenever possible. Tourists visiting the area to fish were dependent on fishing with guides, fishing from public dock areas, or through a resort.

There were a number of small bait shops in the area in the early sixties. Most of those shops of eight hundred to fifteen hundred square feet have been squeezed out of business by large stores with more than sixteen hundred square feet, and which market a wider range of sporting goods and services.

In 1961, to put things into historical perspective, John F. Kennedy became president of the United States, Elvis Presley turned twenty-six years old, and Sam Snead won $5,000 in the Las Vegas "Tournament of Champions" golf tournament. The average income for a family of four was around $5,000, a quart of milk cost about twenty-six cents, and the purchasing power of a dollar was much better than it is today.

The history of the Nisswa Guides' League covers nearly forty years of guiding experience, and as of 2004, more than 41,000 recorded guided trips with customers. Those figures continue to grow with each new fishing season. The league began when Marv and Judy Koep moved to Nisswa and purchased a bait shop—one of many small bait shops in the area at the time. Selling bait was, and still is, a difficult way to make a living. The Koeps discovered they needed to diversify their business in order to stay in operation. Developing a strong relationship with area resorts was key to staying in business during the early years of their bait business.

The formal name of the Nisswa Guides' League was created by Ron Lindner in 1968, the second year that he and his brother, Al, worked out of the Nisswa Bait and Tackle Shop. The name "Nisswa Guides" was changed in

1991 to "Nisswa Professional Guides" and changed back to "Nisswa Guides" in 2004. Marv Koep owned the copyright to the original name. When the Fischers bought the store in 1991, they did not purchase the name, "Nisswa Guides' League" so it was changed. Koep decided to let the guides use the original name again when the store was sold to Bill and Maria Erickson in 2004. Today, it is known as the Nisswa Guides' League.

The first eight guides to be members of the league were Harry Van Doren, Max Slocum, Cully Swenson, Marv Koep, Rod Romine, Ed Jensen, and Al and Ron Lindner. The league has always operated through rules that remained relatively informal. Inducting new members into the league involved a vote at league meetings. This was often, and sometimes still is, an emotional process. New members had to "prove their worth" to the majority of the existing members. Over the years, the size of the league has varied from eight to eighteen members. Currently, there are eleven members in the league. Marv Koep is the only original guide still fishing in the league today.

Except for Al and Ron Lindner, the first members of the league were local guides who were well-known by area resort owners. The guides spent many years on the water learning the area lakes the old-fashioned way—becoming familiar with water depths and land markings. The Lindners came to the area armed with sonar equipment and they learned the area lakes with a skill and speed never before seen by area guides. They fished the area lakes as if they were area natives and came to know the lakes better than most guides because the sonar allowed them to see the real structure of the lakes.

In addition, the Lindners' marketing skills—especially Ron's—elevated the leagues' members to a new status in the print and television media that has not been equaled to this day. During the seventies, the members of the Nisswa Guides' League became household names. Other Nisswa guides, such as Gary Roach and Marv Koep, would become well-known, too, but the stage was set by the early work of the Lindners in forming the league and promoting it across the upper Midwest through workshops, publications, and television shows.

The Lindners' promotional skills brought fishing and the Nisswa Guides' League to the forefront of a rapidly emerging fishing industry. Other fishing pioneers forged new ground during this era, but none had the same impact on the league. In addition, the league was formed about the time the fishing industry began to experience an unbelievable technological revolution in how fishing was done as well as the equipment that was being used to catch fish. Sweeping changes occurred in all areas—boats, motors, fishing rods and reels, fishing line, electronic devices, and even clothing. Some of these changes were not easily accepted by some of the older guides, but over time—after seeing what the technology was doing for guides that used sonar and other pieces of new equipment—most of them accepted the new technology.

There have always been guides who retire, quit, or move on to other ventures, but there was a significant transitional changing of the guides' period that occurred during the early- to late-seventies. Guides, such as Royal Karels and Gary Roach, became new members and brought different skill levels to the league as well as backgrounds from fishing different lakes. Others, such as Rod Romine, moved into new lines of work in the fishing industry. New guides, including Lenny Hodgson, Glen Belgum, Steve Collette, Hank Ebert, and Jim Minerich joined the league during this period and are still current members—providing a core of experience and skilled anglers to the league over four decades.

Rapid customer growth developed during this period because of widespread marketing of the league. With the growth came new opportunities. As other guides left the league to go into fishing-related businesses, additional opportunities were presented to add more new guides.

In the mid-to late eighties, the league grew to eighteen guides. The numbers fluctuated during most of the nineties, ranging anywhere from fifteen to eighteen guides. The numbers dropped slightly in the late-nineties as the tourism industry began changing to reflect an increased focus on golf and other entertainment activities. The Brainerd and Nisswa lakes area's fishing and resort industry saw significant changes in the era of the early 2000s, with a recession and later the impact that was felt following 9/11.

Today, the Nisswa Guides' League enjoys a very good business with a solid core of repeat customers. Some of the families have been fishing with the league since it started. Eleven guides are on the chart now with five or six more who help out when needed. There is also more competition from other guides in the area than probably any time over the past forty years. Some of the bigger resorts now have their own guide services and other independent guides market to the same area as the Nisswa Guides.

The primary mission of the Nisswa Guides' League today is to take customers fishing. Additionally, there are guides who fish tournaments, work at sports shows, promote fishing to children, and participate in marketing boats and fishing gear—much like the guides in this league have been doing for nearly forty years.

Even the telephone number is the same: (218) 963-2547.

Chapter Two
Marv and Judy Koep and the
Beginning of the Bait Business

MARV KOEP WAS RAISED in the small Minnesota farming community of Urbank, Minnesota. He was one of five children, three boys and two girls. His father, Paul, raised minnows in the bait business—mostly sucker minnows. He had one of the largest bait businesses in Minnesota at the time. The Koeps often employed twenty to thirty people during the busiest times of the year. It was common during that era for farm kids to be excused from school to help harvest crops for a week or ten days. Marv was allowed the same excuse to help his dad during the busy minnow season. While working for his dad, he learned the skills of the bait business. Marv attended a small parochial school in Urbank, until he entered the eighth grade, then he went to high school in the neighboring town of Parkers Prairie.

Judy Koep attended a small parochial school six miles down the road in Millerville. She attended high school in Brandon, a few miles from Millerville. Marv and Judy never crossed paths through school activities, even though their schools were so close to each other. They finally met through a parish-sponsored dance and then a special relationship began. (Marv said he was always careful not to let his own kids go to church-sponsored dances, now that he knows what can happen at such events!)

Marv and Judy dated each other in high school. After graduation, they decided that the best thing to do was to leave home and go to the Twin Cities to look for good-paying jobs. Judy got a job with Northwestern Bell and Marv was employed at an upholstery shop. Although they both landed good-paying jobs, they didn't feel at home living in the Twin Cities area.

Their relationship grew. They got married and explored the idea of having their own business away from the Twin Cities. Judy and Marv were married about a year after graduating from high school, on April 22, 1961. They took a three-day honeymoon to Winnipeg, Canada, and reported back to work four days after the wedding.

Pete Link owned a little bait shop in Nisswa on Nisswa Lake. Pete was a minnow trapper and a raccoon hunter. He was also a good bait customer of Marv's dad. Pete had always told Marv that when he (Pete) retired, Marv should buy the business from him. In fact, whenever Marv made a delivery to Pete, he reminded Marv that he should be getting ready to buy his shop. In the spring of 1961, Marv called his dad and said he was going to go into the bait business. His dad was happy to hear that because he always wanted him to go into the business.

Marv and Judy began shopping around to see where they should either buy an existing bait business or start a new one. They considered two locations. One was in Duluth and the other was Link's Bait Shop on Highway 371 in Nisswa. Pete Link had just built a new store and moved from his old location on Nisswa Lake. Marv and Judy decided to buy Pete's store in Nisswa. They didn't have any marketing research to support their decision— it was a gut feeling. Marv figured that with a brand-new, four-lane highway going past the store, someone must expect lots of traffic in the area someday. Later, looking back on his decision, Marv thought he should have bought the shop in Duluth. It had a great existing business and Link's shop wasn't that well-established. The Koeps got lucky with their decision to buy in Nisswa— the store in Duluth was bought up to make room for a new highway. Koeps must have made the right decision—they stayed in their Nisswa location for thirty-one years.

Making money in the bait business was a struggle. The Koeps continually tried to find new ways to increase revenue. The work was hard and the business was very seasonal. It was also dependent on the weather. Fishing-opener weekends were very busy, and then later in the summer, there were periods when business was very slow. Marv was in the National Guard and it seemed as if his two-week guard duty always fell on the trout opener. Judy sold bait all weekend while he was at training camp.

Pete Link had set up the new store specifically to sell bait, with cement tanks for his minnows. He sold minnows wholesale to area resorts and retailed minnows out of his shop. He had a big refrigerator that he used for worms. (Marv added cement tanks as part of his first expansion and ended up with a huge pile of leftover sand. He didn't know what to do with the sand, so he called his dad for advice. "At your age," said his dad, "why don't you just go and play in it?" His dad laughed about that story until his death.)

The first two years were tough ones for young Marv and Judy. Keeping minnows alive was always a challenge. In the early days, bait tanks weren't as good as they are now and losing minnows meant losing money. Their biggest fears were summer storms that caused power outages. Many times, Marv came to the shop after a bad storm to find all the minnows in the tanks dead.

There wasn't enough bait business to make a living, so the Koeps supplemented the good bait months with other business endeavors. Marv's dad was a fur buyer, so Marv began buying furs in the fall. At one time, they had twenty fishhouses they rented on Gull Lake and they also rented snowmobiles. The seasons for both of those businesses were often short and depended on the right weather conditions—proving to be up and down as profitable money-making ventures.

As the bait and tackle business grew, so did Marv and Judy's family. Shelly was the firstborn child, followed by Kevin and Wendy. All three children spent time learning the business since their house was only thirty yards away from the store. Over the years, they got to know everyone who worked at the store as well as many of the customers. Kevin developed into a very good guide and Wendy guided for Lieutenant Governor Marlene Johnson on the Governor's Fishing Opener. This feat left many believing Wendy was a full-time guide. She was not, but people occasionally ask Marv if his daughter Wendy is still a guide.

Judy Koep is a superb angler (there is no such thing as a bad angler in the entire Koep family!). Wednesdays and Sunday afternoons were family time at the Koep home and many of those days were spent fishing. Marv and Judy packed the kids in the car and headed to a distant lake to get away from the store. They went to places such as Leech Lake, Winnibigoshish, and Grand Rapids, Minnesota. They had to leave, because they knew that if they took the day off and stayed home, something would come up at the store and they would have to work. Taking Wednesdays and Sunday afternoons off was a family ritual until the kids got older and began having their own agendas.

Shelly was the oldest child and sometimes the toughest one to convince to go on the trips, but now she looks back and remembers that as one of the best periods of her life. As the kids became older, the competition grew more intense. There were times when the Koeps had to take two boats to the lake on the family day. Judy fished with Kevin, and Marv fished with Shelly and Wendy. By the time Kevin was sixteen years old, he was an accomplished angler. There were days when Kevin and Judy would kick butt in the little family fishing contests with Marv, Shelly, and Wendy. (Perhaps Shelly and Wendy don't remember the old days exactly the same way that Marv does!)

Kevin Koep began guiding before he was old enough to drive a car. His first trip was on Nisswa Lake when he was eleven years old. Marv had customers drive to the lake and put the boat in so Kevin could guide.

The Koeps began selling fishing licenses and sunglasses at sporting shows almost by accident. Marv hired a store manager to take care of the shop, while he and Judy attended the shows. Attending sports shows became a way to add extra income to their business during the winter season and they also helped promote the bait shop during the summer months. At first, the Koeps set up booths at a few area sports shows. The business continued to expand and so did the number of shows they attended. Eventually, they began retailing their business at many of the major sports shows across the northern part of the United States. They were in the Minneapolis show for more than thirty-five years and they also attended shows in Chicago; Detroit; Washington, D. C.; Harrisburg, Pennsylvania; Cincinnati; Cleveland; Detroit; and many other cities. The shows became a good source of income, an interesting way to see the country, and an excellent way to promote the store and the guiding business.

Marv and Judy both have tremendous people skills and a real knack for getting to know people. Over the years, they met many future customers and also became acquainted with some of the biggest names in the fishing industry through the store, through the sports shows, and through their relationships with two other fishing legends, Ron and Al Lindner. Through their friendship with the Lindners, they met people such as Roland Martin, Bill Dance, Ted Williams, and Bill Binkelman.

Nisswa Bait and Tackle didn't become well known statewide until the store began using guides. Marv and his guides established a reputation for fishing excellence and before long, outdoor sports writers and television personalities began giving the store coverage that helped the business grow. (The name of the store changed slightly over the years—Nisswa Bait and Tackle, Marv Koep's Nisswa Bait and Tackle, Koep's Nisswa Bait and Tackle, and later, Koep's Pro Shop. Today it is Koep's Sport Shop.)

Bud Gorham, an area television personality from Channel 7 in Alexandria, Minnesota, became good friends with Marv. He provided good publicity on the store as well as fishing in the area. (Bud was later killed in a snowmobile accident.) He often came to the store to do video fishing reports of the area's action. Bob Brown and Bert Evan were outdoor writers who wrote about the bait shop and its guides. Ron Schara and Dennis Anderson are writers from the *Minneapolis Star Tribune* who have written many articles about Marv and the guide business.

Another early pioneer in the fishing television industry was Virgil Ward. He had one of the early television shows on national television and found his way to Minnesota to fish with Marv on more than one occasion. Marv enjoys the story of the first time he met and fished with Virgil. Virgil didn't know where Nisswa was so he stopped for directions at a gas station in St. Cloud, about seventy-five miles south of Nisswa. The young gas station attendant knew the location of Koep's Nisswa Bait and Tackle Shop, so he gave Virgil directions. Upon Virgil's arrival, Marv told Virgil he was going to take him to a secret lake that was not known by many anglers. He told Virgil that he was quite sure that they could get enough nice fish to make a good show for him and his crew. They drove to the lake, got in the boat, and started fishing. A few minutes later, the young man from the St. Cloud gas station pulled up alongside Marv's boat.

"Hi, Mr. Ward," he said, "I am the guy that gave you directions to Koep's!" Marv couldn't believe it. He wondered what Virgil thought about his secret lake!

On another trip to Minnesota, Virgil wanted to make a television show using the crankbaits he had been promoting on his show—demonstrating how good the baits could be for fishing walleyes. He fished all day with his television crew and never caught a walleye. Stopping into Koep's store that evening, Marv convinced Virgil that they could catch walleyes if they used live bait. Virgil agreed. They went out that evening and caught a nice stringer of walleyes. He never did the show on using crankbaits to catch walleyes. Virgil came back to Nisswa again a few years later and took Marv and Judy out for supper. It was a memorable evening for the Koeps. Marv remembers Virgil Ward as a kind man, a diligent angler, and a real gentleman.

Chapter Three
Doug Kasper

DOUG KASPER WAS A YOUNG BOY in the neighborhood when he got to know the Koeps. He knew Pete Link when Pete owned the former bait shop on Nisswa Lake. Doug worked off and on for the Koeps for about the first two years they had the store. He remembers huge shipments of minnows going from Koeps to Crane Lake in the northeastern part of the state. (Crane Lake was a major drop-off point for the minnow business in northeastern Minnesota. Koep's Bait and Tackle Shop supplied minnows to resorts in the Crane Lake area for many years.)

Doug often fished Nisswa Lake. When Marv needed help, he went to the edge of the lake and hollered for Doug. Goldie was Marv and Judy's dog. Goldie wandered away from the store and Marv often called Doug to find his dog. Doug thought that was great, because while looking for the dog, he got to drive the Koeps' green, 1959 Ford. He wasn't old enough to have a license, so driving that nice car was exciting.

He got to know Harry Van Doren—the first real guide that began working in the store. Harry was a skinny little guy who had lost his wife, Lillian. During the fur-buying season, Doug and Harry skinned muskrats and other animals in the back of the store. Doug only worked at the store for two years, but he remembers the early years and he has many fond memories of Harry Van Doren.

One story about Marv Koep stands out in Doug's memory. At the time, Doug was just a young kid who was probably a little boastful. While Doug was fishing on Gull Lake in a pouring rain, Marv came to the landing with a man who was huddled up and trying to stay warm. Doug began talking smart about the rotten weather and the poor fishing. Marv just grunted something and the customer didn't say anything.

Later that day, when Doug was in the store, Marv asked, "Did you know who that guy was?" Doug had no idea.

"That was Jack Klugman, the movie star!"

Doug was embarrassed about that experience. He also recalls a night when the power went out and all the minnows in the store died. It was a huge financial loss and a stinky mess. As he dug a huge hole behind the house and dumped in the minnows, Doug looked at the house to find Marv and Judy staring in disbelief. It was a real mess!

According to Doug, the retail part of the bait business was slow during the first few years that the Koeps owned the shop. Selling bait and making a lot of money was difficult in the early sixties. But over the years, he watched the business grow. He remained a customer and still lives a few miles from the current store. Doug has many fond memories of Marv and Judy and the folks who worked at the shop over the years.

Chapter Four
Guiding and Fishing
in the Mid- to Late-Sixties

THE MAJORITY OF THE NISSWA BAIT and Tackle guiding business in the early years came from Minnewawa Lodge on Clark Lake, as well as from Harry Van Doren's customers, and business from other area resorts.

Minnewawa Lodge was owned by a gentleman named Papa Potthoff. Potthoff had been an outstanding football player in college, until his career was cut short by an injury. Potthoff bought the resort in 1931, and in the early years, it was only open in July and August—the major tourist season in the Nisswa area in the thirties. Potthoff built a remarkable business and attracted many customers from the St. Louis area. Many of those customers knew Potthoff's football fame and began coming to his resort because they had heard of him in the sports arena. He had developed many business associations that often evolved into attracting new customers to his lodge.

Many of the lodge's customers were doctors, lawyers, and other well-educated folks who really liked to fish—many from Missouri. (Some of those families still return to fish in the Nisswa and Brainerd area.) In the early years, as business grew at Minnewawa Lodge, many of its customers hired guides from Nisswa Bait and Tackle. Papa Potthoff guided customers on Clark Lake, but seldom on other area lakes. He worked closely to line up his customers with Nisswa Bait and Tackle and used its guides to fish many of the other lakes in the Nisswa/Brainerd area.

The guiding business at the bait and tackle store continued to grow. By 1967, six or seven guides worked on and off, depending on the amount of business. Some men guided long enough to realize they didn't like it and got out of the business, but a core of men were regular guides—Max Slocum, Cully Swenson, Harry Van Doren, Marv Koep, and Dick Young. Dick began working for Marv in 1961, hauling minnows to Crane Lake, and he guided part-time when Marv needed extra help. As the minnow business continued to grow, Marv made arrangements with local resorts. He took care of their bait needs, and in exchange, he got new names of customers who wanted to go fishing. It was a nice arrangement for both the resorts and Marv.

Rod Romine was another area guide who worked on his own and often shopped for bait at the shop. He grew up in the area and guided part-time while working as a dispatcher for the local sheriff's office.

Every guide who fished during this period had a favorite lake or a small group of lakes that was his preferred area to fish. Fish electronics hadn't been developed yet, so most guides learned the lakes by spending countless hours and days finding bars, holes, or spots that held fish and marking them from shore—marking depths with anchor ropes, marked fishing line, plastic floating jugs, and other crude devices. A guide became as respected for his knowledge of the lake as he was for his fishing and catching techniques.

Little consideration was given to fish populations or how catching great numbers of fish would affect fishing on a lake in later years. Fish populations were healthy. The focus was on catching fish and eating them. Tourists came from long distances to fish and guides felt it was their duty to make sure they took meat home to eat.

Dutch Cragun, owner of Cragun's Resort, recalls a time when his dad operated the resort. In the spring, loggers and carpenters who were working on projects at the resort went into shallow water on Gull Lake and clubbed northern pike on their heads. Fish were plentiful—when the opportunity presented itself, area folks took what they needed for meals.

Local newspapers as well as radio and television shows promoted the quantities of fish that were caught as well as how big they were. A guide's skill was measured not only by how many fish he and his customers caught, but also by how big the fish were. "Meat is neat" was a phrase often used by local guides to promote their reputations. They didn't see catching and killing fish as having a negative impact on fish populations because the next year there were always more fish in the lake and they were always large and plentiful. No one really had much data on fish populations in area lakes— the information collected from guides and area anglers was the primary means of judging a lake's fishing health. Area newspapers ran weekly photos of stringers of fish caught and nearly every bait shop had a weekly fishing contest to see who could catch the biggest fish.

Tourists who were unfamiliar with the area could catch panfish from shore, but it was difficult to catch stringers of walleyes, bass, or northern pike on a regular basis without hiring a guide or fishing with a local angler. There was not a lot of pressure on area lakes from anglers, beyond local fishermen and local guides, and the fishing populations held up under those circumstances. That changed with the introduction of electronic equipment and new fishing techniques. (Later, those who fished during the sixties learned how little they really knew when they began using electronic equipment and discovered the true contours of the lakes.)

There was some competition for customers during this era, but business for most guides was built on reputation and repeat business. Many families made it a tradition to come to the same resort year after year and got to know the guides as well as the resort owners. Fishing, relaxing, and playing in the lakes were the primary attractions in the lakes area during this period. There were a few golf courses and other things to do, but fishing was the hub of summer recreation in the lakes area.

Chapter Five
Harry Van Doren and the
Beginning of the Guide Service

MARV GOT TO KNOW MANY local fishing guides during his first few years of retailing bait from the store—they stopped in on a regular basis and bought bait. Harry Van Doren, Clarence Luther, Gene Shapinski, and Rums Miller were guides who had excellent reputations as good fishermen. Gene was well known in the area as an expert pan-fishing guide and a tackle producer. One of his specialties was catching crappies. Gene invented the "Quiver Jig," a product that is still in use today.

Marv had owned the store for five or six years when Harry Van Doren's wife, Lillian, died. (Coincidentally, she died in the Brainerd hospital on the same day Judy Koep's father, Tony, died.) Harry's wife was a large part of his guide service—she answered the phone and booked all of his customers. After she died, Harry had no way to book customers.

Harry Van Doren was a Brainerd-area fishing legend. He and Clarence Luther made their living as full-time guides. Both men guided for nearly sixty years in the Nisswa-Brainerd area. (Clarence was never a guide at the Nisswa Bait and Tackle Shop, but like Harry, he was a local legend and a master fisherman.)

Harry was born a few miles away from Koep's store near Lake Edward. He fished the Nisswa area in the summer and headed south in the winter to fish bass. He was good at fishing all species, but he made it clear to customers in Minnesota that he preferred to spend his summer days fishing walleyes. He fished bass and northern pike, but only as a last resort. There were many days when he told the customer that the walleyes were not biting and that they should save their money and come back later when the fish were biting again.

Known for not keeping his boat very clean, the other guides used to kid him by saying that they could tell when old Harry was coming back from the lake because they could see a cloud of flies following his boat down the highway. Harry was also pretty secretive about where the fish were biting and on what lake he was fishing. Heavy smoking took its toll on his health later in life and he suffered from emphysema for many of his final years.

He had a gruff exterior, but a kind heart and he mentored many of the guides that later worked out of the store. Out of necessity, he became the fishing mentor to Marv Koep. At first, Harry did most of the guiding, but there were times when there was more business than Harry could handle, so Marv began guiding, too. Even though Marv had been in the bait business for a few years, he hadn't taken the time nor acquired the skills to catch fish for customers.

Harry showed Marv his secret spots on the lakes and taught him the many techniques needed to become a fishing guide. He taught Marv the science of fishing walleyes. Many of those spots on area lakes are still fished by those of us who guide.

The following article about Harry was written by a friend of mine, Carol Buckmann, for the *Brainerd Daily Dispatch*. She was an avid outdoorsperson who had a keen interest in people who worked in the outdoors. She died too young with way too many unfinished articles yet to be published about the outdoors. I share this article because Carol knew Harry and I think it best illustrates who he really was:

"Fishing was what he loved, it was his life, and for 58 years Harry Van Doren made it his fulltime career. Van Doren died of lung cancer and his funeral was Tuesday. And with his death part of an era died—an era of full-time fishing guides—those who make their living exclusively by guiding. There aren't many of them left. Until Van Doren's death, he and full-time guide Clarence Luther were the last to share this notable acclaim in the Brainerd Lakes area.

But Van Doren left a legacy of fishing skill and knowledge of nature he readily shared with the hundreds of residents and out-of-state visitors with whom he came into contact through nearly 60 years of guiding.

Van Doren, the rail thin man in the olive green union suit had a subtle, quick sense of humor. He ended his guiding career June 20th 1978, the same day he started in 1920 when he was 11 years old.

That didn't mean he stopped fishing. He retired from fishing to fish, to fish with close friends and with people he guided for years, to fish for fun, not money. He had what other angling experts consider the biggest influence, in a quiet way, of anyone in northern Minnesota on the development and use of modern fishing equipment and techniques. His versatility and adaptability and confidence in his ability and knowledge of fishing are what they attribute to his success.

When outboard motors came on the market, Van Doren was the first to have one (before that it was rowing all day). When depth finders were introduced, he was the first dealer. His prime target was the walleye. Through the years, he developed what he found to be the most effective way to fish walleyes, back-trolling with splash boards into the wind, a method that became popular in the mid-60's.

For Van Doren it was a trip in the early morning, another in the afternoon from spring ice-out to fall ice-over and when he was going strong, he had three trips a day and often guided through the night. In the winter, he guided each year on southern reservoirs, Sam Rayburn and Toledo Bend.

"Harry taught me all I know about walleye fishing. Harry could out-fish everybody. When I was guiding, we might get busted, but Harry came in with limits," admits Koep.

Even in the intensive care unit at St. Joseph's Hospital, Brainerd, in his last hours, his thoughts were on fishing. Marv was with Van Doren. He couldn't talk, but he could write and Marv said he surprised him by revealing a well-kept secret.

When Koep was guiding, he'd see Van Doren head for Gull Lake and figured that's where the walleyes were hitting, so he'd go there too. Harry came in with limits, sometimes Koep didn't. In the hospital Koep asked Van Doren: "Where in the heck were you when I was out on Gull?"

Van Doren wrote: "Edward."

"It took me 18 years," said Koep, "to find out he was fooling me. What he'd do was fish Gull and if things were slow, he'd pack up and take customers to Lake Edward.

Van Doren's parents homesteaded a large block of land and lakeshore on the north side of Lake Edward in 1895. The whole family, his father, Orlo, mother, Martha, sisters, Mrs. Clara Wiltshire (now of San Jacinto, Calif.), and Mrs. Herbert (Hattie) Christensen, Brainerd, and his brother Frederick, now of Poteau, Okla. (also a guide here in the early days), loved to fish.

In his boat he carried a big tackle box filled with jigs, jerk baits, spoons and plugs, mostly wooden plugs, many dating back to the 1920s and earlier, many his own designs. But he seldom used it. Instead, in his shirt pocket he carried a small, circular, hard leather case. Inside were four compartments that fold together like a miniature accordion, with an assortment of walleye rigs. Van Doren's innovative combinations of snells, swivels, adjustable floats and small hooks were his secrets to success.

Van Doren's long-time fishing partner and fellow member of the Nisswa Guides' League was Cully Swenson.

Of his fishing persistence, Swenson tells of an experience in 1975 when Van Doren had to be flown from a fishing trip in the Upper Peninsula in Michigan to a Duluth hospital with an acute emphysema attack, an attack that nearly took his life.

But two weeks after being released from the hospital, he insisted on going along on a three-day Canadian fishing trip with Swenson and several others. "He loved to fish. We couldn't get him to stay home," recalls Swenson.

Altogether, the group caught 641 walleyes. "We'd be out in the morning and by afternoon, we'd caught 50 walleyes, catch and release except for eating. But still Harry wasn't ready to quit. He'd point to another spot and say 'Let's go try it,'" Swenson said of his fishing buddy.

When Van Doren retired he and Swenson made a pact. They'd fish at least once a week for muskies and they did. Van Doren's challenge here became the muskies and in the winter it became the striped bass in the south.

"I'll have to find a new fishing partner now. It'll be hard. Harry was the best," Swenson proclaimed. And so, with the death of Harry Van Doren, part of an era died, but he left a legacy of fish, fishing, knowledge and ability that will be discussed in fishing circles here for many years to come."

(*Brainerd Daily Dispatch*, June 1, 1980. Used by permission.)

Two of Van Doren's customers, Jerry and Peggy Wellik, still live on Gull Lake. "Harry was a well-known guide on Gull Lake," recalled Peggy. "He knew the lake like the back of his gnarly old hand. He was a slight man who always smoked a cigarette. Whenever he caught a little perch he swore, ripped it in half, and used it for bait. He was well-known as the best guide on Gull Lake. We were quite fortunate to have him as a guide. We always fished on the sunken island in the widest part of Gull out from Sandy Point."

Harry Van Doren had great influence on the guides that worked out of Koep's. He helped younger guys like Al Lindner, Bobby Collette, Ron Kristofferson, and others. Most of the guides have stories that involved Harry.

Gary Roach probably said it best. "If there is one man I know from fishing that deserves to have his name in the Fishing Hall of Fame, it is Harry Van Doren. He was an unbelievable fisherman and many of the techniques we still use today for fishing came from Harry."

Cully Swenson, another one of Harry's friends, began helping out on the weekends. Swenson was an excellent angler and knew the area lakes very well. Soon a third guide, Max Slocum, was added to the store. Slocum was a meat inspector from the Duluth area. He spent a lot of time fishing the Nisswa lakes area and he began guiding on weekends. He was also an excellent fisherman. And so a new era had begun for Koep's. Their business expanded beyond just selling bait and tackle to providing a guide service. It was a change that had a ripple effect across the country.

Chapter Six
The Lindners Arrive
and a New Legacy Begins

THE YEAR WAS 1967—Ron Lindner and his brother, Al, dreamed of owning their own bait and tackle shop as well as running a guide business. The Lindners' passion in life was fishing. Al was an outstanding fisherman who was knowledgeable in fishing many species of fish and had already won bass tournaments in Illinois and Wisconsin.

Ron, the oldest, had a family of six children. He was a trained survey technician and thought he would try to find a job in that field until they could get their business up and running. Al was single and had just been released from the military after finishing a tour in Viet Nam. He worked as a logger in the woods from time to time, cutting pulp.

The Lindners traveled around Michigan, Wisconsin, and Minnesota, looking for the right area to open their bait shop. They thought the best place to locate would probably be Michigan because they had grown up in the Chicago area and already knew a little bit about Michigan and southern Wisconsin.

They spent time in Minnesota, looking at the communities of Alexandria and Grand Rapids. Both had many lakes and seemed to fit the criteria they were using to make their decision.

The search eventually brought them to the Nisswa and Brainerd area, where they happened to see a photo of Harry Van Doren and Papa Potthoff holding a huge stringer of fish. Ron and Al were impressed with the variety of lakes and rivers in such a confined area. Every imaginable species was to be found—from lake trout to muskies and superb walleye, smallmouth bass, largemouth bass, northern pike, muskies, bluegills, sunfish, and jumbo perch. They believed they could fish here and not even get to every lake or river. Leech Lake was only sixty miles north and the premier walleye lake in the world—Mille Lacs Lake—was a twenty-minute drive to the east. They decided to move to the Brainerd-Nisswa area.

Ron had a family to take care of and needed a job. A local engineering company that was about to take on a big construction project hired him. Ron put a bid on some property on Highway 371, thinking they could build a bait shop there someday, but he didn't get the bid. He took out a loan on 175 feet of lakeshore on the south side of Gull Lake, which cost $19,000. Just after the agreement was signed, Ron lost his job. The engineering company did not get the contract and said they didn't need him after all. Ron kept his land, but ended up taking a job in St. Cloud that first year.

Ron and Al visited Marv Koep's Bait and Tackle Shop and introduced themselves. They told Marv they were excellent fishermen. True, they did not know the area lakes, but they had an electronic box that helped them learn the lakes and they knew how to fish structure. The Lindners said it would not take them long to figure out where to fish. Marv was skeptical. Hiring two unknown guys from Chicago seemed risky.

Harry Van Doren also had doubts. "What do these two city guys know about walleye fishing?" he asked Marv. They weren't convinced about the "structure-fishing" idea either, but in the end, the Lindners sounded too good not to give them a chance.

Any doubts were quickly erased when everyone started seeing the stringers full of fish that the Lindners brought in. Ron was the marketer and many marketing experts consider him to be a true marketing genius. He bragged about his little brother, Al, and Al produced results. Ron took photos of their catches and sent the photos to area newspapers and television stations. The photos began having a real impact on business at the bait shop.

According to guide Rod Romine, Al was such a good fisherman it was unbelievable. Rod told me that he had fished area lakes all his life and he saw Al pulling fish out of spots that no one had thought of fishing before. Al had one of the first electronic flashers ever sold—a red box with the serial number 58. It allowed him to quickly learn area lakes. (Electronic flashers let the operator see the contours of the lake bottom, determine the hardness of the bottom, and also see fish and weed cover.)

The Lindners also experimented with making lures and sinkers. Ron came up with a new style of sinker that he used when fishing. When people asked what they used to catch their fish, Ron and Al said they caught them on a "Lindy Rig." That became the forerunner to the Lindy Rig fishing tackle, which is manufactured today.

Ron Lindner's mind is always thinking of new ways to do things. The second year they were in the area, it was his idea to start a guide league. He thought it was foolish to guide without promoting the business and he also thought it made more sense to work together in the guiding business than to compete against other guides. Ron's philosophy was that there was enough business for everybody.

He made a sign and logos for "Lindy's Guide Service." Marv thought it was a good idea to put the sign in the front of the bait shop. That was the start of the guide league. The guides got together for a meeting in the basement of Marv's house later that season and decided to call themselves, "Nisswa Guides." According to Ron, the first eight guides were Harry Van Doren, Max Slocum, Cully Swenson, Marv Koep, Rod Romine, Ed Jensen (who didn't guide long), Al, and himself. Dick Young also guided part-time. In order to become a member, one had to be voted in by existing guides. The next guides to join were Royal Karels and later, Gary Roach.

Ron sent photos to Bud Gorham, a television reporter in Alexandria, as well as two Twin Cities' writers: Ron Schara with the *Minneapolis Star-Tribune* and Hank Kehborn with the *St. Paul Pioneer Press*. These writers had great influence on the business that the guides generated over the years at the bait shop. Fishing was good and the reputation of the guides began to grow.

Ron recalls that the cost of a half-day trip in 1968 was $12.50. It was never easy to figure out how much to charge for a trip. That was difficult for Marv—he always thought they were charging too much. The customer paid $12.50, bought the gas, and provided the bait. Nightcrawlers and minnows were preferred—leeches were not used much. The customer also paid for any lures that were lost. The guides used eighteen-horse motors and rented their boats from resorts because the accesses on most lakes were not very good.

The competition between guides was also quite fierce. One of Ron's customers said he was amazed at the way it seemed to be more important to impress the other guides with fish caught, than it was to impress the customer. Ron says that Al was the first guide not to clean his own fish. The store began hiring kids to clean fish. One of them was little Ricky Potthoff—fishing was so good that there were days when Ricky made more money than the guides.

Ron used two old cigar boxes for his tackle. He carried his gas and motor in his car trunk on most trips. Ron's favorite lake was Pelican Lake and he also liked to fish Hubert and a few other small lakes in the area.

Catching walleyes became tough mid-summer, so everyone switched to bass, panfish, and northern pike. Most of the guides fished area lakes and stayed away from the Mississippi River because it had a reputation as being dirty. They later discovered that the Mississippi was a real treasure for bass, walleye, and just about every kind of fish.

Around a year later, guides began buying their own boats. Ron recalls that Harry Van Doren built the first splash-guards for his boat from rubber he'd salvaged from an elevator. Soon Al and the other guides built splash-guards on the back of their boats so they could troll backwards without getting water in the back of the boat.

One September morning in 1968, a significant event drew attention to the Nisswa Guides' League. According to Ron, all the guides fishing that morning hit a hot bite and returned to the shop with limits of walleyes. The guides and their customers posed for a picture that showed more than 102 walleyes (seventeen limits!). The picture was seen in newspapers and magazines all over the upper Midwest. Bookings for guides really began to grow after that photo was published.

Ron is the first to say that Al is the best fisherman in the family, but early on, Al was not the best with customers. Ron, Gary Roach, and other guides usually got bigger tips from customers because they were patient and more inclined to socialize with the people in the boat.

"Al was the competitive one," says Ron. "In the early days, he often caught the most fish, which made customers a little upset. Al fished as if he was on a timeline in a tournament. Max, Cully, Gary, and I were better entertainers. Al was often late to the shop in the early years and customers would be pacing and upset. He made a deal—if you don't get your limits, you don't pay. They usually got their limits."

One group of customers took Al up on the bet to catch a limit or not pay for the trip. Al was back with the group, and a limit, in one hour and fifteen minutes. Most customers wanted to catch fish, but they also wanted to have a good experience on the water, too, so the guides who made those bets eventually stopped the practice. Marv Koep remembers many days when Al left the shop with customers forty-five minutes later than the other guides and still would be back with limits before 10 A.M.

Al had developed quite a reputation and usually had open guiding reservation slots should any one cancel a trip. On one stretch, according to Ron, Al guided ninety-five straight days without a break.

Ron recalls that the guides were very competitive in the early days, but everyone worked together and shared information about fishing. The guides got along well and lifelong friendships were formed. The atmosphere changed in later years, with new guides working at the store. Some kept fishing information to themselves and some of the friendships were not as strong as in the early years.

Due to a burning desire to start his own tackle-making company, Ron left the guide league in October 1970. He had already developed a walking sinker that he called the Lindy Walking Sinker, as well as something he called a Dingo Rig. So in 1968, Ron and Al ventured off with a partner named Nick Adams and began the

Lindy Little Joe Tackle Company on the west side of Brainerd. None of the investors had much money and most of the money was borrowed to get the business started. Rod Romine recalled spending many evening hours in the basement at Ron's house—pouring lead, making jigs, and wrapping Lindy Rigs.

Ron and Al sold the tackle company to Ray-O-Vac in 1973. After setbacks, in 1974 the Lindners established In-Fisherman, Inc. In-Fisherman would become one of the most successful fishing companies in the country—publishing magazines, books, articles, producing videos, and television shows. The Lindners sold their company in 1998, and in 2002, they launched a new company, "Lindner's Edge," which specializes in producing television shows. Ron remains a creative force with his new company and fishes with the same passion he did when he first came to Minnesota.

The Little Brother—Al

Al Lindner is an intense fisherman, but an easygoing guy who is fun to be around. For Al, fishing was an obsession, not a leisure-time sport. Like Ron, he is in the Minnesota Fishing Hall of Fame (located at Reeds Sporting Goods, north of Brainerd, Minnesota) and he is also a member of the National Freshwater Fishing Hall of Fame (Hayward, Wisconsin). He never fished to become famous—he fished because of his passion for the sport. He fished at Marv Koep's Bait and Tackle Shop for about five years after Ron stopped guiding to work in their tackle company.

Al's memories of guiding at the Nisswa Bait and Tackle shop are ones that are filled with fun and experimentation.

"Papa Potthoff had a table at the back of the Minnewawa Lodge that was set up just for guides," said Al. "We all got together at noon and shared information about what we did that morning fishing. We talked about patterns on the lakes, what bait was working, and what wasn't working. Some days, a guy had a bad day on a lake and figured the fish weren't biting, then four other boats came in from the same lake with fish. I started to change my way of thinking from those years. We learned that just because one lake wasn't going with fish, didn't mean other lakes weren't good. Each lake has its own period of turning on and we started to pattern when lakes usually had a good bite. We also learned to fish different techniques on different lakes at different times of the year. You would see Pelican Lake on for two or three weeks and then it dipped a little bit—the fish went through a little transition and then Gull Lake turned on. There was more going on in these fishing environments than we realized.

"The wealth and sharing that went on with the other guides during this period was incredible! Incredible! Having such skilled anglers out on the water every day, watching the lakes, and the weather patterns was fascinating, because it wasn't just you on the water. I couldn't wait to get to lunch or at the end of the guide trip to meet with the other guys and find out how they caught their fish, what depth they were at, and what bait they used. Year after year, this information started to show us where to go, and when, and what to use for bait. I know, without a doubt, it was a huge impact on my career in teaching me how to look at water and see fish movements.

"We had no idea that fishing at Koep's would lead to other ventures," recalled Al, "such as Lindy Little Joe, In-Fisherman, and now The Lindner's Edge. We worked with people like Tommy Carlson, who at the time had Carlson's Tackle Company, which is now CSI, now one of the largest tackle companies in the world. Tom used to drive a little truck to Nisswa Bait and Tackle and supplied Marv with most of his tackle out of the back end of the truck. Tom and Marv told me and my brother that we should take some of the tackle and tie it into snells and package some of it. That's how we got started making some of our early tackle."

Al's first real fishing hero was Harry Van Doren. "Harry was a local legend and he was an unbelievable fisherman," said Al. "He was the walleye king! Papa Potthoff was known all over for his bass catching. Harry was the walleye man and Papa was the bass guy! I learned a lot from those guys.

"Harry fished Edward, Gull, North Long, and Pelican. Those were his mainstays. He knew the bite and he rotated lakes with the different seasons. He'd see a dip on one lake and then he jumped to another. It didn't take long to know if a bite was good or bad with eight guys—we shared information and by the next trip we pretty well knew where the bite was. I was one of the younger guys and he really showed me the ropes here and down south.

"I went south a few years during the winter months and lived with Harry. We stayed in a small town in Broadhurst, Texas, and guided out of the Sam Rayburn Reservoir. Harry also used to fish out of Greer's Ferry before going to Texas.

"We fished every day in Texas. We stayed in a two-story house and I never took the time to go upstairs."

Al and Harry were bass fishing on Sam Rayburn one day when Harry, who had serious emphysema, coughed so bad that Al thought he was dying. He took Harry to the nearest hospital and hurried back to the lake to pick up customers. When Al returned to the landing that afternoon, there was Harry's car. Harry didn't have customers that day, but he walked out of the hospital, went to the house, got his boat, and went fishing. Al said Harry was a rare man who was tough and crazy about fishing. Al didn't get to know Max Slocum or Cully Swenson very well, but he has never seen another fisherman like Harry.

Fishing at Sam Rayburn was quite an experience. The number of bass in the lake was unbelievable. Fifteen guides worked the lake and the limit was fifteen bass a day. The ultimate challenge was to do three trips and catch forty-five fish. At the time, there were no size requirements and fish ranged from one and one-quarter pounds to three pounds. Harry had won a number of bass tournaments on the lake and in Texas, he had a reputation as an outstanding bass fisherman.

Al has a Virgil Ward story, too. Virgil was in town shooting a show for walleye fishing—using a new kind of walleye lure. He fished for three days and never caught a walleye. He called Al and Ron and they took him fishing on South Long Lake, east of Brainerd. They caught a great limit of walleyes. Al recalls Ron saying that perhaps they should do their own television show with Nick Adams and call it, Facts in Fishing. Around two years later, the Lindners sold the Lindy Little Joe Tackle Company and began promoting fishing through seminars.

According to Rod Romine, Al was petrified before doing a fishing seminar. "It took Al a long time to be at ease doing fishing seminars and look at him now," said Rod. "He is a natural at seminars as well as an on-screen television personality."

The seminars expanded and soon the Lindners were printing articles and other publications about fishing. Once they sold the tackle business, they discovered they had an interest in the communications side of the fishing business. Soon the In-Fisherman network was born.

One of the first employees of the In-Fisherman company was a young Jeff Zernov. Jeff had worked at Koep's for a short period as a guide and later developed the Zercom Depth finder and the Aqua-Vu underwater television camera system. Gary Roach, too, became one of the early employees of the Lindners and remains one of the Lindners' best friends.

Al Lindner had won two major BASS events and three back-to-back BASSMaster Classics; he has won many more since. He remembers driving home after one of the bass tournaments and telling his wife he was at a crossroads. He either had to spend the time it took to be a good tournament angler or devote his time to producing quality television shows. He decided his love was doing the television shows and from then on, he quit tournaments except for an occasional one just for fun.

His all-time favorite fishing lake in Minnesota is North Long Lake. It has nice sizes for all species. His first boat fit on top of his car. In the early fishing years he rented his boat from Bobergs on Gull Lake. His first real guide boat was a Shell Lake 351 tri-hull. Most of the guides had one of these boats at one time or another. This was considered one of the best boats on the market at the time, but looking at the boat today one would consider it a bathtub. (Eventually, the Lund Boat Company bought Shell Lake Boat Company.)

What is Al's opinion about the current climate of fishing? He thinks fishing for bass, smallmouth, and musky are as good as ever, but he sees deterioration in some of the area lakes with more weeds and more algae. There aren't as many big fish and he accepts part of the blame. Guides in the early years didn't realize the impact they had on lakes. Now they do and that is why selective harvest and catch-and-release are being promoted. Al recommends that today's guides focus less on the harvest and more on education. Don't make the mistakes the early guides did in over-harvesting.

It is hard to measure the impact that Al and Ron Lindner have had on the fishing industry. It is immense, but it has not been without criticism. Many anglers feel that too much education has been provided to too many people by the Lindner organizations. But Ron and Al would argue that everyone has a right to learn and be informed—better decisions are made by an informed angling public.

Ron and Al Lindner are now famous, but they have not conducted most of their business to be famous or even to make money. That was never their goal—they live and breathe fishing. They had a wild side in their younger days, but they matured through it. They are generous people with reputations for acts of kindness and loyalty to friends and employees. They look to the future and not the past to see how fishing can be made better. The Lindners are to fishing what Frank Sinatra was to music—legends that left their marks on the fishing industry and on the history of the Nisswa guides. Al and Ron brought the name of the Nisswa Guides to a bigger stage. Along with Gary Roach and Marv Koep, they were the biggest promoters of the store and the area. They worked with giants in the industry: Bill Binkelman, Bill Dance, Roland Martin, Carl Lowrance, Virgil Ward, and other sport celebrities. They plan to stay in the fishing industry for a long time and if you want a chance to talk to them, keep your eyes open. They will be out there somewhere, fishing on a Brainerd/Nisswa area lake.

Chapter Seven
Dick Young

MANY GUIDES AT NISSWA BAIT and Tackle are not household names, but they were part of the history of the business. Dick Young is one of those people.

Dick moved to the lakes area from Gaylord, Minnesota. He had been involved in a serious traffic accident and needed time to recuperate from his injuries. His mother owned a resort on Roy Lake (part of the Gull Lake Chain). He spent time recovering at his mother's resort and he liked the area so well, he decided to make it his home.

He held a full-time job at the paper mill in Brainerd, and then in 1961, began working part time for Marv—hauling minnows to Crane Lake for distribution to area resorts. Crane Lake was also a fly-out destination for fishing in other lakes in Minnesota and Canada.

As Koep's business grew, so did the demand for more guides. Marv asked Dick if he was willing to help out as a guide. Somewhat shy, Dick was reluctant at first. He said he was "scared to death" to take people fishing on lakes he didn't know that well. But Marv talked him into guiding and before long, Dick spent more time guiding than he did driving the minnow truck to Crane Lake.

Dick worked from 11 P.M. to 7 A.M. at the paper mill and then guided from 7 A.M. to 3 P.M. It was a grueling schedule. (The other guides who worked at the store during his early years of guiding were Ron and Al Lindner, Royal Karels, Lenny Hodgson, Max Slocum, Harry Van Doren, Cully Swenson, Gary Roach, Bert Lindberry, Bobby Collette, Ron Kristofferson, and Rod Romine.)

He liked to guide for walleyes—his biggest catch during his twelve years of guiding was a ten-pound, seven-ounce trophy walleye. Dick did his best to stay away from bass fishing, but some days the walleyes couldn't be found, and like the other guides, he had to fish for bass. He remembers the days when the walleye bite was pretty tough and how Harry Van Doren told some customers he wasn't going to fish that day. Dick marveled at Harry Van Doren's fishing skill. "That guy was just unbelievable! He was the best fisherman I ever saw!" recalled Dick. "Al Lindner was right up there, too. That guy can really catch fish."

His favorite lakes to fish were Gull, Edward, and the Whitefish Chain. Many of Dick's customers were from the local area—the cost for a four-hour, half-day trip was $17.50. His first guide boat was a wooden, cedar-strip boat with a twenty-horsepower, Mercury outboard motor. Within a few years, the Crestliner Boat Company allowed the guides to use boats for a year and then they had the option of buying the boat at the end of the season.

On one of Dick's Gull Lake trips, he was fishing with a married couple. A big storm was fast approaching in the western sky. Dick suggested that they should think about getting off the lake before the storm hit. The husband insisted on staying a little longer, thinking that fish really bite before a storm. They were about two miles from shore when the sky turned green and Dick told them to lie down in the boat and cover their heads with their seat cushions because they were about to be hit by hail. The hail felt like small stones hitting them in the face and arms. Dick got them to shore before the wind hit and the man's wife was furious. She told her husband that that was the last time she would ever go fishing with him.

Dick guided well into the fall each year—probably his favorite time to fish because it was a good time to catch big walleyes. He once guided a player from the Chicago Bears as well as an announcer from the Baltimore Orioles, but he doesn't recall the names of either one. Dick worked at the shop for nearly twenty years—twelve of those years as a guide. He feels the quantity of fishing is still good, but the quality is smaller than it was almost forty years ago.

The main reason that Dick finally quit in 1979 was his inability to keep up the pace on so little sleep, due to holding down the paper mill job along with guiding. He also became discouraged with the emphasis on catching and killing fish. He is happy to see the emphasis today on catch-and-release. Dick lives in the Brainerd area on the Gull River and still enjoys fishing, especially in the fall when the big walleyes start to turn on.

Dick Young may not be a household name in the fishing world, but he was there when the legends and legacies started—he was part of it all. Dick is retired now and still loves to fish. He can be found in the fall on Gull Lake looking for big walleyes. He won't have a big fancy boat with his name on the motor. He will just be sitting in his little boat—concentrating, having fun, and enjoying the moment.

Chapter Eight
Cully Swenson

CULLY SWENSON WAS ONE of the original Nisswa Guides—a modest man who found happiness in the simple things of life. Ray Hollingsworth was Cully's neighbor in rural Nisswa for nearly forty years. Ray and his wife, Norma, lived across the road from Cully and they treated him more like a family member than a neighbor. They ate together, traveled together, and helped each other out. Ray's wife cleaned Cully's home and sewed his clothes. Ray and Cully fished together and hunted together through the years and the friendship with the Hollingsworths remained until Cully's death. (Much of the information in this chapter about Cully comes from the Hollingsworths.)

Ray Hollingsworth grew up on the shores of North Long Lake. His parents owned Old Camp Resort, which is still owned by Ray's younger brother, Collin. Ray was just a kid when he got to know Harry Van Doren. Harry often launched his boat at Ray's parents' resort. Ray knew Harry as a real good fisherman.

Cully Swenson moved to the Nisswa area from Rockford, Illinois. He came to know the area while coming to Nisswa with Virgil Ross, a classmate. Virgil moved to the area and shortly afterward, Cully also moved—attracted by the lakes and large tracts of hunting land. Cully had been married in Rockford, but after about seven years, the marriage fell apart and they divorced. They remained friends, however, and Cully often visited his ex-wife when he returned to Rockford. Cully never remarried and didn't spend much time worrying about women. He seemed to be content working, fishing, and living alone in his trailer house in rural Nisswa. His loves outside of working were fishing and deer hunting.

A big man about six feet tall with massive shoulders and big arms, no one messed with Cully. Even as an older man, he was an imposing figure. But he was also kind and gentle and had a good sense of humor. He was a skilled craftsman and worked as a construction worker, laying cement blocks, framing houses, and other jobs required in his trade. He was also a bus driver and drove for a Brainerd bus company for twenty-seven years before he retired.

Spending a fair amount of time fishing in the area, Cully began learning the area lakes soon after he arrived in Nisswa. His fishing took him from the big lakes in the north, such as Winnibigoshish and Leech, to Mille Lacs at the south end of the guides' haunts. He liked fishing all species, but often looked for crappies and sunfish when the dog days of summer made walleye fishing tough.

Cully's first encounter with Harry Van Doren was not too pleasant. Harry was guiding full time and Cully was getting into guiding. They ended up guiding customers on the same lake. Cully had a good day and Harry did not. Cully got the message that Harry was not too happy about him being the new guy fishing at Koep's. And Harry definitely did not like the new guy showing him up by catching more fish. The resentment soon wore off and Harry and Cully became very good friends. It was a common sight to see the two buddies fishing the same lakes and the same spots all summer long. They also took many fishing trips together to other states and into Canada until Harry's health prevented him from traveling. Harry's death was a big blow to Cully. He often talked about the loss with the other guides.

Ray Hollingsworth's first musky-fishing trip was with Cully and Harry Van Doren. He was fishing with two legends and didn't even realize it. Cully developed an interest in musky fishing and he and Ray took many trips to their favorite musky lake, Cass, about eighty-five miles north of Nisswa. They spent countless hours chasing the fifty-inch fish. Cully's biggest musky was a twenty-five-pound beauty. He was never able to land the big musky, in the thirty-five to forty-pound range, but he enjoyed fishing for the elusive fish until the last few years of his life.

Cully Swenson loved to guide and he fit in well with the new young guides. He also loved spending time with his customers and enjoyed helping them catch fish. Much of his guide business was with satisfied, repeat customers. On one trip, two ladies were making a big fuss about touching leeches and putting them on their hooks. Finally, Cully told them it was strange that they thought nothing of taking dirty, old diapers off little kids' butts, but they couldn't stand to reach into a clean bucket of water and pick up a fresh, clean leech. The women stared at him, agreed that he was absolutely right, and baited their own leeches for the rest of the trip.

He fished out of a Crestliner boat with a thirty-five-horse Johnson motor for much of his last years of guiding. Along with the other guides, he worked with tackle companies, such as Berkley and Lindy Little Joe, helping to promote their products.

Cully guided until around 1982 or 1983. He loved to fish until he reached his early eighties. When Ray Hollingsworth stopped by his house, some days he felt like fishing and other days he didn't have the energy to go.

Ray recalled a special trip with Cully on an early November day. They were deer hunting and the temperature reached about seventy degrees. It was too hot to hunt, so Ray suggested that they take their guns home and go fishing on North Long Lake. Cully thought that was a great idea. They hit the lake and went bass fishing. The bass were on a feeding terror. They had their limit of twelve in less than half an hour. The fish were hitting top water baits and it was some of the best fishing either friend had ever experienced. They fished for another few hours and released the rest of the fish. Ray had no idea how many they caught, but it was an unbelievable fishing experience.

A reporter from *National Geographic* came to Nisswa in the mid-seventies and wrote a feature article about Cully Swenson. Though his name never became famous like some of his fellow guides, he possessed the same passion and fire for fishing as his guiding peers. *Brainerd Daily Dispatch* photos show Cully as a successful angler, with many happy customers holding nice stringers of bass, northern pike, and walleyes.

On an October day in 1999, Cully was driving near one of his favorite lakes when he pulled out in front of a vehicle. He was hit from the side and severely injured. He spent about three weeks in the hospital followed by a stay in a veteran's nursing home. He died from complications from his injuries on November 8th, 1999. Fittingly, in Minnesota, that day is traditionally either the day before, or the day of, deer-hunting opener.

Chapter Nine
Max Slocum

MAX SLOCUM WAS ONE of the original Nisswa Guides. Max's father, Glenn, lived on a farm north of Nisswa on Highway 371, just outside of Pequot Lakes. His father had developed medical skills while working with an area veterinarian and had a reputation as being very good with treating large animals, especially horses. Even though he was not a veterinarian, Glenn built a large customer base and did much of the same work as a vet and serviced a large area in central Minnesota.

In 1943 or 1944, Max was working as a photographer in the animal stockyards in St. Paul, where animals were taken to be slaughtered for processing for table fare and meat byproducts. Max and his wife, Eva, had just purchased their first home in St. Paul when Max's father had a serious stroke. His father was able to get around, but he had lost some of his physical ability on the right side of his body and was no longer able to work with big animals, such as cows and horses. Max decided to help his dad. Even though they had just purchased a home, Max quit his job at the stockyards and moved to Pequot Lakes to help his father. Eva liked their new home and she had a job in St. Paul, so she decided to stay for a year to see if Max liked working with his father before selling their home. Max brought Delores, their only child, with him to Pequot Lakes. Eva worked in St. Paul and commuted to Pequot Lakes on many weekends. A year later, Max and Eva sold their house and the whole family moved to Pequot Lakes.

Max worked with his father until his father's death. He stayed in the Pequot Lakes area and worked as a veterinary technician, but he decided that was not what he wanted to do for his life's work. Max got a job as a meat inspector and moved to Iowa. Later, his meat inspecting job took him to Duluth, Minnesota. His first love was fishing and being around lakes, so Max and Eva bought a home on Sibley Lake in Pequot Lakes. He worked in Duluth during the week and came home every weekend to fish. He fished on holidays and other days he could get off. Eva did not always appreciate his schedule, but she put up with it for many years.

Max started guiding in 1927 or 1928. His first guide trip was with a customer on Lower Hay Lake on the Whitefish Chain. His fish of choice was the walleye. He fished northern pike and bass when he knew he couldn't find any biting walleyes. His daughter, Delores, remembers his absolute passion for fishing.

"Dad would get back to Pequot Lakes and if he didn't have a guide trip, he scouted out an area lake to see if he could find fish," recalled Delores. "He kept track of the weather and where he found fish under different weather conditions. I was lucky to go fishing with him once in a while, but he was usually too busy to take me out much. Dad loved to fish. My mom wasn't real interested in fishing, but he took her out once in a while." Max was also an avid hunter. He hunted ducks in Minnesota and made yearly trips to Canada to hunt deer and moose.

"My dad was a friend to everybody," said Delores. "I remember him talking about fishing with Harry Van Doren and Cully Swenson. He developed a customer base from many area resorts and many of those people booked my dad year after year. He fished a lot out of Potthoff's resort. Two customers became really good friends: J.D.Chastian, who owned a chain of nursing homes and later owned a resort somewhere in the St. Louis area, and the big-band leader, Russ Carlyle. Russ became my dad's best friend and they stayed in contact with each other almost every week."

Max was an established guide before Marv Koep moved to the Nisswa area and started his store. He became one of the original members of the Nisswa Guides' League the first year the league was formed. Gull and Pelican Lakes were his favorites. He fished other area lakes, but he had a real love for Gull and Pelican. According to Delores, Max spent a lot of time fishing from a Lund boat.

Max Slocum was a great storyteller as well as a very kind and gentle man with customers. He prided himself on teaching people how to fish without embarrassing them in the process. Many of the original guides told stories of days when other guides caught more fish, but Max's customers seemed to have more fun. "Dad had many jokes," said Delores. "Some were a little dark in nature and he wouldn't tell them in front of me."

Max worked as a meat inspector until he was about sixty-five years old. No one remembers what year he quit guiding with the Nisswa Guides, but he faded out of the league and began taking more trips with customers out of Breezy Point Resort on Pelican Lake. Jim Wentworth, owner of Fish Lectronics in Nisswa, recalled Max as being one of the funniest guys who ever worked at Koep's.

"Max could walk into a room and tell jokes nonstop for thirty minutes," said Jim.

"He was an entertainer. People loved to fish with Max because they knew they were in for a fun fishing trip, whether the fish were biting or not."

It was a common sight to see Max, Harry Van Doren, and Cully Swenson working a lake together. They were not always happy to have some other boat slip in close to them. They worked as a team, they were good friends, and all three were excellent anglers. But Max could never understand how Harry Van Doren could go south for the winter and fish murky, southern waters after spending so much time on crystal-clear, Minnesota lakes.

Max slowly phased out his guiding business as he got older, but he never stopped fishing until his health forced him to quit. He had just bought a boat from a cousin and decided that he wanted to put the boat on a different trailer. He got a neighbor to come to the boat landing on Sibley Lake to help him make the change. The wind was blowing and either Max slipped and hit his head on the boat trailer, causing a stroke, or he had a stroke that caused him to fall on the trailer. That event was the end of his health and his fishing. He was forced to move into a nursing home in the Bemidji area where Delores and her children visited him nearly every day. Max hated living in a nursing home. His wife had died earlier and Delores had to put him in a facility where he could receive good care. He surrounded himself with his fishing pictures and told fishing stories to every visitor. Max died in the nursing home at the age of eighty-nine. He loved life, loved the outdoors, and really loved fishing.

Chapter Ten
Rod Romine

I HAD THE PLEASURE of knowing Rod Romine and I fished with him on a couple of occasions before his death on June 2, 2003. (He was preceded in death by his wife, Gloria.) Fortunately, I was able to interview him for the book before his death. Watching the videotape and hearing him talk about fishing, one can feel the excitement as he relived his fishing experiences. A member of the original group of Nisswa Guides, Rod was a great individual who truly loved fishing and the fishing industry. He was quite well-known as a guide, a tournament angler, a tackle-manufacturing representative, and an educator.

Rodney was born in Minneapolis in 1932. His family moved to Pine River, Minnesota, and he graduated from Pine River High School in 1950. He was a veteran of the Korean War; serving in the Air Force. For twelve years, he worked as a dispatcher for the Minnesota State Patrol. He began guiding when he was fifteen years old and until 2001 he still guided occasionally.

His father had a big influence on Rod's fishing career. As a young boy, he often fished with his father. His father used burned-out lightbulbs to mark corners of sunken bars and lined up the lightbulbs with landmarks, such as trees and buildings.

Rod used to declare himself the "King of the Whitefish." He loved fishing the Whitefish Chain and many of his early years were spent on Hay Lake, Upper, Middle, and Lower Whitefish, and Gull Lake as well as the waters in the Longville area. (Longville is about sixty miles northeast of Nisswa.) Much of his early fishing was done with artificial plugs such as the Prescott Spinner, Lazy Ike, and the June bug. He prided himself on knowing the structures of area lakes. It was a real shock when he got his first Lowrance red box sonar depth finder. Only then did he realize he didn't know much about the structure in any of the lakes!

Rodney went to his deathbed believing that while fishing on Whitefish one day, he lost what could have been a state-record walleye. When fishing the day before, he had caught a twelve-and-one-half-pound walleye and the day he lost the monster it appeared to be twice as big—in the eighteen to twenty pound class. He had it beside the boat and it got off. It was the biggest walleye he had ever seen and he never saw another one that size.

In the mid- to late-sixties, Rod was an independent guide. He was familiar with the other area guides, but at the time, they were not yet organized—everyone was on their own. He would get trips out of Minnewawa Lodge—many with customers he had fished with in previous years. He knew Harry Van Doren, and like every other guide in the area, he was in awe of his fishing skills. He remembered an early discussion with Harry when Al and Ron Lindner first came to the area. "Those two kids from Chicago won't be catching fish," said Harry. "They don't even know these lakes." He would later eat those words!

Customers fishing with Rod in the early days had to provide bait and pay for the boat that was rented from an area resort. He received $12 or $15 a day. He could still remember a meeting when the guides voted to raise the rate to $25 for a half-day trip. Marv Koep was upset and thought that would put the guides out of business. "Marv didn't think any one would pay $25 for a half-day fishing trip," said Rod.

Rod always had to work guiding around his job as a dispatcher with the Minnesota Highway Patrol at the Brainerd office. Having another job was a point of contention for some of the other guides, but by mid-April, Rod was usually booked for the rest of the summer.

Rod had fond memories of the original group of guides. Everyone helped each other with fishing tips, where to fish, and shared what was hot and what was not working on area lakes. Everyone competed for the fish, but they were professional and respected each other's abilities. Marv Koep gave 10 percent discounts for purchasing bait and tackle and that was an important package to the guides. The Koeps were kind to the guides' families and often took them to Bar Harbor or other supper clubs in the area for special meals over holidays or other times during the year. The Koeps' kindness went a long way in keeping guides loyal and dedicated to working at the store.

As the guide business began to grow, Rod had mixed feelings about the addition of newer guides. He felt some of the "new kids" were not professional in the way they conducted business—hanging catches on the sides of their boats when coming back to the store, being late, or having too much fun playing jokes on each other. He felt that some of them failed to bring the same kind of professionalism to the store as exhibited by the original group of guides. But by the same token, he recognized that some of the new guides had real fishing talent.

The guide business grew so fast, at times Koep's had to turn away business. During those periods, Marv Koep helped out as a guide. Royal Karels and Gary Roach were hired while Rod was guiding, about three years after the league was formed. It was not easy getting into the league because members had to vote in new members or they could not belong to the organization. The guides felt that becoming a part of the league should be for anglers who had demonstrated skill both as fishermen and in handling customers. Voting new members into the league was often a highly emotional event. If everyone didn't agree to a new member, the potential candidate was not admitted. Two area guys that helped out the league during Rod's membership were Don Knold and Jim Miller, area residents who knew the lakes well enough to fill in when extra help was needed.

His first fishing boat was a Crestliner. Later he began using what was to become a guide standard—the Shell Lake 315 tri-hull. Shell Lake Company was based in Wisconsin and was later purchased by the Lund Boat Company of New York Mills, Minnesota. The 315 was the boat of choice by the guides at Koep's in the early years. Now that boat is considered to be a floating bathtub, but it was the most modern boat anyone had seen during that era. Compared to the old, wooden-seated, aluminum boats everyone had been using, fishing out of a 315 was a pleasure.

Rod's notable fishing memories include his first Governors' Fishing Opener when Carl Rolvagg was the governor of Minnesota. And he had fond recollections of Gary Roach and the Lindners. He felt the Lindners earned everything they have received in terms of recognition and success. They were tireless leaders in the early years of the fishing industry, just as they are today. And Rod remembered the addition of new guides, Ron Kristofferson, Bobby Collette, and Bert Lindberry.

Rod recalled when Ron Lindner took Carl Lowrance, the inventor of the Lowrance Electronic Fishing Flasher, fishing on the Whitefish Chain and they got lost. Ron was not familiar with the lake at the time, but he kept talking as if he knew the spots and their location. Finally, as it became time to head home, Ron had to tell Carl he had no idea where they were. After that, Ron earned the nickname, "Silver Tongue."

Along with his good friend, Jim Wentworth, Rod met Carl Lowrance in 1969. Lowrance fished with Rod and other guides at Koep's, and later hired Wentworth to provide technical assistance in developing some of his new electronic products. Before beginning his business in the electronic and sonar-fishing industry, Lowrance was a fruit and vegetable salesman. Carl loved to cook and invited folks from the store to his cabin for some of his tasty meals.

Harry Van Doren, Rod Romine, and the Lindners had some of the first red sonar fishing locators made by Lowrance. These machines revolutionized the fishing industry and the way anglers fished.

According to Rod, Bill Binkelman was an early fishing pioneer who influenced the Lindners as well as other anglers of the era. He was a pioneer of fishing with different techniques and different products. A fishing technique that he had developed was later enhanced by Ron Lindner and eventually became the Lindy Rig.

"Ron Lindner is a creative genius," recalled Rod. "He never sits still, can't sit still, and he is always trying to figure out a better mousetrap. We spent hours in his basement tying jigs and making tackle, and he was always trying to figure out a new way to make another piece of tackle. I don't think he is the fisherman that Al is and I think he would admit it, but he could visualize new ideas better than anyone I ever met."

Rod remembers the Lindners as always creating new ideas and concepts. They were never just fishing guides—they were entrepreneurs. When they began producing different fishing products in the basement of Ron's house, Rod worked evenings helping to assemble the jigs and other products they marketed for the fishing industry.

Eventually, the Lindners started a business called Lindy Little Joe, and in 1972, Rod went to work for them in sales. He also began spending time with them doing fishing seminars and public-relations work. According to Rod, Al Lindner was "scared to death," when making public appearances in the early years.

"He did fishing seminars and he was absolutely mortified to get in front of an audience," said Rod. "Now he is one of the best presenters around." Gary Roach also joined Lindy Little Joe and he, too, worked in sales and began doing promotional and educational work for the company. The friendships that were developed with Gary Roach and the Lindners stayed strong through the years and they remained very good friends until Rod's death.

Rod had great success as a guide, and later, as a company representative for other fishing companies. He said he was a great copycat. He never really invented anything or came up with unique ideas, but he was first in line to try out the new technologies and the new fishing equipment. His association with the Lindners and Gary Roach allowed him to have success as a guide, and later, as a tournament fisherman.

One of the early guides sponsored by the Lund Boat Company in the early days of Minnesota fishing tournaments, Rod's first tournament boat was a Lund S-16. Decals were placed on the sides of the boats and the guides wore promotional material on their fishing jackets. The tournament trend began in the southern United States and worked its way to the north in the late sixties. *Fishing Facts* magazine was a major sponsor of the guides in the early fishing tournaments. Rod quit working for Lindy Little Joe in the mid-eighties. The company had been sold by the Lindners and was purchased by another company. Rod then joined another sports company, Paul Bunyan Wholesale, where he continued to work in the fishing industry.

He lived on a small lake north of Brainerd until his death. When he was feeling well enough, the thing he liked most was to jump into his boat and go fishing. Rod Romine was like the other original Nisswa Guides. He had an absolute passion for fishing and a lifelong commitment to the fishing industry. He was proud to be an original member of the league, honored to be associated with the many people he came to know in the industry, and loved to tell stories about his fishing experiences. He was also proud of the friendships he had made with the Lindners and so many others during his career in the fishing industry. Like the other early guides, he never realized that some of the guides would become household names in the fishing world. He was pleased about that and he smiled whenever he talked about the good old days at the Nisswa Bait and Tackle Shop.

Chapter Eleven
Jim Wentworth

IN ADDITION to Marv and Judy Koep, Jim Wentworth is the one person who has seen it all from the beginning of the Nisswa Guides' League. He began working at the Nisswa Bait and Tackle shop on a part-time basis while he attended Brainerd Community College. Jim's brother, Steve, was an instructor at the college and Marv called Steve to ask if anyone at the college with a background in electronics might be interested in working at the store. Steve suggested his younger brother, Jim, which marked the beginning of a long relationship with the Koeps, and later, with other owners of the store.

The Wentworth family hailed from Iowa. Jim and his two brothers were blessed with great intelligence. Jim had worked for a time for Control Data in Minneapolis. He planned to work part time at Koep's until he found a job in electronics, but he never got away from the fishing industry. Jim began working on electric trolling motors and eventually branched into the electronic sonar business. He is a gifted technician and in the early era of flashers, he developed a reputation for being able to fix just about anything that was broken. He still works out of his own shop, rigging boats and servicing electronic trolling motors and other electronic fishing devices.

In 1972, Carl Lowrance—the man credited with developing the first inland sonar flashers and depth finders—often fished with the Nisswa Guides and stopped by the shop to see if there was any interest in setting up a service center for his new line of sonar units. Carl had started his little company in Joplin, Missouri, and later moved it to Tulsa, Oklahoma. Marv Koep and Jim Wentworth were both interested in Carl's idea, so they started a service center above the bait shop. It was the second service center set up by Lowrance—the first one was located in California. Jim and Marv later collaborated on setting up service centers in Ohio, Indiana, and Missouri. Those centers were later closed—proving too difficult to manage from the home base of Nisswa. Jim and Marv were not prepared for the challenges they faced in administering all the new businesses at the same time.

New boats were not yet rigged with the new electronic equipment in the early- to mid-seventies. Jim Wentworth began working with Al Lindner, Gary Roach, and other guides to modify the equipment to fit the boats. They also made changes on the boats themselves. They replaced the standard boat seats with swivel seats, installed home-made splashguards, and custom-built and installed livewells.

Before long, the boat companies noticed the modifications and began working with the guides to change how their boats were constructed. Many guides got involved in designing style changes on the boats. The hulls became wider and deeper, lengths were expanded, interior layouts changed—the classic fishing boat gradually changed to be more functional and comfortable. The Nisswa Guides were not the only fishermen involved in this evolution, but they were influential in the designs of Lund, Crestliner, and Alumacraft, for example. Based on input from Gary Roach, Al Lindner, and others, Lund Boat Company manufactured a tri-hull fiberglass boat called the Nisswa Guide. The early Lund 315 flat bottom boat has evolved into the twenty-one-foot, model 2025, which was designed to hold a 250-horse motor. Many such designs came from Al Lindner and Gary Roach, who are currently still involved in designing and promoting Lund Boats.

Carl Lowrance learned to appreciate the special gifts that Jim Wentworth had in designing and servicing electronic equipment. He flew Jim to the plant in Oklahoma to work with his engineers in trouble-shooting design and service problems. Through his working relationship with Jim, Carl Lowrance developed a close friendship with the Koeps and many of the guides. Carl fished with the guides and even developed a reputation as a good cook. He was a wonderful man who enjoyed time spent on the water.

Two other major competitors made inland sonar equipment during the seventies—Humminbird units, developed by Tom Mann who had been an employee with the Lowrance Company; and the Ray Jefferson Company. The next major change in electronics technology within the fishing industry was the introduction of the Vexilar paper graphs, which greatly enhanced what anglers were able to see under their boats.

Jim Wentworth, the Nisswa Bait and Tackle Shop, and the Nisswa Guides were very much a part of the technology revolution that occurred during the seventies.

"I look at the changes that occurred in technology over the past thirty years and I can't even begin to imagine what the next thirty years will hold," said Jim. "I think the most important consideration we have in fishing today is not technology, but the preservation of our natural resources. If we don't do a better job taking care of our lakes, air, and forests, technology won't mean much." Jim has fond memories of working with the guides in the early years.

"The fishing in the late sixties and early seventies was tremendous. I saw unbeliev-able stringers of fish brought into the store," he said. "I remember when Al Lindner got customers so mad. He took people fishing for an hour or so, Al brought in eight-een walleyes, and the customers never caught a fish. That is how good he was. Harry Van Doren was great, too. He was just terrible at keeping his boat clean. There were dead minnows, fish parts, and worms all over the bottom of his boat. You could see the flies hanging around his boat a half-mile away, but boy, he could catch fish. Harry was pretty opinionated, too. He told people what was on his mind. His boat was a Ouachita. It was built in the south and it had a stick steering device that was way ahead of its time in many ways.

"The guides always went fishing if they had a day off," continued Jim. "It was like a vacation for them and they were as excited to go fishing as if they were coming to fish from Alabama. All the guides were rodeo guides [wild and rowdy]. Some liked to drink, they all liked to fish, and they all liked to have fun. Max Slocum was a meat inspector, but he was also a veterinarian. He told stories with the best of them and some of his customers liked to fish with him just to go on the water and laugh.

"None of us had any money in those days. I remember when Gary Roach and I went crappie fishing so we could get a mess of crappies and trade them in for a case of beer from one of the guys who had a grocery store up north. We didn't have enough money to buy much in those days. Gary had his whole family living in a little trailer house and money was hard to come by.

"Judy Koep's mother, we called her Al, was a great lady. She lived in the trailer house next to the bait shop and she was usually the first one at the store every morn-ing! The bait shop was the hub of fishing in the lakes area. People stopped at the store from all over the country. You saw license plates from New York, California, Illinois, Florida, and Alaska. We never realized we were in the middle of a fishing revolution. I think Ron and Al did. They saw the value in promoting fishing. They weren't think-ing of trying to become famous, but they did see new ways of promoting the fishing industry and making money.

"That era is gone. The ma-and-pa resorts are gone, the population is changing, and there is more competition for the entertainment dollar. We have golfing, racing, the National Football League, and so many other things to do that fishing is a smaller piece of a bigger pie. We started seeing the changes in the seventies and eighties. The only people making money on the small resorts were the realtors who sold from one owner to another until most of the small resorts were divided into development lots."

Jim has rigged just about every guide boat in the Brainerd-Nisswa area over the last thirty years. He has customers from all over the country. One can always tell when Jim is at work because his laughter can be heard for a block away. At one time, he had five technicians working for him, but he downsized his business and usually has one or two employees during the busiest times of the year. His business, Fish Lectronics, was located at Koep's for more than thirty years before he relocated the business to his home for about two years in 2001. Fish Lectronics is now located back at the original Koep's store site, which is now also a marine dealership. Koep's Sport Shop has built a brand-new store a few blocks south of the original store site.

Jim Wentworth is one of the legends of the Nisswa Guides' League.

Chapter Twelve
Gary Roach—"Mr. Walleye"

SOME OF THE NISSWA GUIDES became household names within the fishing industry—Gary Roach is one. He earned the name Mr. Walleye because he is so good at catching walleyes and later used the name in some of his commercial ventures. Gary is an expert at catching many different species of fish and is well-published as an author of the sport. His national appearances include television shows, sports magazines, and sports shows. His photos have appeared all over the country and he is widely known in fishing circles as one of the premier, freshwater anglers in America.

Gary dropped out of school in the eighth grade. He knew how to read and write, but he wanted to make money and he decided he didn't have time for school. Joining a logging operation in the Brainerd area, Gary made $50 a week cutting pulp for a paper mill. Logging was a common occupation in central Minnesota and the pay was decent, but the work was hard and the days were long. He continued logging for a few years, until one winter the snow was so deep it was impossible to get into the woods. Gary and other loggers were without work. Bored, Gary decided to join the Navy and work for Uncle Sam. After four years in the United States Navy, he finished his tour of duty in 1960.

After returning home, his first job was planting trees for Crow Wing County—mainly around the Brainerd airport—for which he earned $1.50 an hour. Today, Gary and Beverly laugh, marveling at their income from tax reports from those days. One year they made $3,800 and thought they were doing pretty well.

Gary started working at a gas station in northeast Brainerd for owner, Bill Getty. He met his wife-to-be, Beverly Lavoie, at a neighborhood cafe. After working at the station for about four years, his life was turned upside-down one day when he was in a serious car accident. He had a low tire on his car and he drove into the shoulder of the road and the car rolled into the ditch. The car was wrecked and he received serious injuries to his back. Gary spent six months in the hospital and suffered from back pain for many years.

Once he was well enough to work again, Gary bought his own little service station on the east side of Brainerd and he began fixing tires for $1.50 each. He had all the work he needed and soon decided to get a bigger station, so he bought a Texaco station on the south side of town and stayed there for a few years. Business was good and the Roaches were making a living wage, but Gary said he itched to go fishing on Pelican Lake when spring came and the walleyes were in the shallows. Some days, he had his employee, Jake, take care of business while he slipped out to the lake. On many days, the gas station business just got in the way of fishing.

One day, Gary and Jake were working on a car together. Gary was going to finish the job and then have Jake take care of the shop so he could make a service call. The car they were servicing had its hood up and Gary was under the hood checking the generator. For some reason, Jake accidentally put the car in gear and the car pinned Gary up against a workbench that was attached to the wall of the garage. Gary's body was under the hood, but his legs were hyperextended against the car's grill, crushing both legs against the workbench.

Gary was seriously injured and unable to work for a long period of time. He didn't have insurance and every day he stayed in the hospital was another day of bills he couldn't afford. Finally, Gary decided to go home, so he called a taxi and left the hospital. Jim Roach, Gary's brother, worked at the paper mill in Brainerd and worked at Gary's station when he was off duty at the mill. He kept the station going for a few months, while Gary was confined to his bed and couch at home. Beverly worked to earn extra money any way that she could, including selling pop bottles and waitressing with her mother. Gary will never forget the help he got from his brother—through Jim's sacrifice, he and Beverly were able to keep the service station.

Gary's recovery was slow and painful, but he began fishing once his body healed enough for him to be able to get around. He remembers going to Stony Brook—a little river that runs into Gull Lake—and fishing for trout. Throwing his bait in the river, he would lie on his back because it hurt too much to stand and fish. He only rose to his feet if he had a bite. Otherwise, he fished from his back.

Breezy Point Resort was looking for a guide and he took the job on a part-time basis—working around his other job. The resort had a big pontoon boat that Gary used for his guide trips.

One day, Gary's brother-in-law, Butch (Ted) Lavoie, a teenager at the time, told Gary about the pictures of the Nisswa Guides he had seen in the local newspaper. He said the photos made some of the fish look three times bigger than they really were.

"The guides are pretty good at promoting their business," said Butch, "but Gary, you can catch fish as good as those guys. You have to go to the bait shop and talk to Marv Koep. Tell him you are a good fisherman and you want to guide for him."

Gary was reluctant, but he finally decided to talk to Marv about a job. Gary recalled walking into the store, thinking that Marv probably saw him as a little hayseed from Merrifield who didn't know anything about fishing. (Gary grew up in Merrifield, just a few miles north of Brainerd.)

Marv recalled clearly the day Gary Roach walked into the store. Gary asked Marv about a job guiding and he also asked to borrow one of the little, green, fishing electronic sonar devices. Some of the guides at Koep's were using them and Gary wanted to see if they worked. During the conversation, Gary told Marv he grew up fishing on Pelican Lake and he knew it like the back of his hand. Marv loaned him the green sonar flasher and then didn't see him for several days. He began thinking that he was really stupid to let a total stranger use a new piece of sonar equipment and that it was probably the last he would see of the stranger and his equipment.

Around a week later, Gary stopped at the store, dropped off the flasher, and told Marv he was amazed at what he learned about the lake using the sonar device. Gary told Marv the bottom of the lake wasn't at all the way he thought it was. Marv was glad that Gary returned his green box fishing locator, but at the same time, he decided Gary seemed like a pretty nice guy. He didn't know much about his fishing skills, but he decided to hire Gary and see how well he could do as a guide.

Gary had recently finished cutting trees beneath the power lines all the way from Grand Rapids, Minnesota, to Riverton, a small town between Brainerd and Crosby. The company was going to Wisconsin to clear more trees and Gary decided that the work was too hard and he didn't really want to be in that business anymore. He sold his gas station, too, and went to work at Koep's.

Marv told him he needed to be voted in by the other guides as well as following the rules that they had established. Harry Van Doren, Cully Swenson, Max Slocum, Rod Romine, Dick Young, and the Lindners were the core of the group. The guides voted to accept Gary into the league in 1968. He was the second guide voted in by the original members—the first was Royal Karels. Gary remembers being paid $12.50 a day.

In those days, he fished with pretty big tackle. He just called his setup the "big rig." It had heavy line and a heavy sinker. He had a 7½ horse motor and a small boat. He also fished in a secret lake with no public landing. (As promised, the lake will not be mentioned in this book—he still fishes it from time to time.) He fished Pelican and other lakes, but would often sneak down to his secret lake when fishing was tough and many times came back with a limit of walleyes. The lake was only forty-five minutes from the store—only he, Cully, and a few others knew about it. He fished with the old motor and small boat for about one-and-a-half years. The second year he fished, he bought an old boat that came with an eighteen-horse motor and he figured he put more than six thousand hours on that motor before he got rid of it.

"When Gary Roach was a new guide, he took some customers to Pelican Lake," recalled Rod Romine. "He came back with four or five walleyes over his limit. Marv bought a bag of marbles and a small box and told Gary that when he went fishing, he had to take a marble out of the bag and put it into the box every time he caught a fish. 'And when all eighteen marbles are gone, quit!'"

Gary's old, cream-colored Cadillac always leaked oil or transmission fluid. The other guides knew where Gary fished because his car left oil all over the landing ramps.

Like most of the guides, Gary found work in the off season. He was a part-time bartender as well as a piano player in some of the small clubs in the Brainerd area. He and some friends formed a group and played in the winter months. One of the clubs they played was the Wagon Wheel in Merrifield. For a few years, Gary played in the band and bartended in the winter, and guided during the summer months. He enjoyed his years at Koep's—especially working with the Koep family—and he liked working with the guides that were there.

Marv Koep sponsored Gary in his first fishing tournament in 1970 or 1971. It was held on Lake Minnetonka, west of Minneapolis. Marv told Gary he was good enough to fish with the tournament anglers and gave him the money to enter the event. Gary met another angler at the tournament—whose name he has forgotten—who gave him good information about the lake. Gary ended up winning the tournament and he was interviewed on WCCO Radio in Minneapolis. It was his first major win and he became really excited about fishing tournaments. The tournament was a multi-species event and Gary was, by his own account, lucky enough to get into a big school of nice smallmouth bass that put him in the money. Gary remembers that event for another reason—he built and used his first livewell for his Lund boat, which allowed him to keep his fish alive and well until the end of the fishing contest.

Al Lindner had already become a polished tournament angler, but this was a new experience for Gary. He began traveling with Al and fished more tournaments. Gary Roach worked with the Lindners during the early years of their Lindy Tackle manufacturing company—making tackle and also promoting their products. In 1970 or early 1971, Gary quit working as a full-time guide and went to work for the Lindners. In his first year at Lindy, his salary was $6,500 a year.

(The Lindy Company was sold in 1973 to Ray-O-Vac. Ray-O-Vac owned the company until 1979 when the parent company, Electric Storage Battery, put the company up for sale. Nick Adams, one of Lindy's original founders, repurchased the company, moved to a new facility, and expanded the business.)

Gary Roach stayed with the Lindy Tackle Company through different owners and worked for the company for seventeen years. He also continued to work with the Lindners for much of this time, helping them with their new business—*In-Fisherman* magazine and the *In-Fisherman* television show.

Many guides have associations with boat companies and guides have also helped design boats and marine products. Few have been more influential than Gary Roach and the Lindners. Gary and Al began working with the Lund Boat Company in the early seventies. They still help design and promote Lund boats. Lund has a tournament boat that is called the Gary Roach edition. Randy Amenrud, another tournament angler, and Nick Adams also worked with Gary and the Lund staff in changing boat designs over the years.

Gary's relationship with Lund Boats went back to the early years his dad was fishing. His dad owned the family's first Lund boat. Gary began fishing out of a Lund boat when he was ten years old. He got his first new boat in 1970—the fiberglass 315 model. The guides used to call it the "Teddy Roosevelt" boat because it was such a rough rider—also President Roosevelt's nickname. It may not have been smooth riding, but at the time, it was the Cadillac of boats. Gary and Al spent a large amount of time with their promotional work in the south and they were impressed with the design of the bass boats they saw in bass tournaments. They brought ideas back to Lund that included features such as carpeted floors, swivel seats instead of wooden bench seats, and vinyl siding on the boats' interiors. Lanny Orvalla was with the Lund Boat Company during this period and he allowed the guides to have great flexibility in boat design. (Ron Lindner even recalls that Gary Roach had the first handle extension on a real tiller motor to make boat control easier.)

Gary traveled across the United States working in the fishing industry, fishing tournaments, and working with the Lindners and other companies after leaving the Nisswa Guides' League. He met many sportswriters, company representatives, and other tournament professionals over the years and he continues to promote fishing products, write fishing articles, and appear on various television programs.

Ron Schara, a writer for the *Minneapolis Star Tribune* and the producer of his own television show is one of Gary's good friends who also fished tournaments with Gary. Ron wrote the first newspaper article on Gary and Al fishing in tournaments. Gary credits Schara with helping to develop his career in the fishing industry.

Gary Roach has had a real impact on the fishing industry. He has helped design boats for Lund, designed fishing rods for Berkley Tackle Company, and created tackle for Normark Company and Northland Bait and Tackle Company. Gary has been dealt tough blows in life. He underwent open-heart surgery a few years ago and when I visited with him at a boat show recently, he had just gotten out of the hospital the night before, recovering from a gallstone attack. He has no plans to slow down or quit fishing tournaments. He is an amazing man—kind, humble, and caring—one who takes the time to talk to anyone who has an interest in visiting about fishing. He would give a needy person the shirt off his back. The fishing world is a better place because of Gary Roach. He is one of the legends of the Nisswa Guides' League.

Chapter Thirteen
Royal Karels

ROYAL KARELS JOINED the Nisswa Guides' League in 1969. He was the first guide voted in after the original group of guides. Born in Brainerd, Royal's mother divorced when he was only four years old. His grandparents ran a small resort on Shirt Lake (north of Bay Lake, which is east of Brainerd). When Royal was five years old, his mother sent him to his grandparents' resort to spend the summer. They were wonderful people and summers at the resort were a fantastic experience. From his first day at the resort, Royal immediately took to fishing. In the beginning, he learned to fish off the docks. By the time he was seven or eight, he was fishing from a small boat. His grandparents allowed him to fish from the boat as long as he stayed in view. They "cut him loose" when he was nine years old—allowing him to fish the whole lake. It was not a very wide lake, but it was long, narrow, and full of bass. He fished every morning and every evening all summer during his early years until he was sixteen or seventeen years old. (Except for college and his first teaching job in another community, Royal spent his entire life in Brainerd.)

Customers came from Ruttger's Resort on Bay Lake and rented boats from his grandparents—they had about fifteen boats. Royal also sold worms and frogs to the resort's customers. Many of the customers at his grandfather's resort were from the Kansas and St. Louis area and they liked using frogs for bait. By the time he was ten years old, Royal guided customers on the little lake. He had a pretty good feel for the lake and he knew where to catch nice bass. He rowed customers to his best spots and wouldn't charge anything, but most people gave him a buck or two—a lot of money to a ten-year-old boy. From then on, one of Royal's dreams was to be a fishing guide.

"I even thought of guiding when I was going to college," recalled Royal. "My first teaching job was in White Bear Lake, in 1959. I met Bill Erickson there, who wanted to guide, too. He never went on to guide, but he was an avid fisherman."

Bill and Royal hooked up with a couple of other fishing guides, Orin Tutt from Tutt's Bait Shop in Garrison on the shores of Mille Lacs Lake, and Terry Hanson, from the Deerwood area. The four began fishing and took a few guide trips out of Birkland's Resort on Bay Lake.

Royal began catching pretty nice bass on area lakes. He and Bill entered their catches in Brainerd-area bait shop contests and Marv Koep noticed that Royal won many weekly tournaments. He called Royal and asked him to stop by the store to see if he would be a candidate to guide at the shop. In 1969, Royal had an informal interview with Marv and Rod Romine, and then the other guides met and voted Royal into the league—the first member voted into the league by the original group of Nisswa Guides. Royal was thirty-one years old when he was invited to join and he guided with the league until 1978.

Many guides icefish during the off-season. Royal doesn't icefish occasionally—he icefishes nearly every day. Royal grew up learning to fish bass, but his passion now is to fish for whatever is biting. Like Al, Ron, Marv, and Gary, fishing is a passion, not a seasonal fad. Royal feels most customers don't care what they are fishing for—they just want action. He seldom fishes while guiding customers; he just runs the boat. Royal is a big fan of catch-and-release and he has promoted this practice for many years. He would like to see limits reduced on bass and walleyes, but he doesn't care what the limits are as long as people are willing to start releasing fish.

In his first year of guiding, he had a car-topper boat—a small aluminum Crestliner—very narrow and not very seaworthy. By today's standards, it looked more like a canoe. With a 9.9 horse Johnson motor, he made it through his first season in that little boat.

Royal has vivid memories of the early years in the Nisswa Guides' League.

"The younger guys had a lot of respect and admiration for the more senior members of the league," said Royal. "We paid attention to the things that Max, Harry, and Cully said, and we watched what they did on the lakes. Fish photos were really big then, because we never practiced catch-and-release techniques. We were very busy, but we also laughed a lot. My wife, Diane, reminded me that if she wanted to do something with the family, she had me cross out time on the guide chart so we could spend time together. Marv Koep was good at marketing and so were Al and Ron Lindner. Those guys did a fantastic job of promoting our business."

Royal recalled the way fishermen were intrigued with the new fish locators and splashguards for the back of the boats. In 1969, these items were not found on anyone else's boats. People stopped at the bait shop just to look at how the guide boats were organized inside and the different equipment with which they were outfitted. Royal also has a vivid memory of the pressures of coming back to the store with or without fish—wondering how he stacked up against the likes of Harry Van Doren, Cully Swenson, Max Slocum, Al Lindner, Ron Lindner, Ron Kristofferson, and the others.

"You knew that if you didn't produce, you wouldn't look very good against the competition," said Royal. "It made everyone better fishermen. People talk about pressure fishing tournaments today, but I don't think it could be more intense than fishing against fishermen as good as they were during that period of guiding."

Royal had assistance from all the guides when he began working with the Nisswa Guides' League, but Rod Romine really helped him learn some of the lakes that he hadn't fished before joining the league. Rod was an expert on the Whitefish Chain of lakes and Royal recalled one funny trip.

"I had my little car-topper boat with its 9.9 horse-powered motor and Rod and I went walleye fishing up on the Whitefish. I had a woman fishing with me who had a cheap little push-button reel. The wind was really blowing and I had all I could do to fish, while keeping the waves from coming into the boat. The woman in my boat hooked onto a monster. She couldn't even get it off the bottom of the lake. We fought this fish for twenty minutes and Rod is watching from his boat and came over to see what we had. Finally, the woman pulls up a monster tree branch and Rod laughed so hard, he nearly fell out of the boat. There is no way I would take a little boat out on the water in wind like that today. I can still hear Rod's laughter whenever I think of that story.

"Marv Koep used to laugh at me because I loved to fish bass and I would go out into the parking lot to see which way the wind was blowing, before I decided which lake I'd fish that day. I think I was one of the first guides to start leaping to a different lake if fishing was slow. Now it is pretty common to move to a different lake with the same customers if the fishing is slow on the first lake.

"One day, Dick Young came into the store with three customers after an all-day trip to Winnibigoshish. They all had long faces, so I asked what was wrong. They told me that they'd had an unbelievable day of fishing, got their eighteenth walleye, and just as Dick was putting the last fish on the stringer, the stringer slipped out of his hand, and they lost every fish! That happened to me once, so I knew how Dick felt that day!"

Royal's most forgettable trip happened when he was teamed with Ron Lindner while fishing on Gull Lake. He took his customers to the north end of the lake and Ron had his customers rigged to troll Bomber crankbaits along the shoreline of Steamboat Bay on the south end of the lake. Royal fished for four hours and caught two walleyes. He met Ron back on the south end of the lake. When Royal arrived, Ron and his customers where holding an unbelievable stringer of walleyes, northern pike, and largemouth bass. They had a fantastic catch. One of Royal's customers said, "Man, I wished we were fishing with that guy." Royal wanted to crawl under the nearest boat.

Another memorable fishing trip was when Royal took Marv and Judy Koep to the Mississippi River to fish for smallmouth bass. They only caught three fish on the trip, but they were trophies and they mounted all three fish.

His first year as a guide, Royal fished a lot with Gary Roach. Roach rented his boats at a resort on a small lake and Royal brought his little car-topper to the same lake. Gary showed Royal many new lakes to fish.

Carl Lowrance had invented a new electronic device called a sonar flasher in the late fifties. The Lindners had one and so did a few other fishermen, but they weren't very common. One day, when Carl came to Brainerd to visit the Lindners, Ron invited him over to his house for a spaghetti supper. Ron pointed to Royal and told Carl that Royal was one good fisherman.

"If you put that little sonar unit in his boat, watch out," said Ron. Royal was honored by Ron's kind words.

Royal had spent one summer on Gull Lake at the time his mother remarried, so he knew a little about Gull, but not much. When he began exploring the lake with the new sonar, he was amazed at what he saw. Al Lindner pointed out the key spots on the lake. The first guide trip Royal took on the lake was a winner. He was guiding a group on a pontoon and the whole group filled out on one of the spots Al had shown him.

On his second trip to Gull, he had two gentlemen who didn't know each other— one was an airline pilot and the other was an elderly gentleman. They came back to the shop with ten walleyes, averaging two to three pounds. He got those on another one of Al's spots. He especially remembers the trip because when he got back to the store, Harry Van Doren had gotten skunked. Al had a bad morning, too, and they couldn't believe that Royal had such good luck. Although his first two trips were really good ones, he found that he, too, would take his lumps as a fishing guide.

Royal soon learned that Al was a fabulous fisherman, and when it came to walleyes, Harry was the star. As far as Royal was concerned, when talking about guides, none could be compared to Harry. He remembers Harry telling him at one point that he guided for fifty-five consecutive years.

"My fondest memory of the Nisswa Guides is Harry Van Doren," said Royal. "He was a nice guy and a wonderful fisherman. When you think about what Harry did, it was absolutely amazing—he started in Arkansas and then moved to Texas. He really was a walleye fisherman. He knew the key spots and he learned them the hard way, with no technology. If I took one thing from all my years at the shop, it was learning how to guide from Harry. He was the epitome of what a guide could do and he was an excellent storyteller, too.

"Harry also had a great sense of humor. One summer, Harry talked to me about taking one of his customers fishing. It was a guy that Harry had some problems with over the years and Harry didn't want to fish with this guy anymore. He never told me what the problem was, but he asked if I would take the guy to fish the Mississippi River. He said, 'Just get him some walleyes and the guy will be happy.'

"So I took the guy to the river, just below the paper mill in Brainerd. After we'd fished for a short time, the gentleman caught a nice walleye. He was happy, holding the fish, talking about what a nice fish it was, and all of a sudden this green and brown and red stuff began coming out of a big pipe that drained into the river from the paper mill. The man screamed, 'Get me out of here!' I took him to shore and back to the shop. He jumped out of the truck, never paid me a dime, and drove off. I looked over by the store and there was Harry, laughing so hard he was on his knees and tears were running down his face. He thought that was the funniest thing he ever saw and he was glad he was not on the receiving end of it!"

Harry also got Royal interested in fishing for salmon in Lake Michigan. Royal had seen one of the salmon catches that Harry brought to the bait shop and decided to take that trip with his sons. Harry, who was in poor health, told Royal he would take him to the river where he caught the fish and he would show them how to catch salmon using a fly rod. Harry told Royal where to meet him on the river. Harry walked the riverbank and Royal and the boys would float the river in the boat and meet at the designated spot.

Royal was up early in the morning, put the boat in the river, and went to the spot where Harry told him to meet—expecting to wait until Harry could find his way along the riverbank. Royal and the boys got there, only to hear a voice holler, "What took you so long?" It was Harry, nearly too sick to fish, but already on the spot and ready to go.

"The best guides are the ones who can go out and entertain people," recalled Royal, "sometimes getting no fish, but the people want them back the next year anyway. That was Max Slocum—his specialty was telling jokes. He could go out all day and entertain customers. He came back from one trip and had a much bigger tip than Harry and Cully, but he never caught a fish on the trip. Max was a meat inspector as well as an unlicensed veterinarian. He was a very intelligent guy and he fished a lot with Harry and Cully Swenson.

"I learned a lot from Al Lindner about how to figure out a lake and I learned a lot from Gary Roach, too. Structure is much more productive than fishing shoreline. I learned a lot about North Long Lake from Al, who learned a lot about that lake from Papa Potthoff. Papa knew a lot about North Long Lake, too, but I don't know how he learned it so well—I guess from spending so many years on the water." (Interestingly enough, Al considers Royal Karels to be one of the best multi-species anglers in the Brainerd-Nisswa area.)

"Gull Lake is my favorite now," said Royal. "It's a good, all-around fishing lake. I wish I could take more time to fish northern pike in the fall, because it is spectacular. There are some really big fish in Gull. Mille Lacs Lake is right up there, but I have fifteen lakes that I fish on a regular basis and I won't mention the names of the ones I really like.

"I learned almost all the lakes on my own and found most of my good spots by going into bait shops, little country stores, and bars. I fished the lakes and then kept the information to myself. Many of the lakes are small and can't take the pressure of lots of fishermen. For instance, I would hear guys talk about the good crappie fishing at farmer Jones's lake and off I would go. I still find new spots to fish on the big lakes all the time. Those little walleyes hide out all over the lakes.

"I think the Nisswa Guides' League has had an impact on many other parts of the state. I have met people in other areas of Minnesota who started guiding because they got to know Rod, Al, Ron, and others. I can't prove this, but I believe that this league is the oldest in the state.

"Marv Koep also got me connected with fishing companies. When he hooked me up with Lund Boats, I got the use of a free boat through the summer. Harry introduced me to a lure company from Arkansas that made crankbaits. The owner used to send me cases of crankbaits every year. Marv was always very generous to the guides. He handed out a lot of praise in my direction. Ron and Al really helped me, too, when it came to connection with tackle companies. I did very little of that on my own.

"Gary Roach and I did a fair amount of work for Lund Boats. Gary still designs features for their boats and he and I did a convention for Lund in Wisconsin. Eventually, Lund began featuring Gary and the Lindners and I faded out of that market. It was a very exciting period to be a guide. I took great pride in it and loved every minute. In the late seventies, my oldest son, Sam, guided for a couple of years at

Koep's, too. It was a real treat to guide with my son. Now he teaches school in Bemidji and guides every summer in Alaska.

"I guided two different couples on their honeymoons. One was Mark Dorn, the tournament director for In-Fisherman. And once while guiding another couple, I had something in my mouth, a fishing line or a cigar or something, and we had just started fishing using Lindy Rigs. This was one of my first years guiding and the young lady asked me what I do besides guiding. I told her I was sixth-grade teacher, only I didn't say sixth-grade teacher. I said, 'I teach sixth.' Since I had something in my mouth, she thought I said, 'I teach sex,' but I didn't realize I said it that way. We fished together again the next day. While we talked, she realized I had said I taught sixth grade, not sex, so she began pounding her husband on the side of his head. He laughed so hard he couldn't stop and I finally figured out what was going on. The lady was really embarrassed. She whacked him about five times before he quit laughing."

"I also guided Babe Winkelman, who was living in St. Cloud at the time. He was really interested in learning how to fish with plastic worms.

"Somewhere along the line I became good friends with the Fellegys—the best guides I ever knew on Mille Lacs Lake. I fished mostly with Joe, who was one of the premiere guides on big Mille Lacs. He doesn't guide much today. He spends most of his time writing outdoor news for papers and magazines. I used to do a lot of northern pike fishing on Mille Lacs. I have fished the lake for more than forty years. I am probably one of the only guides that fishes the lake without a GPS system. Joe taught me how to fish the mud flats on Mille Lacs. Years ago, he was the first one I saw who went out and fished the flats. I still find the flats by using landmarks and other structures on the lake.

"I will tell you an interesting story about Harry Van Doren's fishing skill. We used to guide a lot at Potthoff's Resort. There were five or six guides at a time, working mornings and afternoons. Our fee was reasonable and the lodging rates at Potthoff's were always reasonable. People almost always took a guide. Harry was the most sought-after guide. One day, I ended up with two doctors—a father-and-son team. They wanted to fish smallmouth on Lake Hubert, so I asked Harry where I should go. He told me to go to the girl's camp bar and fish in fifteen to twenty feet of water with a Lindy Rig and a leech. Man, did we catch smallmouth! The fish averaged three to four pounds. He just knew where to go. Another time, I had a trip with Harry on the Fourth of July—it was blazing hot. I had been fishing bass, that was my preference then, and Marv always tried to line me up with folks looking for bass. On this day, these folks wanted walleyes. Gull Lake is not usually a good spot to look for walleyes on a hot July afternoon, but these guys wanted to fish walleyes on Gull Lake. Harry told me to get Lindy Little Joe spinners, put a weight about three feet from the hook, put on half a nightcrawler, and troll in eight feet of water on the south side of the rock pile. We absolutely killed the walleyes. There was no wind, it was blazing hot, and I never had that happen again. Harry had a knack for knowing what to do.

"Gary Roach and I fished Pelican together a lot. He was an innovator—always trying some new technique. He went ahead of me, trolling spinner baits, and I came behind, casting for bass. He always wanted to try for walleyes and I was trying for bass. I remember fishing with Marv and Gary on Gull. If I got a hit, I'd set the hook right away. When Gary got a hit, he fed the line for two minutes—he had a lot of patience. I think I am a patient fisherman, but I still like to cast rather than fish with a line over the side of the boat."

Royal Karels may have retired from teaching, but he has no plans to retire from fishing or guiding. He is one of the best fishermen in the Brainerd-Nisswa area. He is also known for his great sense of humor. Marv Koep told me that Royal had a habit of being late to the store. One day he was about forty-five minutes late and the customers were really getting upset. Finally, Royal walked into the store and Marv asked why he was late. Royal said his car wouldn't start. Marv dropped the subject and let him go fishing. That night when Royal came back to the store, Marv asked why his car wouldn't start. "Nobody was in it!" said Royal.

Royal Karels still guides, he icefishes nearly every day in the winter, and he loves every minute of his time on the water. He is truly one of the legends of the Nisswa Guides' League.

Chapter Fourteen
Ron "Crash" Kristofferson

I HAVE KNOWN Ron Kristofferson since our days together at Brainerd's Washington High School. Ron is colorful, controversial, and one of the best storytellers I have ever met. He is also a darn good fisherman. Of all the guides that I interviewed for this book, his recollection of the past is the most vivid and perhaps the most entertaining.

After Ron graduated from Brainerd, he joined the Marine Corps. He served in Viet Nam and received a Purple Heart. Shortly after being discharged, he was involved in a serious motorcycle accident and spent much of the summer of 1968 in the hospital. The next year, he went back to college. While visiting a local watering hole in the spring of 1969, he met Al Lindner. Al was fairly new to the Brainerd area and Ron had never heard of him. Al was a young kid, just out of school, much like Ron, and they began talking. Ron still remembers the conversation.

"Well, I have to go," said Al, on a Sunday afternoon in early May. "I've got some people that I'm taking fishing."

"Really?" said Ron.

"Yeah, some people want to go crappie fishing and I am a fishing guide. My brother, Ron, and I came up here to start a fishing service, so I take people fishing."

"What do you do with these people?" asked Ron. Al explained that he took people fishing, tried hard to catch fish, and they paid him when the trip was done. "You take people fishing and they pay you to do that?" said Ron. "That sounds like a good deal. How does a guy get into something like that?" From the first meeting, Ron developed a friendship with Al.

Later that spring, Ron purchased a brand-new boat, motor, and trailer. His goal was to find a way to get into the guiding business. Al Lindner had just bought his first new boat, a Lund model 315. Ron was so impressed with the boat that he bought the same equipment. The cost for the whole package set him back about $600.

Ron began putting out the word that he could catch fish and that he was interested in fishing with the Nisswa Guides' League. He thinks Nick Adams, his father-in-law at the time, put in a good word for him with Marv Koep. (Nick later became one of the founders of the Lindy Little Joe Tackle Company with Al and Ron Lindner.) Nick told Ron to see Marv about getting into the league as a guide, so Ron stopped at the bait shop. Marv said he had a group of three from Indiana that wanted to fish the next day and he needed a guide to take them. He asked Ron if he could go and Ron said he could. They caught their limit of eighteen walleyes. Ron still has pictures of the catch. The writing on the photo says they were caught on Gull Lake, but they were really caught on another small lake in the area. (It was common practice in those days, as it is today, not to disclose the real lake where fish were caught, to keep others from jumping in to the hotspots.)

He picked up a few more trips. Before the summer was over, he was pretty busy as a back-up guide to the main core of guides at the store. He earned $12.50 for a half-day trip—then it went to $15 or $17 for a half-day trip. Ron spent much of the first summer fishing for northern pike. The middle of summer often marks a tough time to catch walleyes. Harry Van Doren used to tell Ron that he could have all the northern and bass trips he wanted. Harry fished bass all winter and was not interested in spending time fishing for bass or northern in the summer. Northern fishing in the late sixties was pretty good, both in size and quality, so Ron made fishing northern pike his specialty. There were many days when the jig and minnow bite on Pelican Lake and other area lakes was excellent.

Marv Koep asked Ron if he had ever tried spoon-plugging for pike. When Ron said no, Marv gave him a couple of Peerless 209 reels and 944 True Temper reels with prestretched, seventeen-pound monofilament line. The line was also color-coded.

"We used to work the shore breaks with that heavy line, pulling spoons, with two people in the boat. Sometimes we wouldn't go thirty yards and we had a fish on the line. On good days, we had our limit of pike in an hour and a half. I left the store at 7 A.M. and returned by 9 A.M. I fished bass, too, but I really liked fishing northern pike. When the bite was on, I focused on walleyes. Royal Karels and Gary Roach were very good bass fishermen and when the walleye bite was slow, they spent a lot of time catching bass. Back then, few guides fished walleyes in midsummer. If you were smart, you didn't spend time trying to get walleyes to bite. It was too hard to make a living at it.

"I remember one day, coming into Minnewawa Lodge—we ate at the lodge and we had a table set up just for the guides—there was an area to pull up your boat if you didn't catch any fish. It was the 'skunk hole.' If you parked your boat by the skunk hole, everyone from the lodge knew you had a bad day. Well, I pulled into the lodge and Max Slocum and Harry Van Doren were sitting in the lot. Harry asked me how I did. I told him I got my limit. He asked me how much money I got and I told him I had my fee, plus a ten-dollar tip. Harry asked Max how much he made fishing walleyes that day and Max said he got his fee and that was it. 'Well Max,' said Harry, 'maybe we better start fishing those snakes.'" ("Snakes" is slang for northern pike.)

Ron recalls that part-time guides had a tough time catching fish because they only fished one or two days a week. It was hard to know where the fish were, at what depths, and what presentations were working.

Ron worked as a guide through a few summers and graduated from college in 1974. He took a job in the retail business, but didn't really like it. He got a management job in retail in January, but by the time spring rolled around, he was itching to guide again that summer. The next year he took a job as co-manager of the Pamida store in Brainerd. The next spring he quit that job, too, so he could guide. The guide bug was strong for Ron and it was hard for him to devote his energies to another line of work.

Ron fondly remembers the early years with the Nisswa Guides. "We had a real sense of friendship—we all got along well and helped each other. I remember later when we added some of the other guides, such as Bert Lindberry. The league changed a little bit as new people were added and some of the older guides were not in favor of adding new guides, but we had too much business not to get more help." Bobby Collette joined around 1972 and then a few other guides were added to the business.

"Harry Van Doren was a mentor to me. He was a special man and he always called me 'kid.' I really respected Harry and I think he respected me, too. I remember the first year I was guiding—I was doing well on a small lake in the Nisswa area. It was only a nine hundred-acre lake, but the bite was really hot. The other lakes were not producing much. Harry would come into the shop at the end of the day, grab a can of pop from the cooler, go out to his truck and pour a little 'bump' into the pop, drink it, and go home.

"Harry knew I had been getting fish for a few days and so he is sitting on a stool, drinking his drink. 'Kid,' he said, 'I have a good customer coming up tomorrow to fish walleyes. He has been with me two years in a row and we have been skunked. You're on a good bite, could you help me out tomorrow?'

"I told Harry where I was fishing. It was a little lake he had never fished—he didn't even know how to get on the lake. So I gave him directions and told him where to go. I told him he needed four-wheel drive to get into the lake and I mapped out exactly where he needed to go. Harry said he would never go to the lake again without asking. So the next day, Harry comes into the parking lot of the store with a big smile on his face—he had a limit of eighteen walleyes. He was my friend for life. In fact, I went to work for the State of Minnesota in 1974, and when Harry headed south to fish for the winter, he had lunch with me before going and he stopped when he got back in the spring. He always wanted me to come south with him and fish the big Sam Rayburn Reservoir, but it never worked out for me with family and my job.

"One of the new guides that Harry did not like in the beginning was Bert Lindberry." [This was verified by Bert himself in his interview with me.] "Bert would tailpipe Harry. He followed him all around the lake, learning the spots that Harry fished. Harry got very upset with Bert. The best advice that I received when I began fishing was from my father-in-law, Nick Adams. Nick told me that whatever you do, don't get Harry mad at you. Don't follow him around on the lake—if he is fishing on a bar, you go to another bar. I thought that was good advice and I never followed Harry around like some of the new guides. Harry was such an expert on Gull, the Whitefish Chain, Pelican, and North Long that it was understandable why the new guys wanted to learn the lake from him. I really liked to fish Gull, Pelican, and the Whitefish Chain, but I also had a lot of small lakes that I fished that I knew from growing up in the Brainerd and Nisswa area.

"I don't remember this guy's name anymore, but one day I had a trip on Pelican Lake. The customer worked for the Mallory Corporation out of St. Louis. I picked him up at Breezy Point Resort and he wanted to fish northern pike. I pulled up to the resort and the guy looked like a guide's nightmare! He had a huge bundle of Fenwick rods with Ambassador 5000 and 6000 reels and an old Kennedy tackle box that folded out, gunnel to gunnel.

"He got into my boat. I said that I understood that he wanted to fish northern pike. He said that he did. I said perhaps he should use my equipment because it was all set up for pike fishing with Bomber lures. The Bomber lures were really doing well for pike and I had good colors that really produced some nice fish. I said I was using Noble trolling line that worked well. The guy said no, he would use his equipment because it was state-of-the-art. He opened up his tackle box and it looked like a portable bait shop, but there was not one Bomber lure in the box.

"I could not convince this guy to try my equipment, so we started fishing. We weren't fishing twenty minutes and 'bang,' I got a five-pound northern. We went a little farther and 'bang' another northern. This went on until I had about a dozen pike and he had none. He just sat in the boat—changing lures, changing colors, and finally said, 'Do you think I could borrow one of those Bomber lures?' I said yes, but you gotta put it on my pole. He used my rig and caught a walleye, then a few bass, and then some northern pike. He couldn't believe how good that lure was. We ended up having one heck-of-a-day fishing.

"That was in July. In October, I was getting ready to go somewhere and a UPS truck pulled into the yard—the driver delivered three huge boxes. On the side of the box was stamped: Bomber Bait Company, Gainesville, Texas. There was a letter in the box addressed to me, and it said, 'Dear Ron, those Bomber Baits were so good that I quit my job in St. Louis to become the national sales manger for Smithwick Bait Company, which is the parent company for the Bomber Bait Company.' The letter went on to say that I would never have to buy another Bomber as long as I was guiding. Later, that gentleman went to work for Lindy Little Joe. I don't remember his name, but a few years later, he was killed in a car accident. About two years later, the fish quit hitting on those Bombers and we had to start fishing with different baits. I believe I still have about twenty-five dozen of those baits at home."

Ron continued with his storytelling. "I gotta tell you about Joe Masik. Joe retired from the meat business. He sold meat to restaurants—McDonald's was a big customer of his. He told me he sold five thousand pounds of meat in one day to McDonald's. Joe lived in Racine, Wisconsin, and he decided to retire on Gull Lake. He got to know the area from selling meat to customers in the Brainerd and Nisswa area and fell in love with the lakes. He was nuts about fishing and stopped at the store all the time. One day, he was talking to Marv Koep and wanted to know the best way to learn how to fish Gull Lake. Marv told him the best suggestion he had was to refer him to me because I would take the time to show him the lake. Marv said that Harry Van Doren was the best fisherman on Gull, but if he hired him, he would just go fishing—if you hire Ron he will help you learn the lake.

"Joe was a regular at the store for many years. He had plenty of money, but he told Marv that he would clean the toilets every day—all he wanted in return was a discount on tackle and bait. That was the arrangement they agreed to and every day Joe came in and cleaned toilets and hung out with the guys.

"Joe hired me to guide him several days, but I still remember the first trip we had together. He asked what we were going to fish with and I told him we would use nightcrawlers. Joe pulled out a bar of Virgil Ward soap and asked if I would wash my hands before I put a nightcrawler on his hook. He had heard that walleyes don't like the smell of humans, so he didn't want the worms to stink. I told him I had a better idea. He could use the soap and put on his own crawlers and I would scratch my nose, itch my butt, smoke my cigar, and see if it made any difference. He agreed. I dropped my line in the water, went about twenty feet, and caught about a four-pound walleye. I flipped the ashes off the end of my cigar and asked Joe what he thought so far. He reached into his bag, grabbed the bar of soap, and threw it into the lake. 'Enough said,' he replied. That was the end of that discussion.

"Joe became a good friend of mine as well as the other guides. He was a great guy and loved to fish. He helped the Minnesota Department of Natural Resources to discover that walleyes spawned on the north end of Gull Lake, in the area we call the Narrows. He came into the store one day with his paper graph and showed us the big arcs of fish he had marked in shallow water. I asked him if he was sure they were walleyes. He said yes, he had dropped a jig in the water and pulled out a four- or five-pound walleye. The guides caught a lot of fish in the shallows that year. When word got out, everybody started whacking the walleyes in the Narrows. Joe was concerned about the impact this had on the walleye-spawning population and he worked with the DNR to close fishing in the Narrows during the spawning period. That area is closed every spring now, in part because of the work Joe did with the Lake Shore Rod and Gun Club and the DNR. Joe has passed on, but he was a fixture around the Nisswa Guides for many years.

"One of the funniest stories I remember about Harry Van Doren involved two businessmen from St. Louis. I remember their names, but I am not sure about the spelling. One was Ollie Guttmann, owner of a trucking company and the other was Bob Meyer. Meyer had a connection to the Crystal Sugar Company. They were big-money people and they hired Harry once or twice each summer. They loved to harass Harry and gave him a hard time. They told him that they wanted to fish for large-mouth bass and Harry said that he would not fish for those carp. Any fool could catch a carp and he didn't want anything to do with it. On this morning, Ollie and Bob gave Harry a line of crap about wanting to fish bass. I was fishing that morning with a group from Potthoff's who liked to party, so I figured they would be a little late. Ollie and Bob finally got Harry to agree to fish bass, but he said, 'Here are the rules. The limit for you two is twelve bass. We get twelve bass in the boat and we are done. Agreed?' Bob and Ollie agreed and headed out to get in Harry's vehicle. Harry looked at me and said, 'I'll fix them!'

"An hour later, around 8 A.M., my customers had not arrived yet. I looked out the store window and here came Harry's Jeep Wagoneer. Harry walked into the store, sat down, and said, 'Well, I fixed them!' A few minutes later Ollie and Meyer walked in, not in very good moods."

"'That damn Harry,' said Ollie. 'He took the boat off the trailer and we get in the boat. He starts his trolling motor, makes about fifteen casts, and has twelve bass in the boat. We never even had our lines ready to fish yet, and he says we're done fishing—anybody can catch a carp!'

"Not many people realized it," said Ron, continuing with his story, "but Harry fished bass all winter down on the Sam Rayburn Reservoir. At one time, he held the record for fish size caught on that lake. I think the limit was fifteen bass per person and he had forty-five bass that weighed around five pounds each (three in the party). It was an unbelievable catch. Harry was also the national bass-fishing champion in 1967. So the guy could really fish bass.

"I have a great Bobby Collette story—it happened before Bobby had his accident and became paralyzed. Fishing was pretty tough, especially walleye fishing. We were fishing together on Sylvan Lake with John Furrow, an old customer of mine. John's wife was twin sister to the wife of the other gentleman. John asked me to take the ladies in my boat and the husbands would fish with Bobby. This was a period when we didn't have livewells in our boats, but I had a cooler that I carried to keep the fish from getting too hot. We put our boats in the water and started fishing and one of the ladies landed a nice, two- to three-pound walleye. Bobby and the guys came by, saw it, and said, 'Nice fish.'

"I asked the ladies if they wanted to have some fun with their husbands and show them how good they were at catching walleyes. I would put the same fish back on their lines and every time the men's boat went by, we would pretend that we caught a new walleye. The ladies thought that was a great idea, so I put the fish on one of their lines and every ten minutes or so, we pretended to catch another fish. The guys began asking what we were using for bait, how deep we were fishing, and all kinds of other questions. Pretty soon they got a little irate. We pulled the same fish in eleven times—it was getting pretty beat up. Bobby was a little irate, too, they did not have a bite, did not catch a fish, period.

"Finally, the trip was over and we pulled up to the landing on the north side of the lake. Bobby came over and says, 'Geez, what were you using? How did you get those fish to bite?' I said the ladies just had the touch—it was unbelievable how they could catch walleyes.

"Finally, Bobby leaned into my boat, opened the cooler, and looked inside to find one, white-colored, beaten-up walleye with the hook and line still in its mouth. He yelled for the husbands to look at the catch. They looked in the cooler and just roared! They had been had. They had a great sense of humor about it and thought that was one of the funniest things that had ever happened to them. Johnny lived on Pine Beach Peninsula on Gull Lake and he told that story to his neighbors for years.

"Another time, Bobby Collette and I were fishing together with a party. They were friends and needed two boats for the fishing trip on Whitefish Lake. Bobby was taking a little nap in his truck—waiting for the customers to arrive—with his feet stuck out the window. I went behind the truck, unhooked his boat trailer, and put a piece of wood under the trailer tongue to keep it level. The customers arrived and Bobby jumped out of the truck, raring to go. He planned on being the first one to the boat ramp. That was part of the deal—be the first one to the ramp. Harry had already gone, so he had beaten both of us, and Max Slocum was already on his way, too.

"Bobby loaded his pickup with his half of the party's gear and I loaded the other half into my truck. I got out of the driveway first and Bobby was right on my tail. He didn't know it, but his boat was still parked in front of the store. I got to the Bertha Lake Marina first and jumped out of my truck to watch what would happen next. Bobby looked behind him, to back in his boat, but it was not there. 'My God,' he said. 'My boat came off!' One of the guys in the truck said, 'No you left it at the store!' Bobby said, 'What do you mean I left it at the store?' The guy said, 'We thought it was odd that you put all that stuff in your boat and took off without it, but we thought you had another plan in mind.' Bobby figured out that I pulled a trick on him. He didn't say anything, but hurried back and got his boat—about a fifteen-minute drive.

"Three days later, I was fishing with a husband-and-wife team on Gull Lake. It was windy and the water was rough. I started taking a little water into the boat. We didn't have bilge pumps then, so the water had to be scooped out by hand. Water began to cover the bottom of the boat, and all of a sudden, the woman let out a blood-curdling scream. I looked down and there was a dead cat floating out from behind the gas cans! You can imagine how bad it looked—it was a road-killed cat, as flat as a pancake!

"I came into the store at noon that day and there was Bobby Collette. He asked me what I caught that morning. I said it was kind of slow, but I caught one catfish. Bobby got a big grin on his face and I knew he had gotten even with me for the trick I had pulled on him a few days earlier."

Ron recalls his days with the guide league as a period of great fun and wonderful friendships. He was impressed with what good fishermen the guides were and how they helped each other become successful. He remembers Royal Karels as an outstanding bass fisherman. After the Lindners left, he thought that Gary Roach was the best multi-species angler he had ever seen. Ron had great experiences as a guide and met some wonderful people. He fished with Ralph Emery, of country music fame; Shot Gun Red, from the Grand Ole Opry; and many other celebrities during his tenure with the league.

Retired from his work as an employee for the State of Minnesota, Ron still guides in the Brainerd area. Most fall days, when the walleye bite begins getting hot, I see him on the water. He spends a part of his winter months in Florida fishing with his good friend, Ron Lindner.

Chapter Fifteen
John Wetrosky

JOHN WETROSKY NEVER GREW UP thinking he would be connected to the fishing business, yet he became acquainted with some of the biggest names in the fishing industry by being in the right place at the right time.

John grew up in Iowa, and with his family, spent about twenty years vacationing on Pelican Lake. His folks loved the area so much that they bought the Hawkeye Resort on Jones Bay of Pelican Lake, which they still own today. John wanted to make a living in the outdoors. He didn't know what that would be, but he loved hunting, fishing, and any activity that involved nature. He graduated from college at twenty-two, with a degree in wildlife management.

In May 1970, Marv asked John if he wanted to work part-time at the store while he looked for a job with his new degree. John worked eighty hours the first week. Marv was still doing a huge business, selling minnows to Crane Lake. One of John's first jobs was hauling minnows to Crane Lake once a week. It was a five-hour drive one way—it took all day to haul the minnows up north. John recalls hauling thousands of gallons of minnows a day to the distribution point on Crane Lake. He often picked up minnows from Marv's brothers—Les, Phil, and Joe—in Urbank, about a two-hour drive from Nisswa. Sometimes there were twenty trucks lined up to get bait in Urbank. Marv was a stickler for keeping fresh minnows and he wanted the best-looking bait in his tanks at the store.

While John was helping his folks at their resort, he got the idea of selling tackle at the lodge. When he talked to Marv about selling fishing tackle from the resort, Marv said he had a better idea. Let Marv sell the tackle from his store, and in turn, Marv would refer customers to the Hawkeye Resort. John and Marv agreed. From then on, the tackle business stayed at the store and customers looking for lodging were referred to Hawkeye Resort.

When John began working at the store, there was quite a collection of guides:

Harry Van Doren, Max Slocum, Cully Swenson, Al and Ron Lindner, Bert Lindberry, Bobby Collette, Ron Kristofferson, Dick Young, Royal Karels, and Rod Romine. John worked at the store for eight years, much of that period as the store manager. He guided sometimes when there was a greater demand for guides than there were guides available, but John had no burning desire to be a guide. He would rather fish alone on his free time or go fishing with friends. John married Jackie Silbaugh, a young woman from Pine River, in 1975. They still own and operate Silbaugh's Department Store in Pine River.

1970 was a transition year at Nisswa Bait and Tackle. The Lindners were beginning to make fishing tackle—John remembered Rod Romine and Gary Roach helping the Lindners assemble tackle in the basement of Ron's home. Electronic devices were emerging as important tools in fishing and tackle was becoming more sophisticated. The guiding business was robust. Area resorts were doing well and the bait-and-tackle business was good.

John has many memories of the guides. He recalled the Lindners as great providers of information about fishing to anyone who asked for and needed help; Harry loved fishing for walleyes, but he hated fishing for bass because he did that all winter; Cully fished bass and walleyes; Royal loved fishing bass; and Gary Roach fished anything that would bite a hook. The guides were especially helpful to each other and John remembered how they teamed up to make everyone's fishing trips as successful as possible.

When John began working at the store, a half-day guide trip was $17 and a full-day trip cost $35. By 1978, his last year at the store, the prices had doubled. Guides only took two people in a boat during that era because most boats were not designed to fish more than three people. During John's years of employment, the biggest fish to be registered at the store were a fourteen-pound, six-ounce walleye and a twenty-eight-pound northern pike.

There were not too many other guides in the area at that time. John sold bait to Clarence Luther and Gene Shapinski, but when big conventions came to area resorts, it was a scramble to find extra guides to help out. John recalled that from time to time some local residents would get mad at the guides—saying they put too much pressure on the local lakes—but for the most part, the guides were accepted as a business that was good for the local economy.

Like others, John was also amazed at Harry Van Doren. "Harry fished Pelican at night—before any electronics were available. He marked some of his fishing areas by placing lighted lanterns on top of mud and sandbars. Then he trolled on and around the bars catching walleyes. He knew the lakes so well—it was unbelievable. When other boats came by, he slid off the bars, and made it look like he was fishing in deeper water. Guides like Harry had years of knowledge about the lakes that tourists never had time to learn—they were amazed at his knowledge of fishing. Harry was working on one lung before he got really sick and died, but he fished on days when some of us wondered if he would get back alive. When one fished with Harry, it was on his terms. He was the boss in the boat. People used the bait he selected, fished the way he told them to, and it usually paid off with nice fish. Harry liked to have a daily shot of Jim Beam whiskey. He went out to his truck after his afternoon trip and poured one drink of whiskey before going home. One drink was all he usually ever drank."

John and Harry got to be such good friends that Harry even went with John and Jackie on their honeymoon to Michigan. It was a tough time because Harry was having serious health problems, but he toughed it out and they had a great trip together.

"Harry knew just about everyone who was an important part of the fishing industry at that time—Carl Lowrance, a great guy; Bill Norman, a tackle manufacturer; Tom Mann; and Forrest Wood, who designed and built Ranger Boats. Carl Lowrance loved to cook and he stopped in and invited guys to come over, just so he could cook."

John recalled an occasion when Dick Young came back from a trip with a stringer of walleyes and each fish weighed between two-and-one-half to four pounds. John was amazed at the size of the fish and Dick shrugged it off, like it was no big deal. "Dick was a good fisherman, but so humble, it was hard to know if he had a good day or a bad day on the water."

According to an account that Harry told John, Pelican Lake was not a great walleye lake in the fifties and sixties, but it got better over the years. Billy Fawcett, owner of Breezy Point and a Hollywood personality, privately stocked walleyes in the lake to try to enhance the walleye fishing.

John met many other celebrities at the store; Tony Dean, of television fame; Jerry McInnis, from the Eagle Claw Company; Babe Winkelman; television personality, Mac Davis; Chuck Ross of WCCO Radio; Buck Perry; Ron Schara; and many others.

John did some early work with the Lindners when they started *In-Fisherman*, a magazine that eventually became a national publication, and later evolved into a national television series. The Lindners felt it was important to educate anglers about fishing, so much of the early work by the new company was spent putting on fishing seminars. The first seminars, which were conducted at Cragun's Resort on Gull Lake, were often attended by as many as 50 to 150 people. John taught classes on using depth finders. Later, the seminars were held at other area resorts and the local college. At one of the seminars, John met a young fellow named Dan Sura. Dan eventually went to work for the Lindners, and he, too, became an outstanding fisherman and on-screen television personality.

Another young fisherman that John recalled working with at Koep's for a short time was Jeff Zernov. Jeff later worked for the Lindners and then began his own business making Zercom depth finders and Aqua-Vu underwater cameras.

"Papa Potthoff had a secret recipe for cooking fish that was really good. I don't think anybody found out what was in the recipe, but Gary Roach came close when he marketed his own recipe years later. Gary is one of the few guides that cooked rock bass. Nearly everyone else threw them away as junk fish, but not Gary. The way he cooked rock bass, people really liked them. He called them 'Pelican Lake Trout.' For years, the guides met at Potthoffs for lunch and often provided the fish for the noon meal. Gary often provided Pelican Lake Trout.

"All the guides overslept, every one of them. It was my job to get them to the store on time. The first trip of the day was 7 A.M. and the second shift was 3 P.M. I spent a lot of my career calling guys at home and getting them out of bed. Harry talked people out of going fishing when the fish weren't biting. He didn't think they should waste their time and money when the bite was off."

John recalled that Nisswa Bait and Tackle was the only place for anglers to buy the early, unique fishing products, such as Fenwick Rods, Lowrance depth finders, and Mister Twister plastic fishing baits. For a while, Marv Koep had exclusive rights to Mister Twister products, but later Burger Brothers got into the product.

Early Shell Lake boats later became Lund Boats. They were the best fishing boat on the market until the mid-seventies, when Lund and other companies began making smoother-riding V hulls. Crestliner and Ranger Boats also made bigger boats and smoother-riding boats. Guides began spending more time on the big waters of Mille Lacs and Leech because it had become safer to fish from the bigger rigs.

John had a knack for remembering names and he established many lifelong friendships while working at the store.

"In the early seventies, the opening day of fishing at Nisswa Bait and Tackle Shop was really something. Cars were parked on both sides of Highway 371 for a half-mile in both directions. We hired guys to direct traffic, so we could keep everything moving. It was the place to be on the opening weekend. We had so much bait in those days that a power outage would kill thousands of gallons of minnows. We also sold thousands of leopard frogs. One day, when Kevin Koep was sent to catch frogs, the mosquitoes were so thick he could hardly see to catch frogs. He got some mosquito spray and sprayed everything in sight. The next morning, all the frogs were dead. A lot of the fisherman in those days only fished with frogs, especially many of the anglers from the south. I also remember when guys began fishing with mud puppies or salamanders, as they are most often called.

"Ron Kristofferson was fishing with a ten-year-old boy who whined a lot. Walleye fishing was slow, so Ron was going to try to catch the party some northern pike. The boy kept asking to fish for walleyes, so finally Ron said, 'Let out ten more feet of line.' When the boy did, Ron said, 'Okay, now you're fishing walleyes.' The boy was happy!

"I recall that Royal Karels was the first guide to ask people to release fish. He knew the resource was limited and felt he had a responsibility to protect the fish in area lakes. He always came into the store looking like he had just gotten up. His shirt-tail was always out and his shoes were never tied. Royal was a funny guy. One summer day, the fish were not biting anywhere. He met his customers at the store, got out the biggest minnows we had in the bait tank, bought some huge bobbers, and headed out the door. I asked him what he was fishing for and he said they were going lake trout fishing on Trout Lake. I knew Royal had never fished lake trout. Later that day, he returned to the store with his customers and not a single fish, but those folks had a great time fishing with Royal. They spent all afternoon watching the monster minnows pulling the huge bobbers around and waiting for a huge trout to bite.

"Max Slocum was a great storyteller. Many times, customers came back from fishing with Max, and no fish in the boat, but they said it was one of the best times they ever had fishing. He was a very entertaining man—folks loved to fish with him.

"One of my best fishing stories happened one day when I opened the store. We were really busy and Marv overbooked the guides. A party came to meet their guide on the afternoon shift and there was no guide available. The customer was a vice-president of Westinghouse and Marv needed a guide so I took the folks fishing. We fished for a couple of hours and never had a bite. I could tell the customers were getting restless and a little disappointed, so I suggested trying a small lake close by to see if our luck would change. The guys wanted to fish until 4:30, when it would be cocktail hour. We got into the walleyes about an hour before they wanted to quit. We were landing double and triples and we got our limit and were off the water before 4:30. I'll never forget that trip because I never wanted to fish that day and it turned out to be one of the best fishing days I ever had."

At one time period during John's tenure as store manager, three guides were wheelchair-bound: Henry Ebert, Bobby Collette, and Mike Olsen. That was another unique feature of the Nisswa Guides' League in the seventies. But their excellent fishing and guiding skills were all that really mattered—their perceived disabilities didn't hold them back.

John has very fond memories of working at Koep's. He saw the fishing industry go from cane poles to high-tech equipment. When he began, there were many area resorts and by the time he left, the number had greatly decreased. John doesn't believe there are as many anglers today as there were more than thirty years ago, plus, the competition for the angling dollar is greater today.

"Working at Koep's was a great experience that I wouldn't trade for anything I have ever done. It was a great family business and everyone who worked there was like family. None of us ever expected that so many famous people would eventually come out of that little store."

Today, John works in Pine River. He and Jackie operate Silbaugh's Department Store and John is the executive director of the Pine River Chamber of Commerce.

Chapter Sixteen
John Jensen

JOHN JENSEN (all his friends call him "J.J.") became the second store manager to manage the Nisswa Bait and Tackle Shop for Marv Koep after John Wetrosky made a career change.

John Jensen was a native of Pipestone, Minnesota, and moved to Brainerd after graduating from high school in 1975. He entered a one-year, recreational equipment management program at the Brainerd Area Vocational Technical School. He graduated from the program in 1976 and began an internship program at Koep's.

Marv and John Wetrosky asked John if he was interested in a job interview for a full-time position. John was very interested and went to Marv's house for an interview. The year was 1976 and long hair was in style. John had hair down to his shoulders and never gave it much of a thought. John was just about through with the interview when Marv left to attend another meeting.

After the interview, Jensen went home. That evening, he got a phone call from John Wetrosky. Wetrosky told him he could have the job if he got a haircut. John said he would get a haircut and take the job. Later, Wetrosky told John Jensen that he told Marv he didn't think that they could tell John to get a haircut because that would be job discrimination. "He will get his hair cut if he wants the job," replied Marv.

John remained store manager for almost twelve years. In 1987, he left the store to take a new job selling fire-protection equipment, which he is still doing today.

"I had a wonderful run working at the Nisswa Bait and Tackle Shop. Marv and Judy Koep were absolutely wonderful people to work for all those years. I got to know Harry Van Doren, Max Slocum, Cully Swenson, the Lindners, and all the guides and celebrities associated with the business. We used to have pretty good parties back in those days because everybody worked and played together.

"I went to Brainerd and played cards with Harry Van Doren. I even went on a fishing trip to Canada with Harry, Kevin Koep, and my girlfriend. Harry was getting a little frail—he had quit guiding by then. One night, he was sitting in the front seat of the boat and he got a walleye bite. He set the hook, fell onto the floor of the boat, and bounced back up like he was ten years old. He threw his bait back into the lake and said, 'I am going to get that SOB!' Harry was the king of the fishermen—he was a legend. He was one of the most remarkable fishermen I ever knew. I know Gary Roach, the Lindners, and some of the other guys that worked with the Nisswa Guide League were great fishermen, too, but they were all gone before I began working at the store.

"We used to sell bait wholesale when I first started. We also bought a lot of furs during the trapping season. We sold our furs to Marv's dad, who had a huge fur business in the Urbank area.

"I can remember Royal Karels coming to the store late—he was known for that back in those days—and his customers would be steaming mad. By the end of the day, he had them eating out of his hands. He was a charmer and one heck of a fisherman.

"When I began at the store, local people came to see what fish were being caught and to find out where the fish were biting. That part of the business grew and a few years later, Jim Wentworth began doing his traffic control skit on the opener to keep traffic moving. We'll never see anything like that again because there are too many stores and too many stations selling bait, but boy, it was a sight to see in those days."

The Koeps had a trailer house east of the store parking lot and that was John Wetrosky's home when he was the manager as well as the home of John Jensen and later, Keith Ament, the third manager after Jensen left. It was a great place to live for being close to work, but it was also a knock on the door away from the store. Each of the managers had customers who came looking for bait at 3 A.M. That was not always a fun part of the job!

Marv bought a boat for the store that could be used by employees who didn't have a boat or it could be rented out from time to time. Motors were also available for rent by the day or longer. It was through the use of store equipment that John got to do a lot of fishing.

John remembered the day Marv drove home from Lake Edward (some say this happened from Pelican Lake) with his outboard motor running. He told John he thought a motorcycle was behind him.

"I met a lot of interesting people who came to the store—Mac Davis, Roland Martin, Jimmy Houston, Bill Binkelman, and Chuck Ross, who was an announcer on WCCO Radio in Minneapolis. We did a lot of work with Tom Carlson who owned CSI, probably the biggest wholesale sporting goods company in the fishing industry in our part of the country.

"Kevin and Shelly Koep used to get stuck a lot. The public ramps weren't as good as they are now because few were tarred or concrete. When Kevin was on Lake Edward, he drove along the ramp in the water with his Jeep and floated his boat off his trailer—that way he never had to get out to unhook his boat. One time, he got buried in the mud and called the store to have someone help him, so Marv told me to pull him out. I took my four-wheel drive truck to the lake and I couldn't move him, so we got a wrecker. We got the wrecker stuck, too. It was quite an ordeal—getting everyone out of the lake that day."

John saw lots of big fish during his years as store manager. It was before the catch-and-release ethic began and most people were awed to see stringers of big fish. One guy came into the store with a limit of fish from Mille Lacs Lake and every one of the fish was more than eight pounds.

"The Nisswa Guides were known all over. There wasn't a bad fisherman among them and Harry was the chairman of the board. I still can see him in that Kenzie Craft boat with the rear-tiller handle. He had a sixty-five-horse Mercury motor with a twenty-horse kicker motor. It wasn't fancy, but it fit his personality. Every one who worked at the store was like family. We had great times together and that is a part of my life that I will always cherish."

John travels over the northern half of Minnesota on his current job and often meets people who recognize him from his days of working at Koep's. He lives in the Nisswa area and still fishes from time to time, but he has also taken up golf and now spends more time playing golf than he does fishing.

Chapter Seventeen
Keith Ament

KEITH AMENT, known by all as "Perky," became the third manager of Koep's after John Jensen left to take a new job. Perky grew up in Bluegrass, Minnesota, about forty miles northwest of Brainerd, where his family operated a dairy farm. Perky was one of seven children, with three sisters and three brothers.

He loved to fish—he spent his youth fishing the Leaf and Red Eye Rivers near his family's farm. His tackle box was an old, metal, Band-Aid box with spoons and plugs he used for casting into the river. He went to the nearest large town, Wadena, and spent fifty cents at the Coast-to-Coast store or the Gambles store to buy new spoons. His dad made his first fishing rod—a five-foot piece of plastic tubing with a fishing reel taped on it and eyelets—which worked fine for casting the rivers. His family loved to spear for suckers and redhorse in the spring. The guys would walk in the river and spear and the ladies had the fires going to cook the fish and the other foods that were brought along for the event. Many of the speared fish were smoked and eaten later.

Perky watched the Virgil Ward television show on Saturday nights. Virgil Ward was one of his fishing heroes. Perky thought Marv Koep sponsored the shows, but he didn't know anything about Marv Koep or the Nisswa Guides when he was a youngster. (One of his highlights of working at Koep's was meeting Virgil Ward.)

Perky graduated from high school in 1979 and went to the Brainerd Area Vocational Technical School—enrolling in the sporting goods sales and management course. He graduated from the program in 1981 and that spring, Marv Koep talked to the class about the sporting retail business. Marv said if anyone in the class was interested in a job at the bait shop to call him. Perky took the offer and interviewed with Marv; John Jensen, who was the store manager; and Shelly Koep, Marv's daughter, the assistant store manager. Perky didn't know anything about the bait and tackle business nor did he know anything about the Nisswa Guides' League, but he got the job and began working as a clerk in the spring of 1981.

Perky remembered thinking how odd it was to fish with the tackle that was being sold at the store. Live bait, Lindy Rigs, light tackle, and light line were all new concepts to him. He also didn't know anything about the lakes or where to fish them. He was just a river angler who used a half-dozen plugs or spoons to catch fish.

"I bought a fourteen-foot Shell Lake Lund boat, borrowed one of the store's motors, and began fishing Roy and Nisswa Lakes. I began to get the hang of fishing lakes, which was something I never had the chance to do when I was growing up on the farm. Marv was great. Many weeks, we went fishing five nights after work. Marv told me my shift was up—we were going fishing. I also fished a lot with John Jensen, Hank Ebert, Bobby Collette, and Kevin Koep. Those guys taught me how to fish and where to fish, and that helped me guide customers about where to go when they asked for help at the store.

"I got to know the guides really well as well as some of the older guides who were retired, such as Clarence Luther. Clarence stopped in the store a lot to talk and see how fishing was going. Joe Masik was another person who took me fishing a lot. He was a kind man who never had a bad thing to say about anyone. If he said we were going fishing for the day—he meant for the day! We left at 4:30 A.M. and wouldn't come home until dark.

"I think the hardest part about working at the store was the days when the power got knocked out. I remember many times when we got all the guides together at the end of the day, took their trolling motors, and hooked them up to aerators to try and keep the minnows alive until power was restored. In those days, we had $6,000 to $7,000 worth of minnows in the tanks and if we saved 50 percent, it was worth $3,000 to $3,500.

"We were still selling bait wholesale when I started working at Koep's and it was a challenge to keep bait alive. Marv made the trip to Crane Lake in those years. He worked at the store all day, drove to Crane Lake, came home early the next morning, got a few hours of sleep, and was back at it the next day.

"I was also involved in buying furs for Marv. We bought furs locally and hauled them to Paul Koep, Marv's dad. There was a real art to buying the right furs and I learned a lot about that from Marv.

"We used to have a lot of fun at the store. One time, John Jensen and Mark Bateman, a clerk at the store, came in with serious looks on their faces and told me to get the electronic scale. That usually meant someone had a big fish. I got the scale, turned it on, and went out to their boat. They told me to weigh the fish in the livewell.

I opened the livewell and a seagull flew out at my head. I just about had a heart attack. It was dark out and we all learned something that night—sea gulls won't fly in the dark. The crazy bird was still there early the next morning and didn't leave the parking lot until it began to get light. A lot of the guides also used to hide fish under the seats of each other's cars, and in a few days, the cars smelled so bad it was almost impossible to get into them.

"One afternoon, a tall, lanky guy came into the store and wanted me to look at a fish he had caught. He was really serious and I didn't know what to expect when I got to his boat. He caught a walleye and he wanted to know if it was big enough to enter in the contest we had every year. He opened the livewell and took out the biggest walleye I've ever seen. I couldn't believe it—it was a monster! We took it into the store and weighed it. It weighed fifteen pounds and six ounces. I told the guy that it was the biggest walleye I'd ever seen, that he would get a trophy (we gave any one who caught an eight-pound walleye a trophy), and he would surely win the contest. He showed me the rest of his fish—he took five more walleyes out of the livewell that were all more than ten pounds—some were near twelve pounds. This guy was not bragging and he was very serious. He told me he only fished two weekends each fall and only kept the fish he caught during those weekends. We took about forty pictures of that fish and it was in all the area publications. We never did take pictures of the rest of his fish, but that was an unbelievable catch of trophy walleyes. I have never seen a walleye bigger than that to this day.

"We were shooting a television show for one of the fishing shows and it was a hot day, really hot! We had about three guide boats and a boat with television cameras. The fishing was just terrible. Finally, someone got a three-pound northern pike. We used the pike for about six different scenes with six different people pretending to catch the fish. By the time we were finished, the fish had a forty-five-degree bend in its tail from being on and off the hooks so much. We finally wrapped up the day and we couldn't wait to get off the lake and get away from that little northern pike.

"We took a lot of pictures of people with fish and many years later, the people came back to the store to remind us of the memories they had fishing with the Niswa Guides. Marv and Judy Koep were the greatest people I ever worked for and I had a great experience working at Koep's.

"The store was sold to the Fischer family in the fall of 1992 and the Fischers had two boys and some other folks they brought with them, so my job was eliminated. I understood that was part of the sale, so I moved up the road and worked at the Oasis

Sport Shop for a little more than two years before I got a job at the paper mill in Brainerd. The Fischers were great people, too, and did a nice job after they bought the store."

Perky still lives in the Nisswa area with his two young daughters. He lost his wife, Terri, to cancer at the age of thirty-six. He loves to fish with his two girls and he currently works in the Nisswa area where he harbors many great memories of Koep's and the Nisswa Guides' League.

Chapter Eighteen
Bert Lindberry

KNOWN BY THE NAME on his boat—"The Happy Hooker"—Bert Lindberry was born in Hopkins, Minnesota. He graduated from high school in 1963 and moved to northern Minnesota and attended Bemidji State University in 1967. Bert got a degree in elementary education and landed a job teaching in the Brainerd school district. He retired as a teacher, earning an excellent reputation as an outstanding teacher.

Bert always had an interest in fishing. His father died when he was only twelve years old. He did a lot of fishing as a young boy, but he didn't have the equipment to fish many areas, except on bridges and offshore along lake edges. He did fish Minnesota's largest lake, Red Lake, as a young boy.

He became fascinated with the Nisswa Guides' League through reading the articles and seeing the many pictures of fish in the newspaper. He decided he wanted to learn the lakes and see if he could get into the league. He heard getting an opportunity to join the group was tough—he knew he needed to learn a lot more about fishing as well as learning a lot more about area lakes.

Bert got a job in the summer of 1967, working for the Coca-Cola Company. He delivered pop to area stores and resorts—much of his route wound around Gull Lake and the Whitefish Lake area. He built a new home on East Twin Lake, north of Nisswa and whenever he had a chance, he began fishing the lakes in the Brainerd-Nisswa area.

Figuring the best way to learn the area lakes was to learn from the best fishermen in the area, he came up with a unique plan to accomplish his goal. He would follow the best fishermen and learn the lakes by watching where they fished. He, like many others at the time, had heard of the legend, Harry Van Doren as well as Max Slocum and Cully Swenson. He figured the best way to really learn the lakes was to see where these three and other guides fished. His basic plan was to find out what time of the day the guides hit the lake and "follow them" with binoculars from his Coca-Cola truck.

While doing this, he learned that Harry liked to fish the middle and north end of

Gull Lake. He followed him by watching from his route to Grand View and other resorts on the north end of Gull. He also learned where Harry, Max, and Cully fished when they went to the Whitefish Chain. It was not always easy to find them with binoculars, but he managed to do it. He got a pattern down for the guides—learning where they usually fished in the mornings and where they fished in the afternoons.

Harry was not open to just anyone fishing in his spots. Max and Cully were two guides that fished with Harry from time to time, but he did not appreciate others tagging along and he made no secret of that. Bert didn't care—he had guts and a strong desire to learn the lakes, so he figured it was worth taking the chance of getting some of the guys mad at him for following them around the lakes.

Bert later purchased a boat, an S-14 Lund, and actually followed Harry from spot to spot on the lakes—a feat that made Harry furious! Harry had no time for Bert in the early days of knowing each other. He made it clear that he didn't like Bert and he didn't want Bert hanging around him or following him on the water. Bert shrugged off the bad feelings, kept fishing near Harry, and learned the lakes and the techniques that the guides were using. He became a good fisherman by being a copycat. He was not ashamed to admit that was how he learned to fish and how he learned the lakes.

Bert spent a lot of time around the bait shop when he wasn't working. He was also catching fish. Marv Koep took notice. One day, he asked Bert if he was interested in quitting his job with Coca-Cola and coming to work at the store. This was the day Bert had been waiting for—the day he had worked so long to achieve.

Getting into the Nisswa Guides' League was a matter of being voted in by the other guides. This was, and still is, an area of controversy for the guides. It is important to have guides that know how to fish and who can work well with customers. Sometimes guides have some skills, but not the whole package—putting the wrong person into position could hurt business and the reputations of all the guides. There has always been a fine line between the owners of Koep's (at this time, Marv), and how decisions were made about the guides. Marv needed help, but the guides didn't want Marv to ask other fishermen to be guides without their approval. From time to time, there was bound to be disagreement about who should be fishing.

Bert began taking trips out of the store as a part-time guide after Marv asked him to work at the store. One day, Bert got a letter in the mail—he could no longer guide at the store until he had approval from the guides' league. This posed a problem for Bert, who had angered Harry and others because he had followed them around to learn the lakes.

It was around 1970 or 1971, and Gary Roach was leaving the league to work for Lindy Little Joe. Bobby Collette and three other guides were going to the group to see if they could get the votes to join the league.

Bert knew getting enough votes to get into the league was an uphill battle. He figured that if anyone could help him get in, it would be Harry Van Doren. Yes, Harry. He met him in the parking lot on the day the guides met to vote and he asked him for his help. He told Harry that he knew he made him mad by following him around the lakes, but that it was he, Harry, who taught Bert everything he knew about fishing.

"Harry, because of you, I am now a pretty good fisherman," admitted Bert. "I owe everything to you for how I learned the lakes and how to fish. I would really appreciate your vote tonight, it means a lot to me."

Bert and Bobby Collette were voted in; the other three were not. Bert was told that it was Harry who convinced the other guides to vote for him. He and Harry became close friends after that event. Bert later went on fishing trips with Harry to Lake Michigan and other places that Harry liked to fish. They remained good friends until Harry's death. Bert was a Nisswa guide for twenty-eight years—one of the longest terms of any of the early guides.

He had one of the very first Lowrance fishing sonar units—the red box. He later sold it to a collector. He bought his first green box, a more-advanced sonar unit, from Marv for $129. In the early years, these devices separated the guides from the general fishing population. Bert's first fishing boat was a fourteen-foot Lund with a ten-horse motor. He taught during the school year and guided during the summer months.

Over the years, Bert fished with entertainer Mac Davis and his son, he fished with Governor Harold Levander, took two or three trips with movie star Paul Newman—a gentleman who really likes to fish—and he fished with a number of the Minnesota Vikings players. He fished a lot with a young man and his father from St. Cloud. The young man's name was Babe Winkelman—now a well-known outdoor television personality. The Winkelman family had a cabin on Hay Lake on the Whitefish Chain.

Working with the Alumacraft Boat Company, Bert helped them design pedestal seats. He later fished out of Crestliner and Ranger boats. Royal Karels' son, Sam, guided a little during the early years that Bert fished and he thinks Sam still has one of the original Lund Shell Lake boats.

Bert had two lakes that he considered his favorites—Edward and Pine Mountain—both close to Nisswa. Pine Mountain is north of Nisswa, in the city of Backus. He still fishes big Mille Lacs Lake with only a flasher or sonar unit. He does not need a GPS system to get around the lake. He used to fish the big lake a lot, many times with Royal Karels.

Joe Fellegy was a fishing guide on Mille Lacs Lake. He is also an author of books and newspaper articles. Royal Karels grew up knowing the Fellegy family. Joe Fellegy and his brother, Steve, are both well-known and well-respected fishermen from the Mille Lacs area. Bert had the same disrespect for giving Joe space on the lake that he did for Harry Van Doren. Joe operated a launch on the big lake, using only a compass and land sights. Royal, too, learned the lake this way and still doesn't use navigational equipment for finding the reefs and bars on the lake. (Mille Lacs is Minnesota's second-largest lake and this feat is quite remarkable—being in the middle of Mille Lacs is like sitting in the middle of the ocean.) Joe is a fishing legend who has an uncanny ability to find reefs and bars on Mille Lacs. Joe and Royal are two, of only a handful of anglers, who can visually find their way around the lake.

Bert knew that following Joe and Royal around the lake was the best way to learn the water. Joe was as furious as Harry was to have Bert tagging after him around the lake. (Joe had disdain for any fisherman who followed him around the lake, as he references many times in his book, *Mille Lacs: Thirty Years on the Big Lake.*)

One day, Bert and Royal were fishing Mille Lacs for walleyes. Royal always stayed a distance from Joe out of respect, but Bert figured the lake was big enough that he could squeeze in next to a launch and there would still be plenty of room. According to Bert, Joe was steaming mad that he was fishing next to him. It wasn't long before one of Joe's customers dropped a fishing rod over the side of the launch. Joe was hot about that, too. A short time later, Bert hooked onto something. He pulled it up and sure enough, it was the rod from Joe's boat. Joe asked for the rod back and Bert, being brash and gutsy, said he wouldn't give the rod back because he was tired of Joe being mad at him. Bert didn't think Joe believed that he would keep it, but he did, just to make his point. He said he never had another conflict with Joe after that. (Of course, this is one side of the story.)

When he first began guiding, Bert recalled earning $27.50 for a half-day trip. He saw the change from many resorts, mostly small family resorts, to the trend of fewer resorts and fewer people fishing. Many other summer events have grown in importance, especially golf, which has gotten huge in this area over the past twenty years.

He fished 100 to 130 days each season during his best years with the Nisswa Guides' League. Like many of the other early guides, he feels that the quantity of fishing is still excellent, but the quality, or size, is not what it once was.

Bert still fishes for fun and he lives on East Twin Lake where he has a bicycle business. He occasionally stops in and visits Koep's to share a fishing tale or two—he has lots of those!

Chapter Nineteen
Bobby Collette

THE COLLETTE NAME has long been associated with the Nisswa Guides' League. Bobby was the first of four brothers who guided with the league over a period of four decades. Out of five Collette boys, the other three brothers who worked at Koep's were Steve and Tim, both full-time guides, and Mark, who helped out when there was a shortage of guides.

Bobby Collette and his brothers grew up next to the Shady Lane Resort on North Long Lake, north of Brainerd. Their father worked in employment services for the State of Minnesota. The Collette boys recalled that their dad took them fishing a lot when they were young kids. There were six people in the boat because all the boys went fishing and everyone loved to fish. None of them remember getting lines tangled, each person knew what he was supposed to do, and they all got along with each other. Fishing was a big deal—each brother looked forward to spending time on the water with their dad.

Bobby began helping out at Shady Lane Resort when he was fourteen years old. He cleaned fish, kept the boats clean, and did general clean-up. He got to know the lake quite well from fishing with his father and spent a lot of time on his own fishing for bass and northern pike.

His first trip as a guide out of Shady Lane was with a catcher from the New York Mets or the New York Yankees. He doesn't recall the man's name, but he remembers being paid one dollar per fish. Lazy Ikes were his main bait. He didn't have a depth finder so he fished the lake the old-fashioned way—using landmarks to locate his favorite spots. Until he got his first job in the sporting industry at King's Sport Shop in Brainerd, Bobby guided for a while at Shady Lane Resort.

When King's Sport Shop burned, later that year, Bobby got a job at Perry's Sport Shop in Brainerd, where he began getting guide trips. While working at Perry's, Bobby met Ron Lindner. They became friends and Bobby began fishing with Ron occasionally. One day, Ron and Bobby had planned to go fishing. Ron stopped by the store and told Bobby that he couldn't go fishing that day, but his brother, Al, could go. Bobby had never met Al, but he never turned down a fishing trip so he and Al went fishing on North Long Lake.

Bobby thought he knew North Long Lake, so he was curious to see what Al Lindner would do on "his lake." In his mind, Bobby was a born fisherman. He knew this lake like the back of his hand and he doubted that anyone could show him very much about it. On his first trip with Al Lindner, he was shocked.

"I think Al wanted to show me how well he could fish, but he also wanted to show me something about the lake. I was completely amazed. He was unbelievable at catching bass! He took me to seventeen different spots on North Long that I had never fished. He didn't fish for numbers of fish—he fished to try new techniques. He was constantly trying a new plug or a new technique to see how fish responded.

"One day, we went fishing to catch a limit of bass. Al put on a Bomber 400 crankbait and in eleven casts, he had eleven keeper bass. He told me to catch the last one! I don't think it took him eight minutes to catch those fish. He began fishing that day with Texas rigged worms and he caught a bass in about two feet of water. He knew the fish were suspended, so he put on a shallow-running crankbait and sure enough, that was the depth of the fish. I saw him do things like that many times. That was back in 1968 or 1969. There was less fishing pressure then, but it was still remarkable how Al could catch fish. He is a remarkable fisherman."

Bobby was friends with the Lindners for a few years before becoming a guide and he remembers many nights in Ron Lindner's home, tying tackle for Lindy Little Joe. He later worked for the Lindners, selling tackle around the upper Midwest. At one time, Lindy Little Joe had tackle centers in all the Sears stores in the greater Chicago area—Bobby recalls at least fourteen Sears stores that were connected to the company. He also conducted fishing seminars in a number of cities and often worked in the Milwaukee, Wisconsin, area with other fishermen, such as well-known musky guide, Spence Petros.

He began guiding for the Nisswa Guides' League in 1972 and he fished out of Koep's until 1987. His first summer as a Nisswa guide, Bobby fished for thirty-six days without a break.

One year, when he was scheduled to fish a tournament with Al Lindner at Watt's Bar in Tennessee, Al called Bobby at the last minute and said he needed him to work a sports show at a Sears store in Chicago. Bobby went to Chicago and Al won the tournament. Bobby still wonders what would have happened to his career if he had fished the tournament with Al, instead of working the sports show.

Due to the Lindners' fishing influence, Bobby chose to quit college. He had been attending Brainerd Junior College, but he kept getting opportunities to work with the Lindners. The fishing industry was more exciting than college, so he quit and stayed in the fishing business.

He began working part time for *In-Fisherman* magazine and television in the spring of 1975. Later in his career, he also worked for Jeff Zernov, who guided at Koep's for one summer and then went to work for the Lindners. Zernoff founded his own companies, which produced Zercom sonar units and later, the underwater television system, Aqua-Vu.

Bobby developed a special friendship with Harry Van Doren. Harry took a liking to Bobby and helped him out when he began guiding. Bobby's first trip as a Nisswa Guide was to Lake Edward. He and his customers only got two walleyes. Harry took Bobby aside after that trip and gave him advice that Bobby never forgot. He told Bobby that he would catch walleyes on Lake Edward if he fished the bottom in sand—stay out of the muddy areas of the lake. The walleyes would only be in the areas where the bottom was sandy and hard. It was good advice.

Harry and Bobby became good friends for the rest of Harry's life. For a number of years, Bobby Collette and Harry Van Doren were the only Nisswa Guides who worked all year in the fishing industry. They fished Minnesota during the boating season, hunted together in the fall, and fished the Sam Rayburn Reservoir in the winter. Bobby spent parts of eight winters fishing in the south as well as selling tackle.

"Harry loved to fish in eighteen feet of water," said Bobby. "We used to kid him and tell him his flasher was stuck at eighteen feet."

Bobby recalled that Harry was on a team of bass fisherman that won a world championship. "I think the team was made up of Harry, Jerry McKinnis, who has a fishing show on ESPN, Bill Dance, and Glen Carver. Glen has since died, but I think he was perhaps the best fisherman on the team.

"Harry won a jacket from that championship that he always had in his truck. He said I could have the jacket when he died. Someone thought it was turned over to the historical society, but I have never been able to find it. I always thought it would be nice to find it and give it to the Fishing Hall of Fame. Harry knew more about fishing than any person I ever met. He held the Sam Rayburn record for bass and maybe still does. He had six bass that weighed a total of ninety-four pounds.

"I took Harry fishing on his last fishing trip—he wanted to go one more time. He was so sick, I thought he was going to die in my boat on the lake. We put in at a local resort and I even asked the resort owner what I should do if he died on the lake. It was a resort where Harry had been living and the owner said Harry had taken care of all the funeral arrangements. He said, 'If Harry dies and the fish are biting, keep fishing! If not, bring him back and we will take care of him!' Harry made it, but he was in tough shape," recalled Bobby.

In the summer of 1973, Ron Kristofferson got a call from the bait shop that said Bobby Collette had been in a bad accident. Bobby was fishing with customers and they decided to go swimming at an area resort. Bobby broke his spine diving into the lake. Ron took the fishing trip the next morning and then drove to the University of Minnesota, in Minneapolis, to visit Bobby.

"I walked into the hospital room and saw Bobby lying there in a body stocking," said Ron. "I guess we were all in total shock—I just couldn't believe it. Bobby and I fished together all the time and I couldn't imagine that he was now paralyzed."

Bobby's days of walking were over. The next summer he was back guiding on the water! A number of years later, he developed an infection that caused him to lose his fingers and toes, but he never allowed his spirit to become handicapped.

"Ron Schara, the writer from the Minneapolis newspaper, wrote an article about me," recalled Bobby. "He mentioned that as far as anyone knew, I was the first guide in the United States in a wheelchair." Bobby didn't let his accident stop him from doing the things he loved. He still fished, hunted, and enjoyed the outdoors as much as before.

After the accident, Bobby began fishing out of a Lund Tyee. His first Lund boat was model 311, which was equipped with a twenty-horse Chrysler motor. He paid $311 for the whole rig. (In the mid- to late-seventies, the Lund Boat Company played a big part in the Nisswa Guides' League.)

Through the years, Bobby has fished with many good fishermen, such as Roland Martin, Hank Parker, among others. He considers Al Lindner to be the best angler he has ever seen. (He also considered Al and Ron's dad, Art—affectionately known as "Pops"—to be the worst fisherman he ever saw. He thought that was a piece of information the readers of this book would enjoy knowing!)

He has fond memories of the Nisswa Guides' League and recalled that the guides had fun playing tricks on each other. Some of the older guides did not think it was professional. One of the guides found a roll of banana labels and stuck the labels on a stringer of small walleyes. It was not uncommon to have boats unhitched in the parking lot or to have plugs taken out of the bottom of the boats before guides headed out to the lake. "The guides had a lot of fun—usually at the expense of someone else."

When Rod Romine came into the bait shop with his hat off and white gull crap all over the top of his head, Cully Swenson laughed and said, "The gulls sing for some people, Ron!"

One morning, Bobby got a call from Ron Kristofferson, asking him if he could take customers for him that morning. When Bobby asked why he wasn't fishing, Ron said he had to figure a way to get his boat out of the back of his Bronco. He had hit the ditch and rammed the boat into the back of his vehicle.

Bobby loves fishing for northern pike and bass, especially when walleye fishing is slow. He doesn't have a favorite lake, he just tried to go where there was a hot bite. Bobby remembered that Gull Lake was really good for huge fish in 1967 to 1968 as well as 1969. Bobby is retiring this year and plans to head south to a warmer climate. Time will tell if the Minnesota lakes will call him home again. His legacy is forever etched in the history of the Nisswa Guides.

Chapter Twenty
Fritz Potthoff

FREDRICK POTTHOFF, OR FRITZ as he was known by most of us, was the son of Papa Potthoff. Fritz was born in St. Louis, Missouri in 1927 and moved to Nisswa with his parents in 1931, when Papa Potthoff bought Minnewawa Lodge on Clark Lake. Fritz worked at his dad's resort when he was just a young boy. He helped his dad by guiding on the lake when he got old enough—his first guide trip was in 1937—and he also worked around the resort wherever help was needed. Fritz went to grade school in Nisswa and graduated from St. Thomas Military Academy in St. Paul. He served in the United States Army after World War II and graduated in 1951 from Cornell University in Ithaca, New York, with a degree in restaurant management.

He took over the operation of Minnewawa Lodge from his father and operated ifor nineteen years, before selling the business in 1972. He fished with the Nisswa Guides full time after selling the lodge. When his health began failing, he cut back on the number of trips. I still fished a few trips with Fritz until about 2000 or 2001. After that, he didn't feel well enough to fish and retired from the guiding business.

I fished with Fritz off and on for about eleven years before he quit guiding. Having grown up fishing Clark Lake, he really enjoyed fishing bass and northern pike. He fished for walleyes, but they were not his first choice. He just loved to put on a big sucker minnow and try to land a big pike or slide into the weeds to hook a nice bass.

Fritz's father, Papa Potthoff, guided until about 1967. Fritz also recalled the days when Cully Swenson was a handyman at the Alaskan Lodge. Cully guided for the lodge when he began guiding and then later worked at Koep's store. It was difficult to contact Cully Swenson because for many years he didn't have a phone. Someone would have to call a neighbor and they would run over and leave a message at Cully's house.

Clarence Luther was another area guide. "Clarence was the main competition for Harry Van Doren in the early days," recalled Fritz. "Both of those guys were good and both of those guys guided full time."

It was difficult to get on the lakes in the fifties. There were hardly any public accesses. The only way to get on a lake was to go through someone's private property.

Fritz recalled the glory days of Breezy Point on Pelican Lake. "That place was crawling with movie stars, such as Clark Gable. Many people went to Breezy Point just to see the movie stars. Billy Fawcett owned the place then and it was really humming."

Most of the trips Fritz took in the early years were for bass, but he also did a lot of crappie fishing. He didn't have a favorite lake, but he enjoyed Clark and Hubert Lakes. One of Fritz's fishing trips in the early years was pretty scary. He had a fourteen-foot Larson boat and he was caught in a storm on a small lake. He didn't get off the lake in time and the waves sank his boat as he headed to shore. The old boats didn't have built-in flotation and it was easy to sink one.

Other guides that Fritz recalled from 1972 were Lenny Hodgson, Bert Lindberry, Bobby Collette, Ron Kristofferson, Royal Karels, and Jeff Zernov.

Fritz fished with many of the customers who had gotten to know the area through his dad's resort—many from the St. Louis area. He fished with some of the same families until he retired from guiding.

Never one to seek the limelight, Fritz was a kind and gentle man—quiet, well-mannered, and always ready with a smile for a friend. His deep, raspy voice could be distinguished from across a room. Many loyal customers asked for Fritz when they returned to Minnesota. Unlike some of the more "famous" guides, he didn't invent anything, he was never on radio or television, and he didn't have much to say about himself, but he was an important part of the legacy of the Nisswa Guides' League. Fritz died on December 14th, 2003, from chronic obstructive pulmonary disease. When I interviewed him for this book in 2001, he didn't even have a picture of himself fishing or catching a fish. He was "just" a humble fisherman.

Chapter Twenty-one
Nick Adams

(The Minnesota Fishing Hall of Famer reflects on the fishing industry and his experiences with some of the Nisswa guides.)

NICK ADAMS IS A LEGEND in the fishing-tackle industry. He was inducted into the Minnesota Fishing Hall of Fame in 2001. He has never been a member of the Nisswa Guides' League, but he has been associated with members of the league since it began.

In 1968, along with cofounders, Ron and Al Lindner, Nick started the Lindy Manufacturing Company. Many of the Nisswa guides became associated with the business, including Jeff Zernov, Gary Roach, Rod Romine, and Harry Van Doren as well as others. The Lindy-Little Joe Company became a springboard for some of the guides as they expanded their careers into other aspects of the fishing industry. Ron and Al Lindner were the first of the Nisswa Guides to work with Nick Adams. Later, other guides, such as Rod Romine and Gary Roach, worked for Nick as sales representatives and educators.

Born in the Brainerd area in the early thirties, Nick grew up fishing with a father who had a passion for the sport. His family was the first Greek family raised in the Brainerd area, where his father and mother, Steve and Kalliopie, were in the restaurant business. Nick worked much of his younger life in the restaurant business, as did his brother, John.

Nick grew up fishing Gull Lake and considered it his home on the water. In his teen years, around the mid-1940s, he began guiding and developed a reputation as a good fisherman. With his father as his teacher, he acquired skill in fishing the lake—learning its structure by using cane poles as crude depth finders. He built up a clientele over the years and had customers who hired him as often as four days a week. He was asked a time or two to consider joining the Nisswa Guides' League, but he never had time to seriously consider it.

His parents wanted him to become a medical doctor. That is also what Nick thought he would become after graduating from Brainerd Junior College. From there, he attended the University of Minnesota, where he completed two years of pre-med. He finished his first two years of medical school in 1954 and decided he didn't really want to be a medical doctor, but he had a keen interest in pathology and cancer research, so he moved to California and enrolled at the University of California-Berkley. He spent time at Berkley as a research assistant doing cancer research and also served as a lab assistant. He then moved back to Minnesota to continue his true passion, which was pathology.

In 1962, tragedy hit the Adams family. Nick's forty-year-old brother, John, died of an illness, leaving a wife and three children. His brother had opened the Starlite Club, a nightclub in the Brainerd area. Nick made a commitment to his brother that he would stay and help the family run the nightclub until the family could manage it on their own. His college career was put on hold until his brother's children were old enough to help with the club. Nick never returned to college or pursued his interest in pathology, but looking back, he harbors no regrets about the direction his life took.

Nick met Ron and Al Lindner at the Starlite Club. They stopped in occasionally to socialize and sometimes played a little poker. Nick knew a little bit about them, such as that they loved to fish and they were into guiding. Ron had a large family of six kids and Al was still single.

One night, while Nick played poker with Ron and Al, Ron said they were thinking of starting a business—selling new ideas in the fishing industry. Ron wondered if Nick was interested in talking to them about it. Nick said he would like to see what they had in mind. Ron invited Nick out to his home for dinner the next day. Nick met Ron's wife, Delores, and their kids, and had an enjoyable time.

Nick was almost ready to leave when Ron brought out a sinker—one that Nick had never seen before. Explaining how the sinker went over rocks and maneuvered around uneven obstacles on the lake bottom, Ron asked Nick what he thought of the design. Nick saw the sinker as unique, but not much different from how he fished with a barrel sinker held in place with a lead split shot.

Nick asked Ron how much money he thought he needed to get this business started and Ron said $50,000. Nick thought he could raise the $50,000 if they could come up with $150,000 worth of purchase orders for the product. If all else failed, he figured that would be enough to cover the $50,000.

"The amazing thing," recalled Nick, "is that none of us had any idea what we were doing. We had no business plan, no marketing plan, and we weren't manufacturing most of what we sold—just retailing the products. Our two main items were the walking sinker, which we called the Lindy Rig, and a jig that Ron developed called the Dingo Jig. None of us had any money. I had seven kids, Ron had six, and to be honest, we didn't know where our next dime was coming from!" Nick borrowed the $50,000 from his folks. At the time, Ron and Al were guiding at Koep's, so in the early period of the new endeavor, the new business began as an evening job.

In one week, Ron and Al sold the purchase orders that Nick asked them to sell. Most of the orders came from U.S. Tackle in Chicago. They began their venture in the five-hundred-square-foot back room of Lakes and Rivers Bait Shop, owned by Harley and Liz Collette. Ron's wife, Delores, helped tie rigs and served as secretary. They bought lead molds, purchased swivels, and tied their own snells.

The early years were tough. Nick served as the chief executive officer, Al promoted the business, and Ron was to be the creative force behind the company—writing articles and developing promotional ideas. Nick recalls that each of the three partners drew a salary of about $300 a month. To promote themselves and their products, they went to every kind of fishing event they could find. They worried that another company might try to duplicate their products. They only had a few items that were unique, so they looked over their shoulders continually, to see who could try to move into their niche in the marketplace.

Two years later, the company moved to a larger facility in Baxter, outside of Brainerd. They hired five female employees and the company began to grow. The partners developed a relationship with the Lund Boat Company. Each year, they got Lund Boats from the company and their contribution to the partnership was helping to market Lund boats.

Occasionally, Ron Lindner talked about selling the company. One day, a Lund board member asked if they were really serious about selling the business. The three partners discussed it and decided they weren't ready to sell, but they decided to keep their options open, in case they changed their minds. One problem the company continually struggled with was that they really didn't have any assets. Their business consisted of products that were assembled, but not manufactured by the company itself—most of the manufacturing was done by subcontractors.

The Lindy Manufacturing Company registered for the largest, regional, retail event in Chicago. The American Fishing Tackle Manufacturing Association's spring trade show was the place to be to promote fishing tackle. The Lindy folks got a basement booth about as far from the main action as could be imagined. A representative from Ray-O-Vac Company stopped by their booth and asked if Lindy would put the Ray-O-Vac logo on their spinnerbait blades.

Ron pulled out a label and put it on spinner bait and said, "Like this?" The salesman said that was perfect—just what he was looking for. He told the Lindy guys he would get back to them.

A month later, Art Anderson, a vice president from Ray-O-Vac, called and asked if Ron, Al, and Nick were interested in selling their business or working together in some way to produce fishing tackle. The Lund Boat Company heard about the potential sale and expressed interest in buying the company, but the guys decided that Ray-O-Vac had a national sales impact—at the time, Lund was only regional. They decided to sell the Lindy business to Ray-O-Vac. In April 1973, the purchase was made.

Nick had also developed a strong friendship with Jim Fladebo—the owner of Mille Lacs Manufacturing—whose brand name was Little Joe. Nick felt the business would be enhanced if it added manufacturing to its assets. Since the Little Joe brand was known for quality and innovation, Nick convinced Ray-O-Vac to purchase the business in December 1973 and the name of the company became Lindy-Little Joe. Ron and Al stayed with the company until 1974, when they began working full time on their newer venture—*In-Fisherman* magazine.

Ray-O-Vac experienced some major business losses with the Lindy-Little Joe company. Electric Storage Battery, Ray-O-Vac's parent company, was not in the fishing business at the national level. In 1979, they decided to sell the Lindy-Little Joe company, along with some of its other divisions, and focus on the battery end of its mission. Nick Adams was contacted and allowed to make an offer for the business—a gesture he appreciates to this day. Nick formed a business partnership and bought back the company in 1979.

It was a good purchase for Nick and his partners, but the business was not always easy. "We had some touchy times, getting this company to become successful," recalled Nick. "The first few years were difficult. The event that got us over the hump was being awarded a large contract to develop a lure for the Minnesota Lottery. That was the turning point. It gave us exposure and opened new doors for our business."

In 1992, Nick met Don Anderson—owner of Thill Floats. Don was interested in selling his company, so later that year, Lindy-Little Joe purchased Thill Floats and added the product line to the company's inventory, which greatly enhanced company sales.

The company built a new facility in the Brainerd industrial park in1982. Since 1982, there have been a number of additions to the building and the company is still located at the industrial park location.

Nick Adams is a fishing legend. He has been with Lindy-Little Joe for about thirty-five years and he loves to create new fishing tackle ideas. Two of Nick's creations are the Sure-Loc hook and a Slip-on Walking Sinker. He can be found in his upstairs office at Lindy-Little Joe—next to the office of the company's president, Ted Takasaki. Takasaki, a professional tournament fisherman, was named the president in 1999. Lindy-Little Joe remains one of the industry leaders in the fishing tackle business.

Nick has developed many lifelong friends in the fishing business, such as Rick Welle of International Falls, who began tying jigs for the company more than thirty years ago and he still ties jigs today. Nick maintains a close relationship with the Lindners as well as other early employees of the Lindy-Little Joe Company who ventured off on their own to become successful.

Like others I interviewed for this book, Nick told me some stories I decided not to print. (In some cases, stories I promised not to print. Some of them were absolutely hilarious.) Here are a few that made the cut.

Nick was not a Nisswa Guide, but he was always around the store buying bait. He also encountered the guides on Gull Lake, where he spent most of his time as a self-employed guide.

"I never saw anyone from the old school that could fish walleyes like Harry Van Doren," said Nick. "He had a knack for finding fish like no one I ever saw, until Al Lindner came along. Al was new school—he was unbelievable at finding walleyes and other species, too. I saw Harry on Gull Lake, anchored in about three feet of water, casting crankbaits into about fifty feet of water. He was catching fish suspended over the deep water. This was years before anyone knew that walleyes would suspend over deep water. I thought he was crazy, until I watched him catch about six fish.

"Our company hired Harry to fish the Governor's Fishing Openers in Wisconsin. Wisconsin was a tough market for us to get into and Harry always found fish—even on a lake he'd never been on before. He always did well when fishing in Wisconsin.

"Ron Lindner was never very good at finding walleyes. He was a great bass fisherman, but he struggled to find walleyes. Ron had a real passion for bass fishing and he could stay on the water from sunrise to sunset without taking a break.

"Gary Roach could fish any species and he had patience like no one I have ever seen. He found a school of fish and sat on top of them until they decided it was time to bite. Great guy! One of the most down-to-earth men I have ever been around. One time, Gary and some customers slipped into a small private lake that was posted with "no trespassing" signs. The owner of the land yelled at them to get off his lake. Gary wouldn't leave, figuring that the guy didn't own the lake. Suddenly, the guy is shooting at them! Gary left."

Nick recalled the time he fished with his good friend, Jim Fladebo, in a Burger Brothers tournament in the mid-seventies. (Burger Brothers was a Minnesota sporting-goods business that was later sold to Gander Mountain.) Randy Amenrud, Gary Roach, and Al Lindner were also fishing the tournament. Nick and Jim bet $100 that they would finish higher in the tournament than the other three guys. On the first day, Jim and Nick came in second—and only about four ounces out of first place. Nick didn't remember exactly what place everyone finished, but he and Jim placed very well and the other three didn't fare as well. None of the three were very happy about how the tournament ended and none of them came up with the money they owed Nick and Jim. Nick figured that none of them had $100 they could come up with at that time of their lives.

About a week later, in the Grand Rapids, Minnesota area, Gary and Al were promoting business with a sports shop owner who was Nick's good friend. Nick bought two sympathy cards, put $100 in each card, sent them to the owner of the sports shop, and asked him to give the cards to Gary and Al. Nick never heard another word about the tournament and he never got the money back, which was fine with him. That was the last time he can remember having a side bet on a tournament with those guys. However, Nick was in many tournaments over the years where he had the same luck that those guys had in the tournament.

Nick fished a number of Governor's Fishing Openers. They used to be tournaments, but now they are media events. Nick won the Governors' Cup one year, along with Hank Kehborn, a writer from the Twin Cities. Hank was a great guy, but he liked to have a good time and he was out a little too late the night before the opener. The tournament started from Breezy Point at 7 A.M. Nick waited until about 8 A.M. and there was still no sign of Hank, so Nick went to his room and got him up. Hank was in no hurry to go on the water—he wanted to eat breakfast.

By the time they left Breezy Point, it was after 10 A.M. They drove nine miles to Gull Lake, where Nick planned to fish. But Nick got lucky. He found a school of large walleyes and they had a limit of beautiful fish by noon—making it back to Breezy Point for the weigh-in by the 1 P.M. deadline. They won the tournament. Hank always wanted to fish with Nick after that experience.

They didn't do as well the next year. They had about twenty minutes to go before the end of the tournament and Hank said he was hung up on a log or something. He couldn't get his hook free and Nick told him to break the line, it was time to quit anyway. Hank pulled and suddenly the line came free, then he found that something was fighting at the other end. It was a walleye that weighed more than nine pounds. So Hank got the trophy for the biggest fish that year.

Nick had an unusual fishing trip with Ray Hody, president of Ray-O-Vac. Ray wanted to fish Mille Lacs Lake, even though the wind was really howling. Nick was worried about how rough the lake would be, but Ray insisted. He reassured Nick that he had been on lots of big water and he could take the pounding of Mille Lacs. A few miles out on the lake, the waves were coming over the side of their boat. Ray was tough—he insisted they stay and fish. They caught some nice walleyes, but the wind blew so hard that Nick had to head to shore about fifteen miles from where they left the boat trailer. Ray was knocked off his seat a number of times on the way to shore, but he never complained. A few weeks later, Ray wrote Nick a nice letter, saying that was one of the best fishing trips he had ever been on—he would never forget that trip and neither would his butt!

He also had a close relationship with the Collette family, and Mike Olson, one of the other wheelchair-bound guides who worked at Koep's. "All the Collette boys were good fisherman," said Nick. Mike Olson and Bobby Collette were both fishing at Koep's at the same time. Mike Olson was one of Nick's closest friends until Mike's death in 2004. Mike and his wife, Sandy, lived close to Nick on Gull Lake. Sandy is still a working taxidermist.

Nick had the honor of fishing with many dignitaries over his career. He fished with Hubert Humphrey, Governors Wendell Anderson and Youngdahl, and many media celebrities.

Like others who have fished the area for many years, Nick sees a decline in the quality of most fish species, but not quantity. "It used to be common to find fifteen- to twenty-pound northern pike or nine- to eleven-pound walleyes in many of our lakes. They aren't as common as they used to be," said Nick. "I've also seen a great decline in the quality of large panfish."

He fishes whenever he gets a chance. In the winter of 2004, he caught and released the biggest and most gorgeous walleye of his life. He figured it weighed more than fourteen pounds. If he had it to do over again, he probably would have kept it.

Nick thought he was going to be a doctor, but he ended up in the fishing business and he has absolutely no regrets. He is a wonderful man who holds a place in history with the some of the legends of the Nisswa Guides' League.

Chapter Twenty-two
Lund Boat Company

MANY BOAT COMPANIES have been involved with the Nisswa Guides' League since it was first formed. There were years when all the guides had access to boat contracts—other years, just some of the guides received boat deals. In the early years, many of the boat companies used guides to promote their products. Bert Lindberry once worked with Alumacraft to help design boat layout. Other boat companies worked with different guides to design boat features for anglers. In the eighties, when tournament fishing began to grow in popularity, boat companies became more selective about who could get free boats or boats at wholesale cost. Lund, Ranger, Alumacraft, Tuffy, Crestliner, Yar Craft, and Warrior Boats all had connections to the guide league over the years, but none has had a longer connection to the league than Lund Boats. Al and Ron Lindner and Gary Roach worked with the Lund Company in the early days of the Nisswa Guides' League—Al and Gary continue to work with the company today. Lund sponsors Pro staff members of the Nisswa Guides' League.

The Lund Boat Company has produced boats for more than fifty-five years. Howard Lund and his family moved to New York Mills from California in 1946. He decided to start a sheetmetal shop and was soon installing furnaces in the community. In 1948, he built the first Lund boat—an aluminum duck boat—in his garage. Howard kept the boat strapped to the top of his car and nearly everyone who drove through town saw it. A boat salesman from Minneapolis stopped one day and asked how he could get a boat like that. When he found that Howard Lund built it and was willing to build more, he ordered fifty boats. With that order, Lund American was created. The business began in Lund's garage with three employees. A year later, they expanded to a Quonset hut and fifteen employees were added. The company became Lund Metalcraft and for two years, its employees produced seven boats a day. When a local company, York Industry, went bankrupt, Howard Lund purchased its building and changed the name of the company from Lund Metalcraft to Lund Boats.

Until his retirement in 1980, Howard Lund tested every model of boat to make sure they were seaworthy. He took them to nearby Rush Lake on windy, rough-water days and tried to tip them over. Once some people who didn't know Howard were watching him on the lake. They called the sheriff and reported that "there was a crazy man out on the lake." When the sheriff arrived and discovered it was Howard Lund, he told the onlookers that this was his usual activity.

In 1977, Lund's seventy-six employees produced around twenty-five models of boats. Today, they have more than five hundred employees and more than one hundred models of boats.

In early 1978, when Lund introduced its Mr. Pike 16 model, circumstances for the company began to change. At the time, this was the first deluxe, multi-species fishing boat to be produced for the American market. The Mr. Pike featured a flat-carpeted floor; soft, comfortable, deluxe, pedestal seats; and side-storage compartments as well as other deluxe features.

Larry Lovold, president of Lund Boats and member of the Minnesota Fishing Hall of Fame, believes the Mr. Pike caught everyone's attention and helped Lund Boats become an industry leader. "The boat was the turning point for Lund Boat Company," said Larry. The next boat to make big waves in the industry was its tiller model called the Pro Angler, which became the standard that the industry began to copy.

Both the Mr. Pike and the Pro Angler became high-volume sales models and gave Lund the confidence to develop its first truly, big-water fishing product, called the Tyee. "The first 5.3 Tyee was built in 1982," said Larry. "This proved to be a very popular boat with dealers and customers. It was also the first big-water fishing machine produced, which offered a full windshield for customer cruising. It was often fitted with twin, fifty-horse motors. One of the first Tyees was owned by Howard Lund."

Lund's big-water line continued to expand into larger models, including the eighteen-foot Tyee and the twenty-foot Baron models. These models led the market as well, and paved the way for dealer development. In the late-eighties, the first tournament model, the Pro V, was introduced. Today's tournament models consist of seventeen, eighteen, nineteen, and twenty-foot boats, all of which comprise a significant percentage of Lund's gross sales. Larry Lovold credits the tournament models for much of Lund's growth and notes that Al Lindner and Gary Roach continue to have input into the design of the Pro Vs.

The Lund Boat Company has more than 350 dealers representing its product line across the United States and Canada. Lund has employees in New York Mills, Minnesota, and it also has a sister plant in Steinback, Manitoba.

Lund Boats has become a major sponsor for fishing tournaments. Tournaments help boat companies expose and market their products to a growing number of anglers who are entering tournaments that now have payouts in excess of $100,000.

Gary Roach and Al Lindner, two of the original Nisswa Guides, continue to work with Lund Boats. That kind of product loyalty is seldom seen in the sporting world today. The relationship remains a big piece of the legacy of the Nisswa Guides.

(Portions of this chapter reproduced by permission from the New York Mills Herald, Sunday, August 9th, 1998.)

Chapter Twenty-three
Jeff Zernov

JEFF ZERNOV DOESN'T FIT the mold of most of the anglers in this book, but in 2004, he became the fifth member of the Nisswa Guides' League to be inducted into the Minnesota Fishing Hall of Fame. Unlike the other guides, he didn't begin fishing at a young age with his parents or grandparents and he didn't have a burning desire to fish when he was a child. He grew up in the Milwaukee, Wisconsin, area and even though he fished with the Nisswa Guides' League for about two years, through three summers, most of the fishing was done as an "outsider" or nonmember.

Jeff's interest in fishing began in 1964 or 1965 when he was fourteen or fifteen years old, after his parents bought a summer home on Okauchee Lake, outside of Milwaukee. Before that, he fished a little as a youngster, but not a lot. Once he became interested in the sport, he developed a real passion for it. As history would show, he was in the right place at the right time to become involved with some of the greatest pioneers and technological advances ever seen in the fishing industry.

Bill Binkelman, who became a fishing mentor to many anglers, especially freshwater anglers, was also from the Milwaukee area. Binkelman was working as a clerk in a sportshop called the Boston Store, when he began writing an area fishing tabloid, called *Milwaukee Fishing Secrets*. The tabloid was distributed free in the store. Binkelman wrote about his weekend fishing trips and promoted fishing tackle such as Jack Crawford Jigs and spoon plugs that were available in the store. His publication later became *Fishing Secrets*, and eventually, *Fishing Facts* magazine.

Binkelman kept his boat at Ray Schroeder's Lodge and Jeff drove his family's boat across the bay and joined Binkelman at the lodge for fishing trips. In the late sixties and early seventies, Binkelman was a pioneer in many areas of fishing—paving the way for identifying new ways to fish and how to find fish on different structures in lakes and rivers. He helped revolutionize the way anglers started to think about where and how to catch fish. He was a big influence on the Lindners and other cutting-edge anglers who also did a lot of experimenting during the sixties and seventies.

Jeff Zernov lived near the Boston Store, where he came to know many unique anglers through his relationship with Binkelman. When he was sixteen years old, Jeff got his driver's license and joined the Okauchee Fishing Club. Through his work with the club, he met Jim Ralstad, an editor for *Fishing Facts* magazine, and also Dan Sura, a member of the Milwaukee Walleyes Unlimited Fishing Club. Dan and Jeff fished together in Wisconsin, and on several occasions were invited by the Lindners to fish in the Minnesota Governor's Fishing Opener. (At the time, Dan Sura worked for the Johnson Wax Company. He later joined the Lindners in many of their ventures and he currently works for the Lindners' Fishing Edge Television Company.)

He met Al and Ron Lindner when they came to Milwaukee to give a presentation to the local fishing club and he got to know them better when they were still living in Chicago. He also became acquainted with Marv and Judy Koep while they were doing sports shows in the Milwaukee area. Later, Jeff did in-store promotions for Lindy Little Joe at Koep's store. His fishing connections developed as quickly as his passion for fishing—by the time he was eighteen, he was a full-fledged fishing fanatic.

Jeff caught the attention of the Lindners and others by winning some of the big fish tournaments sponsored by the Okauchee Fishing Club and the Milwaukee Walleyes Unlimited Club. While he was a senior in high school, he even wrote a fishing article for *Fishing Facts* magazine.

After Al and Ron Lindner moved from Chicago to Brainerd, Jeff maintained contact with them. When they started their new tackle company in 1972, they offered him a job as their first employee. Jeff was nineteen years old and his title was Field Promotional Specialist. Later, Gary Roach, Rod Romine, and Ted Capra were also hired. Jeff's primary role as a field specialist was to take customers fishing and show them how to use a Lindy Rig. He worked for the company during the week, and through his association with Marv Koep, began getting weekend guide trips at Koep's Nisswa Bait and Tackle. He got trips off and on during the summer months, with more trips in the fall, when the guides who were teachers returned to school.

Most anglers in the greater Milwaukee area had heard of the Nisswa Guides' League. The members of the league were featured in area newspapers and magazines and were considered true fishing legends. Writers from Milwaukee went to Brainerd to fish with Al and Ron Lindner, Gary Roach, Harry Van Doren, and others, and returned to Milwaukee to write about their fishing experiences. It was great press for the Nisswa Guides as well as good marketing for others in the fishing industry that were associated with the guides.

Jeff and the other field staff were laid off during one of the sales of the Lindy Little Joe Company in the summer of 1974. Jeff learned much about structure fishing from working with Binkelman, the Lindners, and others, and he used the knowledge to learn the lakes in the Brainerd area. That summer, he guided full time, right into the late-fall, November fishing season. He guided for twenty-six days in a row, mostly fishing for bass. Getting voted into the Nisswa Guides' League during this period was no easy task and Jeff was never formally voted in as a member. He kept taking trips, and one day, the guides told him to start joining them for lunch at Potthoff's. Until he quit guiding to go into other ventures, Jeff was an unofficial member.

He always felt the need to produce when he was working as a guide at Koep's. There was a lot of pressure on each guide to catch fish, take pictures, and promote oneself—competition was pretty keen. Customers knew who was catching fish from the weekly photos in the local newspaper. Jeff felt less pressure when he was finally invited to sit at the guides' table and share information with the other guides. Ultimately, the pressure to catch fish and take pictures was one of the reasons he decided to quit guiding. Catch-and-release was not being practiced at the time and Jeff began feeling guilt at harvesting great numbers of fish on so many area lakes.

As a guide, Jeff's first boat was a Lund 315 with a twenty-five-horse motor—he later purchased a Tuffy boat. The Lund 315 was not a safe, big-lake boat. After Ted Capra nearly lost his life while fishing on Canada's Eagle Lake, Jeff decided to get a different boat for fishing the bigger waters of the state. (Ted had gotten caught in big winds on Eagle Lake and capsized. Ted and his son held onto gas tanks for two hours before being rescued.)

Jeff developed many interesting observations during his years of fishing in the area.

"Ron and Al Lindner are an equation where one plus one equals three," said Jeff. "Ron is a master at marketing and Al is an outstanding angler. I don't think they would have been as successful if they had not worked in tandem all these years. Bill Binkelman, the Lindners, and other pioneers learned that the keys to fishing were structure and biomass. Find the bait and you find the fish. In the early years, few anglers had sonar and this technology put the early users in the driver's seat. Those of us who fished with sonar were doing things other anglers were unable to do. Now this technology is at everyone's fingertips. With GPS, lake maps, and other technologies, anglers can download information on their computers and know in minutes what used to take a lifetime to learn.

"Fishing is still very good today. Many lakes are being supplemented by the DNR and I think the numbers of fish are still in the lakes, but the sizes are not as large as they were in the sixties and seventies. Many of those structure fish that we used to catch are gone and now we see more fish that are relating to the weeds or suspended in deeper water. The fish are definitely more educated, too. They have seen a lot of bait and it has changed they way they behave. I remember when Harry Van Doren talked about fishing out of Sandy Point Resort on Gull Lake in the days before motors. He fished only as far away from the resort as he could row and still get back in time. Now we have big boats and big motors—distance is not a deterrent to where anglers can go. Not many people went nine or ten miles to the mud flats on Mille Lacs in the fifties or early sixties. Now that is a fifteen- to twenty-minute drive.

"When I think of the best fishermen I have been around, I think of Harry Van Doren. He guided for more than fifty years and was totally dedicated to the sport. One time, a man who was unable to get into or out of a boat came to fish with Harry. Harry parked his boat under a tree, got a block-and-tackle, hoisted the man into the tree, lowered him into the boat, and did the same in reverse after the fishing trip. That was how dedicated he was to taking people fishing.

"One day, I fished with Harry on Gull Lake. He was casting a Mepps Bucktail for northern pike. As he reeled in his plug, a northern pike grabbed it and jumped out of the water with the plug in his mouth. In a flash, Harry hit the free spool on his reel, let the northern take the bait and turn in mid-air, and go in the opposite direction. Harry set the hook and nailed the northern. It happened so fast, I couldn't believe he had the frame of mind to let the northern bite the bait, turn, and set the hook. It was quite a show of fishing skill."

According to Jeff, Al Lindner is another unbelievable fisherman who never lost his passion for fishing and still fishes around 320 days a year. "I learned to work the opposite shorelines that Al Lindner worked," recalled Jeff. "Al is right-handed, so he liked to work with the shore to his port side. That way he could read his flasher and scope out the shorelines for points and inside turns. I worked from the starboard side so we wouldn't cover the same area. We found fishing spots in hours that probably took local fishermen a lifetime to learn without the electronics.

"Royal Karels was considered a bass expert in the sixties by bass anglers all over the Midwest. Although Royal took a little break from fishing, now he fishes with the same passion he had thirty years ago.

"Another man who is an absolute scientist and fishing expert is Joe Fellegy. He understood patterns on Mille Lacs Lake as well as any angler I ever saw. He had a reason for the layout of rods and reels on his launch. He knew where to find fish on the mud flats, on rocks or shorelines, and he knew where to find suspended fish. His knowledge of the lake without electronics is legendary and he remains one of the true fishing legends of our time.

"I enjoyed fishing North Long Lake for bass, and Gull, Pelican, and Edward for walleyes. I still try to go fishing three or four days per week, but I fish to experiment rather than to catch fish to take home for a meal. I really enjoy the challenge of trying to outsmart the creature at the other end of the line."

Jeff left guiding and joined the Lindners as an equal partner in the development of *In-Fisherman* magazine. He sold his share of the magazine four years later and started a new company, Zercom. The Zercom company developed many products, some of which were fishing sonar equipment. The company developed into a $22 million company with more than four hundred employees. Jeff sold the company, did some real estate projects, and in 1998, started another new company, Nature Vision. It went public in 2004 and produces many products including the Aqua-Vu Underwater Camera, Bird-Vu, Buzz Stick Rods, and other products used in the outdoors. The underwater camera is a product that has virtually changed the way anglers see the bottoms of lakes. Jeff is currently Nature Vision's president.

Jeff's time with the Nisswa Guides' League was short, but his impact—both on the fishing industry and the legacy he continues to develop—is huge. Jeff was a nineteen-year-old kid when he began guiding. By his own admission, he was an outsider to the Nisswa Guides' League and he was not accepted into the league with open arms until near the end of his guiding experience. Looking back at the era, Jeff appreciates how good the guides in the league were as well as the effect they had on trends in fishing.

He also looks at that period as the invention of fishing as it is today. The techniques and technology that were introduced to anglers during the late sixties and early seventies revolutionized the way people fished. Secret fishing spots on lakes that took anglers years to find could now be found in hours or days and the fishing haunts of all lakes became public information in a short period of time. The big fish that had hiding spots on most lakes were exposed to a wider group of anglers and many of those big fish got caught. According to Jeff, it was not just an era of technology and innovation, but it was also an era of information. All anglers had access to new information on how to catch fish, where to catch fish, and how to track down trophy fish. In the sixties, it was believed that about 10 percent of the anglers caught 90 percent of the fish. Now novice anglers have access to remote "secret" spots by simply buying a lake map, downloading the spots on a computer, and marking the key areas on a Global Positioning System device.

Jeff Zernov was there for the technology revolution in fishing. He has also demonstrated that he is one of the truly unique innovators in the fishing industry. He has registered more than twenty-five different patents. As was mentioned at the beginning of this chapter, he was inducted into the 2004 Minnesota Fishing Hall of Fame as the fifth member of the hall to have been in the Nisswa Guides' League. He has rubbed shoulders with many of the legends of fishing and by his induction into the Minnesota Fishing Hall of Fame, he has earned his spot on the list.

Chapter Twenty-four
Lenny Hodgson

LIKE MANY OF THE GUIDES that have fished for the Nisswa Guides' League, Lenny Hodgson grew up in the fishing world. By the time he was four years old, he was already fishing at his grandfather's cabin on Balsam Lake, north of Nashwauk in northeastern Minnesota. Lenny grew up in the small town of Calumet in the northeastern part of Minnesota, a region containing some of the state's iron ore pits.

His grandfather was a longtime guide in the Longville area, which is north of Nisswa and surrounded by many lakes. With his grandfather, Lenny fished the Lake Winnibigoshish area all through his youth as well as the lakes around Longville.

Attending the community college in Grand Rapids for two years, Lenny finished his bachelor's degree at Bemidji State University, and later completed his master's degree from St. Cloud State University. His first and only teaching job was in Brainerd, teaching at the elementary level.

Lenny began his guiding career at Deerwood Sports Shop in Deerwood—about fifteen miles northeast of Brainerd—and he fished lakes east of Brainerd, such as Bay Lake, Clearwater, and Crooked Lakes. While coaching wrestling, Lenny became acquainted with Marv Koep, whose son, Kevin, was a wrestler.

In 1974, Lenny began guiding from Koep's. Lenny's family used to rent a cabin on Gull Lake every summer. He didn't know the lake well as a kid, but he learned it better when he connected with some of the guys at Nisswa Bait and Tackle after he moved to the area. At the time, in the history of the guides, Max Slocum was winding down his guiding career and was taking a few trips from his home. The Lindners had left the shop, but Harry Van Doren and Cully Swenson still guided. Cully was having some problems with his heart and he, too, was slowing down. Royal Karels was also guiding at the time Lenny joined the league. Lenny got to know Gary Roach and learned to appreciate the great fishing skills he possessed.

Harry and Max taught Lenny the locations of the special fishing spots on the lakes, which made it easier for him to fit into guiding. Lenny still has customers from the St. Louis area that began fishing with him in 1974. Old Joe Masik also helped Lenny to learn Gull Lake. All the help he received was important, but spending countless hours on the water is mainly what helped him become a knowledgeable angler.

Lenny paid $383 for his first real guide boat, motor, and trailer—a sixteen-foot Crestliner with a twenty-five-horse Mercury on the back. It didn't come with a flat, wooden floor, so he built his own floor for the boat. He also fished out of a number of Lund boats during his guiding experiences.

A versatile guide, Lenny covers many lakes during the fishing season, including Gull, Hubert, North Long, Round, Leech, Mille Lacs, and other small lakes. In the early eighties, he began seriously fishing muskies.

When Shelly and Kevin Koep were in their early teens, he took them fishing a lot. His most memorable customers over the years were former University of Minnesota basketball coach Clem Haskins and his family, and Kirby Puckett, the great baseball player from the Minnesota Twins.

"Kirby was a hoot," said Lenny. "He registered at Grand View Lodge under an assumed name. I never knew who I was fishing with before I picked him up on the water. He had one request—don't tell anyone who he was until we were done fishing in a couple of days. Kirby was one heck of a bass fisherman. Never kept any fish and boy, could he set the hook."

One of Lenny's scary fishing moments occurred on Mille Lacs Lake. Lenny and his customers were fishing about nine miles out on one of the big mud flats. "We had a slight breeze coming out of the south and then the wind switched to the northwest. I had a thirty-five-horse motor at the time and I thought we should head home, in case the wind picked up. Boy, did it pick up! I had the customer lie on the bottom of the boat and we pounded against the wind all the way back to the landing. We were soaking wet by the time we got to shore. It was a scary trip. And another year, I got caught on Pelican Lake in one heck of a hailstorm that was a scary experience, too."

His most unusual catch was a padlock that had a key in the keyhole—the hook caught the key. And one customer caught two, two-pound bass on the same lure. Each bass was hooked with a different treble hook and both fish put up a fight. When two bass came in on the same lure—especially bass that large—no one in the boat could believe their eyes.

In Lenny's experience, overall fish sizes are smaller now than thirty years ago, but it is hard to compare quantity—fishing is still very good. Water quality on area lakes is better, due in part to central sewer systems that divert sewage away from the lakes. He has also seen more customers supporting catch-and-release—happy to have the experience of catching the fish along with the satisfaction of letting them go to fight another time.

A nice, thirty-two-inch fish was the biggest walleye that he ever released. And he has caught area bass that weighed up to six pounds, which is a nice bass in Minnesota. A multi-species fisherman, Lenny's first love is bass fishing. His favorite lake is North Long, one of the premier bass lakes in the area.

Lenny can remember past years when the Nisswa/Brainerd lakes area had more than four thousand seasonal homeowners, according to the local postmaster's statistics. In 2004, there were fewer than eight hundred. The area continues to grow and more families have chosen to live in the area all year around.

A couple of Lenny's stories involve boat motors. One morning, having just finished a morning trip, Marv drove to the store with the motor still running on his trailered boat. He had been fishing on Pelican Lake, backed the trailer in the lake, loaded the boat, jumped in the truck, and drove about twelve miles with the motor still running. For some reason, the water pump didn't burn out.

Kevin Koep wasn't as lucky. While loading his boat on the trailer, he forgot to trim the motor. He drove about fifteen miles with the prop dragging on the tarred highway. His motor shaft was quite a bit shorter by the time he reached the store—the bottom had completely worn off.

Lenny served as mayor of Nisswa for a number of years and continues to serve on the Nisswa city council. I have fished with him for about fifteen years. He is one of the real class acts in the fishing industry. The true mark of a good guide is his amount of repeat-client business. Repeat customers make up most of Lenny's business. Without seeking the limelight, he is as good an angler as many of the well-known names in the fishing industry. In the spring of 2004, Lenny retired from teaching. Now entering his thirtieth year as a guide, he plans on guiding as long as he is able. Lenny is a true professional on and off the water—he represents fish guiding the way it should be.

Chapter Twenty-five
Mark Lee

MARK LEE IS A BORN FISHERMAN. He is now in his later forties, but his fishing experience suggests that he is much older. Born in Brainerd, Mark grew up on Gull Lake's Wilson Bay. He is the only son in a family of five kids and none of his sisters became involved in fishing, so when it was time to fish with his dad, Bob, and his uncle, Perry, he got a lot of attention. Uncle Perry owned Perry's Sports Shop in Brainerd, where some of the Collette boys guided. Mark's dad was a building contractor, so Mark learned the construction trade working with his father.

Mark's dad and his Uncle Perry, his father's brother, loved to fish, and usually included Mark in most fishing trips. Mark had access to a boat as a young boy and learned where to fish on Wilson Bay, and later, on the south end of Gull. He didn't own electronic equipment, so he learned the lake by marking shoreline features and marking water depths with various pieces of equipment. He went to school with Jim and Bill Lindner, two of Ron's sons, and spent a lot of time fishing with the Lindner boys who lived on Steamboat Bay, which was also on the south end of Gull.

In his early days of fishing on Wilson Bay, Mark saw one other man who knew many of the same spots that Mark was fishing—Nick Adams, the Minnesota Fishing Hall of Famer. For a long time, Mark's only real competition on some of those spots was Nick.

"I really respected Nick Adams as a fisherman, because he learned those spots long before I knew them," said Mark. "He learned them the old-fashioned way—he spent time on the water. And I also learned a lot about fishing from the Lindner family. They had developed a little scientific publication about FLP: Fish, Location, and Presentation. That scientific approach is what I still use today and it works for all species from panfish to lake trout. I owe a lot of my fishing success to the Lindners."

Mark got his first taste of guiding by catching northern pike at the mouth of the Gull River. He knew where to catch good-size fish and he took the fish to the little resort at the mouth of the river and he showed the resort customers the fish he had caught. Every once in a while, they asked Mark to take them to the spots where he caught the fish—soon he was guiding for fun and a small amount of money.

He began his formal guiding career when he was sixteen years old. He started taking trips out of Perry's Sport Shop in Brainerd and Garrison Creek Marina on Mille Lacs Lake. In 1973, Mark went to his dad to see if he would cosign a loan so he could get a boat, motor, trailer, and a car. His dad was reluctant and said he would talk to Mark's mother.

"I remember lying in bed that night and I could hear my mom and dad talking about the loan," recalled Mark. "My dad didn't want to cosign my loan, but my mother said they needed to give me a chance to see if I could be successful. Dad finally gave in and said he would cosign." Mark borrowed $1,050 from Brainerd National Bank and bought a Tuffy boat, a twenty-five-horse Chrysler motor, and spent $125 for a 1963 Chevrolet Impala. He was in business!

Mark got quite a few trips out of the Garrison Creek Marina. He learned some of Mille Lacs Lake while fishing with his dad, and he learned more of the lake by spending time on the water.

"I didn't always know what mud flat I was fishing on, but I got to know Mille Lacs and usually did pretty well on the big lake. I learned to fish Mille Lacs with my flasher. That was the only way to really get to know your way around all the structure on that lake. I knew who Joe Fellegy was—I knew his boat. I stayed away from Joe because he had a reputation as a launch driver who didn't want other boats following him to his spots. I respected that and usually stayed away from his boat."

Bobby Collette convinced Mark to stop at Nisswa Bait and Tackle and talk to Marv Koep about guiding. Marv gave him a chance to see what he could do. Mark began guiding at Koep's in 1974. Marv talked to Mark's customers to see what kind of a job he did. They were nearly always happy fishing with Mark—he caught fish. Mark was a success. After his first year at the shop, he began taking 240 to 250 trips a year. He became the number-one guide on the chart and held the position until he made a career change in 2000.

Mark learned a lot about fishing by listening to some of the older guides, but most of his skills came from his association with the Lindners.

"I got to know Harry Van Doren very well," said Mark. "I visited him at his trailer house and we spent hours talking about the area lakes and different ways that we fished the lakes. Harry didn't use the Fish-Location-Presentation approach to fishing, but he was a great fisherman. He was more likely to go to his favorite spots and work the break lines or humps. He didn't start by looking for fish, he just went to his spots. If he didn't get a bite or a fish, he moved on to another spot. Harry liked the south and west sides of North Long Lake and he really liked the north end of Gull Lake.

"I think I gained Harry's respect by fishing the same lakes he did and sometimes coming in with more fish than he had. He could see I knew what I was doing and he often came to me to see where I had my luck. That worked the other way, too, when he had more luck than I did. We developed a good relationship working together.

"I didn't know Max Slocum, but I knew Cully Swenson very well. Cully wasn't the fisherman that Harry was, but he was a kind, wonderful man who could tell funny stories all day long. When we would get rained out, we all went back to the store and listened to Cully's stories. He was hilarious.

"I remember hearing that Max Slocum had gotten into some kind of disagreement at the store and he finished his guiding career at Breezy Point, although that was towards the end of his career. I don't think he guided too much after that.

"Marv Koep took photos of the fish that were caught during the summer and he used the photos to develop marketing material for the next year. It was to a guide's advantage to catch as many big fish as he could so he had better pictures in the next year's marketing brochure. There was also a fishing contest every year. Customers looked at the photos and requested the guides they wanted. This was especially true when the customers were new and didn't know any of the guides.

"I guided at Koep's for almost thirty years. I fished during the fishing season and did construction during the winter months. I always remembered what Harry Van Doren had when he died—a beat-up truck, a beat-up boat and motor, and two lots on Lake Edward. That was all he had to show for more than fifty years as a full-time guide. I have seven children, and my wife and I decided that I had to get a better-paying job, at least for the health insurance, so about five years ago, I took my name off the chart and moved to the Twin Cities metro area. It was something I had to do for my family, but I have not stopped fishing, nor I have I stopped guiding. I love to fish and I love guiding. I don't see myself ever quitting, but I am my own boss now. I run my own construction company and I can take off when I want to. I fish in the Twin Cities area, Brainerd area, and Lake of the Woods. I fish about two days a week in September, three days a week in October, and four days a week in November. I will probably never go back to full-time guiding because I don't think I could take the pounding anymore, but I plan to keep guiding at the pace I am keeping up today.

"I made lifelong friendships guiding. I got to be really good friends with Steve and Bobby Collette. We remain close today. Bobby and Steve are absolute fishing experts. Steve and I were friends in high school. He was always the little, short guy and I was always his big, tall buddy. We have had an unbelievable friendship over the years. Sam Karels, Royal's son, was also a guide at Koep's for about three years. He was a great 'hook,' too, and really knew how to fish. He still works as a guide in Alaska.

"I owe an awful lot to Marv Koep, too. I was with Marv when business was great and I was there when times were tough. On more than one occasion, I had to go to Marv and ask if I could borrow money—sometimes it would be for five hundred dollars. He never asked me why I needed the money or when I was going to pay it back. He just gave me the money. I always paid it back and I always offered to pay some interest, but he never accepted more than the amount I borrowed. He was great to me and I'll never forget that. I lobbied hard to get Marv listed as the number-one guide when I left. He had already sold the store and was working as a full-time guide. I was happy when the other guides put Marv at the number-one spot.

"I have a few experiences that I remember as being funny. One time I was guiding on Mille Lacs and the wind was blowing pretty well. One of the customers got motion sickness and he was throwing up over the side of the boat. I offered to take him to shore because it didn't seem like the wind would die down but he insisted on staying and fishing. Finally, I told him to drink a can of cola and see if it settled his stomach. He drank it and within five minutes he did what I guess is called 'projectile vomiting.' He threw up the cola, straight out of his mouth, for at least thirty feet. I have never seen anything like it. His stomach calmed down and he got better and fished the rest of the day.

"On another trip, Glen Belgum, Steve Collette, and I were fishing with three boatloads of customers who wanted a shorelunch. We'd been catching bass and walleyes and some of these guys didn't want anything to do with eating bass, but they wanted the walleyes. A few of the guys didn't care what kind of fish they ate—they just wanted a shorelunch. Steve and Glen came up with the idea of cooking the bass first and telling the guys they were eating walleyes. So they cooked the fish, beans, and potatoes, and served them up—telling everyone they were going to eat the walleyes first. The whole crew ate the bass like they were starving to death. Then Steve served the walleyes, but told them they were the bass. Those guys made faces and put down the fish, saying it didn't taste as good as the walleyes. The jig was up, the guides told them they had already eaten the bass and were turning up their noses at walleyes. Steve,

Mark, and Glen had a great laugh out of that trip, telling the customers they were phony about what kind of fish they really liked!

"Gary Roach used to fish a little lake where my grandmother lived. She got mad, seeing him on this little lake all the time. One day, she said she was going to shoot at him if she ever saw him there again. She never did, but she was sure mad. A guy on Lake Alexandria did shoot at Bobby Collette one morning. I don't remember how that story ended up, but Bobby never got hurt. I had a few experiences on the lake with what I called water rage, where a boater took a run at me and my customers because he thought we were fishing his spot. That was always scary.

"Kevin Koep was one of the best fishermen I ever fished with. I was really disappointed when he quit guiding. He was good at catching fish in areas where no one else ever fished. He was what we call a "good stick! He was definitely good enough to be a tournament angler.

"Steve Collette, Glen Belgum, and I fished together as a team for many years and we had great fishing experiences. I really enjoyed fishing with the Nisswa Guides' League. It was, and still is, a prestigious organization. I was proud to be a member.

"Fishing has changed a lot over the past thirty years. It used to be a lot easier to catch four- or five-pound fish, but the nice thing about fishing today is that most of those fish are put back into the lake. I always liked fishing the big lakes like Gull and the Whitefish Chain. I seemed to get my biggest fish off of Whitefish, but Gull Lake is still a phenomenal lake to fish. I still love guiding, I love the people experiences and the experience of being on the water. I have never gotten burned-out or tired of guiding. I plan to guide as long as I am healthy enough to keep doing it." Mark spoke earnestly, and the look in his eyes was that of a unique person with a passion for what he is doing. Mark has been featured in a book or two and he is often referred to as "Mr. Gull Lake," but his fishing skills work on every lake he fishes.

I consider Mark to be one of the finest fishermen I have ever seen. Like Steve Collette, Marv Koep, and some of the other legendary guides, Mark Lee can be found on the water nearly any time of the year. He will be the tall, lanky guy in the big Ranger boat—just enjoying himself!

Chapter Twenty-six
Henry Ebert

HENRY "HANK" EBERT began his guiding career at Koep's in the spring of 1976. He was asked to help guide for the Governor's Fishing Opener that year and started getting trips off and on during the spring and summer seasons of 1976. Before long, he was fishing full time—putting in more than one hundred days a season on the water. Hank fished as a full-time guide until 2003 when he "retired," and now he only guides occasionally.

Hank grew up in Minneapolis near Lake Harriet, one of many small lakes located inside the city limits. Fishing was part of his family's history. His grandmother owned a resort on a small lake near Mille Lacs Lake. He spent many summers working and fishing at his grandmother's resort, where he developed a lifelong interest in fishing as a very young boy.

His aunt and uncle owned a resort on upper Gull Lake. Russell and Roger Ebert were Hank's two cousins who grew up at the resort. Roger loved to fish and he taught Hank where to fish in the Brainerd-Nisswa area. (I was in the army reserves with Roger and Russell Ebert and both became well-known for racing snowmobiles and cars. Russell became a teacher at the local technical college and developed a reputation as a top mechanic and engineer working for Dick Trickle on the NASCAR circuit. Roger enjoyed a brief career as a snowmobile racer for the John Deere company.)

Roger Ebert was a good-looking, fun-loving guy that everyone enjoyed being around. He and Hank were like brothers. They had the same interests, the same wild streak, and enjoyed being outdoors. Roger took Hank to Mille Lacs Lake, Winnibigoshish, and many of the lakes in the greater-Brainerd area. Hank got to know area lakes quite well just by spending time on the water with Roger. They fished, trapped, hunted, and just spent a great deal of time together.

Hank served in the army and was stationed in Viet Nam. He got through his tour of duty in Viet Nam without a scratch. He was not as lucky after he returned home— a very serious motorcycle accident in 1970 nearly cost him his life and left him paralyzed from the waist down.

Because of his cousin, Roger, Hank decided to move to Brainerd in 1971. As fate would have it, Roger, too, had a serious snowmobile accident a few years later, and was killed when his snowmobile hit a tree. Roger's death was a tremendous shock to Hank as well as the entire community.

Hank did not allow his accident to stop him from doing the things he loved, including fishing, hunting, trapping, and competitive archery. Customers who fish with Hank are amazed at his fishing skills, especially his uncanny accuracy at casting lures under and around docks and boats when fishing for bass. His custom-built van allows him to get in and out of the vehicle and he usually has a customer or another guide help put his boat in and out of the water. He rolls his wheelchair to the boat, slides into the boat, and is ready to fish.

Chuck Cargill was a longtime trapping partner with Hank and told me he never saw anyone with better trapping skills than Hank. "He could skin a beaver or mink as fast as anyone I ever saw," said Chuck. "He can set traps and catch animals with the best of them."

For many years, Hank made his living by guiding in the summer and trapping in the winter. The Nisswa Bait and Tackle Shop still bought and sold furs when Hank first started working there—he did a lot of his business through the shop.

There was a period when three wheelchair guides worked at Koep's: Bobby Collette, Mike Olson, and Hank. Mike mostly did trips on Mille Lacs Lake, but Bobby and Hank fished the same lakes that the other guides did.

Hank's first guide boat was an eighteen-foot Starcraft with a thirty-five-horse Johnson motor. In the seventies, he fished tournaments, but later he quit tournaments and concentrated on guiding. Hank remembers the mid- to late-seventies as an unbelievable period for fishing.

"It was nothing to go to Gull Lake and get a limit of northern pike or walleyes," said Hank, "and Mille Lacs Lake was tremendous, too. When I first began guiding, I didn't have a livewell, so I used stringers and pulled them over the side of the boat. One time, I had three customers fishing on Gull Lake and we were one short of a limit when the stringer came untied and floated away. I told the customers not to worry—we would still get our limit. We started over again and we did get another limit. We didn't catch monster pike, but they were nice in the five- to twelve-pound range. Pink-and-white Fuzz-e-grubs were real hot bait for a few years. It was a blast working the weed edges for pike and bass because the fishing was so good."

Hank fished a lot with the celebrity drag racers who came to race at Brainerd International Raceway. He got to know some of the racers like Don Prudhomme, Raymond Beatle, and Shirley Muldowny—racers who were the best in the business at the time.

One summer, while fishing Mille Lacs, Hank got caught in a violent storm. He and his fishing partner put in on the south end of the big lake and went all the way to the north end to fish. The storm had very strong winds and Hank wondered if he could make it back to the other end of the lake. The waves were so big that boats disappeared between waves. He made it back, but two other fishermen didn't. They drowned when their boat capsized.

During the early years that Hank was guiding, many of the guides used Lund boats. The boats were built in New York Mills—just an hour's drive from Nisswa—and the company had an arrangement that allowed the guides to buy direct from the factory. Later, some of the guides began fishing out of boats manufactured by other companies. Eventually, other companies worked out agreements with the guides and the close connection to Lund Boats was terminated.

I asked Hank how he has seen fishing change since the early seventies and he feels that the quantity seems to be pretty good, but the quality and the size are not the same. He once caught a stringer of six northern pike that weighed fifty-four pounds. He doesn't think the pike are as free-roaming as they were thirty years ago—they are more concentrated on break lines and sunken structure because the lakes don't have the weeds that used to hold bait fish and predators. Cabbage weeds are thinned out of most area lakes and those weeds were excellent for holding fish.

Hank would like to see the fishing limits in Minnesota changed to three bass, three walleyes, and two northern pike. One species he thinks is better now than ever is the musky. He was fishing on Mille Lacs a couple of summers ago and saw sixty fish in one day—that was unheard of thirty years ago on Mille Lacs. The musky fishing has also been excellent on Leech Lake, Cass Lake, and other musky waters in Minnesota. Hank loves fishing musky and his favorite lake today is Mille Lacs.

He has seen many changes in the guide business since his first years of guiding—perhaps the biggest change is that there are fewer small resorts in the area. The bigger resorts use their own guides—often summer employees, who, in Hank's opinion, don't know the lakes very well. He thinks the guides that fish at Koep's today are still some of the best in the area.

One of my funniest stories involving Hank occurred around six or seven years ago.

We were fishing with about twenty guide boats together at Madden's on Gull Lake. Hank was running a little late. He put his boat in at a landing at the resort, then joined all the guides and our customers at Madden's Lodge for breakfast. Everyone was assigned customers to fish with, and after breakfast, we headed out to get into our boats. Hank had been working on his boat the night before and forgot to put the plug back in the bottom of his boat. When he got to the water, his boat had sunk! It was not completely on the bottom of the lake, but it was underwater and it took quite a while to pump the boat dry.

Hank lives in Nisswa and doesn't trap anymore, but he has not lost his zest for fishing. He can still be found on the water every summer, doing what he loves to do—fishing!

Chapter Twenty-seven
Steve Collette

STEVE COLLETTE IS THE YOUNGER brother of Bobby, and like Bobby, has an addiction to fishing. The first thing one notices about Steve is his size. He is not tall in stature, but he is a giant on the water. He is one of the best fishermen I have ever been around in the years that I have worked at Koep's.

Like Bobby, Steve, too, recalls spending much time in the boat with his dad and brothers when he was a youngster. His family lived on the Mississippi River before they moved to North Long Lake. Steve remembers that his dad had a real passion for fishing. He spent quality time on the water teaching his sons how to fish and how to have patience when on the water. Steve's mother honked the car horn to signal to the boys when it was time to quit fishing and come home. If they hadn't been chased off the water, they would have spent all their free time there.

Steve began guiding at Shady Lane Resort when he was only twelve years old. Like his brother Bobby, he worked around the resort and started picking up trips because he knew the lake so well.

As a young boy, Steve bought bait and hung around the Nisswa Bait and Tackle Shop. Through this connection as well as his brother, Bobby, he eventually started getting trips out of the bait shop. In 1976, he began as a part-time guide and then went full time in 1977. Bobby also helped to get Steve's good friend, Mark Lee, into the guides' league and these two young anglers both developed into exceptional fishermen. Mark and Steve attended high school together. It was not easy for them to get accepted into the league. They joined the league on a trial basis and had to prove themselves worthy of getting the votes to become members. They were voted in as full-fledged members and stayed on as full-time guides for nearly twenty-five years.

Steve has vivid memories of working at the bait shop in the early days.

"The opening day of fishing at the store was pure chaos—traffic was lined up on both sides of Highway 371," recalled Steve. "Marv hired people to direct traffic around the store so there wouldn't be accidents. People stopped in at noon to see what the guides brought back from the morning fishing trip. There weren't many other guides in the Nisswa and Brainerd area back in the late-seventies. Many tourists came to the store to see fish, to look at the photos on the wall, and talk to guides about where to fish. There were days when you could hardly get into the store because there were so many sightseers hanging around. It was like a television studio!"

When Steve began fishing at Koep's, Harry Van Doren was winding down his career, but Harry still spent many days hanging around the store because he missed fishing and being with the guides. Steve really liked Harry and got to know him through Bobby's connection with the old guide.

Steve guided at Koep's full time for twenty-seven years. Then he began doing more work in the building construction business and guiding on a part-time basis, something he is still doing today. Four hours on the water are considered a trip when guiding and one summer Steve had 245 trips—a number he believes is still a record for the Nisswa Guides' League.

Even though he now has his own construction business, Steve guides whenever he gets a chance. It is not uncommon to see him fishing on a Wednesday or a Friday during the week. Somehow he manages to get away from the construction business to slip in a trip or two. He "reads" lakes well. He has fished the area so long that he knows the different lakes' cycles of when the fish are most likely to be biting.

His first, real fishing boat as a guide was a Tuffy. He had a twenty-five-horse Johnson motor and he remembers paying $1,700 for the boat and $770 for the motor. His next boat was a Lund Pro Angler.

Steve has a good sense of humor and he remembers some of the funnier stories about fishing at Koep's. Sam Karels, Royal's son, scraped a dead skunk off the road and put it into Dick Young's livewell. Dick went fishing, caught a fish, opened his livewell to put the fish into it, and almost fell overboard from the smell. He thought Bobby Collette was responsible for the trick, so when he finished the morning trip he stuck the skunk in Bobby's livewell. Later that afternoon, Bobby opened up his livewell to put a fish into it and almost died from the smell!

One of the tricks Steve pulled on his storemates happened after a three-day trip to Canada with some old customers. They landed twenty-four monster pike—ranging in weight from sixteen to thirty-one pounds. They put the fish on ice, brought them back to the store, took photos, and told everyone they came from Gull Lake. People were amazed. The men eventually confessed that the fish were from Canada, but they had a great time playing that joke at the store.

Steve learned the area lakes by spending every summer guiding and fishing new spots on different lakes. Since he grew up on North Long, he expanded his fishing range each summer. One special summer customer, Fred Kibbler, brought his children and hired Steve for days at a time. He stayed at an area resort, met Steve for breakfast, and told him the lake he wanted to fish that day. Fred was a great customer and he also provided Steve with the opportunity to explore new lakes on a regular basis.

He has fished with many television and radio personalities, members of the Minnesota Vikings, and other celebrities during his guiding career. He has seen many changes during his tenure on the water—fewer family resorts, more guides, many more sporting stores, and more people heading to Canada and other northern destinations to get away from the urban growth.

He thinks fishing is still very good on the area lakes, but the sizes of fish are smaller today. His favorite fish is the walleye, but he enjoys fishing all species.

Steve is a young man, but he is Old School when it comes to fishing. He learned the lakes the hard way—by spending time on the water. He fished as a young boy and began guiding as an early teenager. When he sees people on the water today who call themselves guides, he wonders how much they know about fishing or the area lakes. Electronics has opened up the lakes to people who didn't have access to many fishing spots before and he thinks some of those folks are taking advantage of customers.

Guiding part time at Koep's, he operates his own building construction business in the Brainerd lakes area. He still has a passion for fishing and is the first to admit that he misses being on the water full time—a day pounding nails will always take a backseat to a good day on the lake. Steve offers a unique connection to the early guides at the Nisswa Bait Shop because he was there in the earlier years and still guides. Steve, like brothers, Bobby and Tim, is an outstanding angler.

Chapter Twenty-eight
Tim Collette

TIM COLLETTE IS THE THIRD brother in the Collette family to have been a full-time guide for the Nisswa Guides' League. Mark Collette, a younger brother, also guided part-time at Koep's. Tim is probably also the most humble and quiet of the three Collette boys who guided full time. During our interview, Tim claimed he didn't have much to say that was interesting—he just fished and worked. Tim, too, has a reputation as an excellent fisherman. Like Bobby and Steve, he began fishing on North Long Lake. When he was fifteen years old, he began working at a resort, which later became known as Sullivan's Resort. He guided one or two trips per week until he worked his way into the guides' league when he was around sixteen years old.

Tim was thirteen years old when he began working with his brother, Bobby, the summer after Bobby's accident. Bobby had purchased a Lund Tyee and started guiding on Mille Lacs Lake. Bobby was the guide and boat pilot and Tim became the deckhand. He assisted customers with bait, netted the fish, cleaned up the boat, and helped in other areas where Bobby needed help. He earned $5 a day—which was thought to be good money for a kid back then. He had a great summer working with Bobby and he learned the big lake really well.

When Tim began working at the Nisswa Bait Shop, he was just a young guy, still wet behind the ears. The guides working at the store at the time were Harry Van Doren, Cully Swenson, Max Slocum, Dick Young, Hank Ebert, Lenny Hodgson, Bert Lindberry, Marv Koep, his brother Steve, Royal Karels, and Mark Lee. He worked with the Koep brothers in the minnow business and he recalled how busy the store would be at certain times of the year, such as the fishing opener when the bait shop was like a modern-day shopping mall.

Tim's first real guide boat was the 315 Lund that was almost a "required" fishing boat in the early- to mid-seventies. Tim's fishing career as a guide at Koep's began around 1977 and he worked as a guide for fourteen years, but the last two years nearly finished him off physically. He had a family and was working full time at the paper mill in Brainerd. The paper mill, which has since closed and reopened under new management, once offered some of the best wages in the area. Tim worked the day shift at the mill and took afternoon shifts at Koep's.

"I think Marv figured that because I was a young guy, I could work without a lot of sleep," recalled Tim. "Some days he booked me for both an afternoon and a late-evening trip on the water. Some days I went to work at the mill at 7 A.M. and got home at 10 P.M. I finally wore down and decided I had to devote more time to my family, so I quit guiding in 1991. I think I only took about twenty trips the last year I guided.

"Dick Young worked at the mill, too. Like me, he put in some long days. Dick would sneak in a nap whenever he got a chance because he worked the midnight shift a lot. He got off work at 7 A.M. and headed to Koep's to pick up customers for the morning trip. Dick slept in his truck whenever he had a break between a morning and an afternoon trip. He slept with his feet sticking out the window. We tied his shoes together, so he rolled around for a few seconds, trying to figure out what happened to his feet. It was probably a mean trick to pull, realizing how tired he was, but we used to have a great time playing jokes on Dick."

Tim also recalls pulling some good jokes on Bill Lindner, Ron's son. "Bill came in from a trip and we flipped the transducer on his boat upside down. Then he went fishing again and couldn't get his flasher to work. He took it into Jimmy Wentworth, who had the electronic repair shop, to see what was wrong. You could hear Jimmy laughing a block away!"

One day, Tim fished a small lake with Lenny Hodgson—they both had customers in their boats. The sky began growing dark to the west and it looked like a storm was forming not too far away. Suddenly, the anglers in both boats began seeing sparks snapping at the end of their rods.

"One of the customers in Lenny's boat was totally bald on top, but he had long hair around his ears. Within minutes, the hair on the sides of his head was sticking straight out. There was so much static electricity in the air, it was scary. Lenny looked at me and said, 'I'll meet you at the landing—now!'"

Tim became an accomplished guide and prided himself in knowing key fishing spots on many area lakes. He fished little-known lakes, such as Tomato Bob's, Turkey Bass, and Bonnie Lake. His most famous customer was probably singer Mac Davis.

"Mac often fished with his son, Scotty," recalled Tim. "Mac loved to fish and he liked to be away from other boats. He liked to sing in the boat and have fun. He usually brought along his own refreshments and really enjoyed being on the water."

Tim's favorite fishing lake in the Brainerd-Nisswa area is Gull Lake, but today he spends more time fishing the prairie lakes in western Minnesota. "I don't like fishing in crowds. Fishing in the early- to late-seventies was a quieter experience in the Brainerd area than it is today. The prairie lakes in the western part of the state remind me of how it used to be thirty years ago. Fishing is still good in the Brainerd area, but there is a lot less pressure on the lakes to the west and that is where our family spends the summer fishing months now."

His career changed a few years ago when the paper mill in Brainerd closed. Tim, like more than six hundred other employees, lost his job at a facility where he thought he would be working for the rest of his life. He went back to school at Central Lakes College in Brainerd and worked on getting a degree in criminal justice and natural resources with plans to become a conservation officer for the State of Minnesota. He would be a good one. When Tim graduated in 2004, he was named the outstanding student of the year, plus he knows a thing or two about the outdoors!

For fourteen years, Tim had been a part of the Nisswa Guides' legacy. The sparkle he gets in his eyes when he talks about fishing shows that he still gets excited when the fishing opener rolls around. Tim Collette was one of the real gems of the Nisswa Guides' League. Guides like Tim give guiding a good reputation!

Chapter Twenty-nine
Glen Belgum

IMAGINE GROWING UP in the small farming community of Kensington, Minnesota, fishing for carp and bullheads, and ending up in the first, organized, fishing guides' league in Nisswa, Minnesota. That is exactly how it happened for Glen Belgum. Glen was raised on a farm and was able to jump on his bike and ride a short distance to the Chippewa River. There he fished for carp, bullheads, and anything else that would bite. That was how his interest in fishing began as a young boy.

After graduating from high school, Glen moved to Bemidji, Minnesota, where he attended Bemidji State University and graduated with a teaching degree. During his four years at Bemidji, he began developing a real joy and special interest in fishing.

In 1972, Glen got married and he and his wife lived in Prior Lake, in southern Minnesota. Glen fished area lakes and always stopped at the bait shop in Savage to get bait and tackle. One day, in the summer of 1974, he landed a lunker bass that weighed seven pounds and four ounces. It was a monster! The guys at the bait shop had never seen a bass that big and neither had Glen. The next day he landed another monster— a six-pound, twelve-ounce pig. The bait shop owner told Glen he had customers who would pay to fish with him for a chance to catch fish like that. That was the beginning for Glen. Next thing he knew, he had his first guide trip out of that bait shop.

Glen remembers his first trip as if it were yesterday. He picked up the customer at the store and the first thing the customer told Glen was that he had just gotten a divorce and his doctor told him he needed to develop some hobbies and try to live a less-stressful life. Then the guy began to cry. Glen wondered what he had gotten himself into.

Despite how the trip began, they had a great fishing trip, caught a lot of bass, released them all, and developed a lifelong friendship. The lesson Glen learned is that guiding is a lot more than catching fish—it's about treating customers right and making sure they have a good time on the water.

From left; Ron Lindner, Carl Lowrance, and Al Lindner with a nice walleye catch.

The legendary Harry Van Doren and two nice walleyes.

Bert Lindberry with his original Nisswa Guides' League fishing jacket.

A young Jeff Zernov with a stringer of largemouth bass.

The ever-smiling Marv Koep.

Nick Adams with a trophy lake trout.

Lenny Hodgson with a caught-and-released Minnesota musky.

Steve Collette and a summer lake trout.

Early photo of Nisswa Bait Shop.

Tim Collette with a trophy largemouth bass.

Tom Briggs and a nice stringer of crappies.

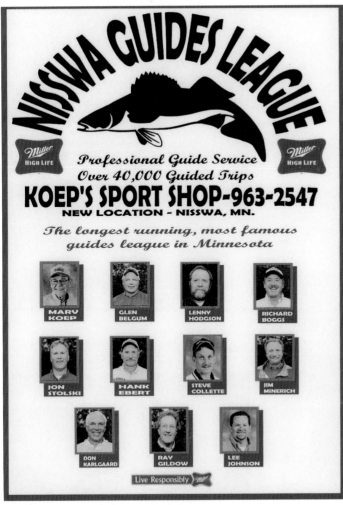

2004 poster of the Nisswa Guides.

Fun-loving Randy Hansen and a king salmon.

A minnow truck at the Koep operation in Urbank, Minnesota (2004).

Jim Minerich (right) and the late Minnesota Governor Rudy Perpich.

The current owners of Koep's Sport Shop, Maria and Bill Erickson (back row, L-R), with their children, Cassie and Billy.

Minnow traps from Phil Koep's Urbank bait business.

John Wetrosky, a long-time store manager for Marv and Judy Koep.

An inside view of Phil Koep's Urbank minnow business, 2004.

John Jensen who became store manager after John Wetrosky.

Mike Zauhar (left) and customer, Glen Frey, of the band, The Eagles.

The always-classy Fritz Potthoff.

Fritz Potthoff's truck stuck at a landing. Maybe "swamped" is a better description!

Bad day at the landing for Fritz Potthoff's truck and trailer.

Bobby Collette outfoxing another walleye.

Store manager, Keith, "Perky," Ament with a stringer of walleyes and northerns.

"Mr. Walleye," Gary Roach with a beautiful lake trout.

Dick Young with a summer walleye catch.

Rich Boggs, Nisswa guide and professional tournament angler.

Hank Ebert and a monster northern pike caught on a jig and minnow.

Glen Belgum and a dandy musky.

Paul Coventry and his trophy musky.

Don Karlgaard and a nice, released walleye.

A bundled-up Jon Stolski and a Gull Lake northern pike.

Mike Hager doing what he loved most—catching walleyes.

Robbie Rasinski and frequent Koep's customer, Brian Tabata.

The old pro, Royal Karels, and a forty-nine-inch musky that was released to swim another day.

The good-natured Cully Swenson and a seven-pound walleye.

(Front) Everyone's buddy, Joe Masik, and (back) Joe Fraune, retired Minnesota regional fisheries director.

An early view of Nisswa Bait store and sign.

The great storyteller, Max Slocum.

The living legend, Marv Koep, National Fresh Water Fishing Hall of Fame legendary angler.

The late part-time guide Mike Olson and his wife, Sandy.

Bob Hanson, Minnesota's Fishing Ambassador.

Mark Lee in a rare moment off the lake.

Judy Koep and one of her many trophy catches—this one is a musky.

Lee Johnson (left) and customer, Tim Besch, with a Minnesota musky on its way back to the lake.

The 1977 Lund 315 deluxe—this is the same model owned by Marv Koep and other guides.

Kevin Koep (left) and Minnesota Governor Tim Pawlenty.

Max Slocum (back row, center), Al Lindner (back row, left), Ron Lindner (front row, left), and Marv Koep (front row, right) and customers with seventeen limits. Cully Swanson is also in the middle of the group on the right.

Ron Lindner working some bass.

Al Lindner and a stringer of walleyes.

From left: Clint Russell (world champion blind golfer), Fritz Potthoff, Karl Kohlbry, Papa (Fred) Potthoff, Harry Van Doren, and Doc Sunby.

Koep's Bait Shop as it looked in the early nineties.

Harry Van Doren working in his "office."

The singing days with Nashville songwriter, Ronnie Rogers (center), Gary Roach (right), and one unknown player.

Rod Romine with two nice catfish.

Harry Van Doren (center) and two happy customers with a heavy stringer of walleyes.

A limit of walleyes caught by Jeff Zernov (left) and Al Lindner in August 1973.

Gary Roach with Gary Bedell, founder of Berkley Tackle Company.

The author and his secret dynamite approach to fishing with Jack Nelson.

Glen Belgum and a trophy released walleye.

The first Lindy Pro Team. Left: Cully Swanson, Rod Romine, Randy Amenrud, and Gary Roach.

Robert Rasinski

Royal Karels

Gary Roach and a 13$\frac{1}{2}$ pound walleye.

Bobby Collette

Hank Ebert

Guide boats lining up at Koep's to meet customers.

Nisswa guides and their customers. Back row, second from left: Cully Swenson. Back right: Royal Karels. Lower left: Bert Lindberry.

Jon Stolski

Jim Wentworth

The versatile Bobby Collette.

Jeff Zernov, Al Lindner, and Marv Koep.

Lee Johnson

Left: Dutch Cragun of Cragun's Resort, Ron Kristofferson, and a Cragun's employee.

Kevin Koep and a nice king salmon caught with a fly rod.

Marv Koep, Al Lindner, and Rod Romine.

Before long, Glen and two of his friends had a nice little guiding business in the Prior Lake area. Glen taught school, his wife was an airline stewardess, and he and his friends were doing more than one hundred trips a summer—venturing as far north as Lake Minnetonka.

In the summer of 1977, Glen and his wife moved to the Brainerd area. He had heard of the Nisswa Guides and the Nisswa Bait and Tackle Shop, so he stopped in and asked Marv about helping out as a guide. Glen got his first guide trip at the bait shop in 1978.

"Harry Van Doren was winding down his guiding career when I began," said Glen. "His health wasn't very good, but he still fished a little. Cully Swenson, Mark Lee, Marv, Bert, Lenny, Royal, and his son, Sam, were all guiding when I started. Harry told me about years in the fifties and sixties when it was impossible to catch a fish on Gull Lake. Harry liked to fish Winnibigoshish and I remember him coming back from some trips with limits and he was using the old, green-box, Lowrance fish locators. He was a great fisherman right up to the end of his life."

Glen had one of the Lund Sportsman's model 315 fiberglass boats. In 1974, he owned a boat, trailer, and a twenty-five-horse motor, and he paid $1,200 for the whole outfit. When Glen first began guiding, the boats were made for two passengers, plus the guide. Then the Tuffy Boat Company built an eighteen-foot fishing boat for the guides that allowed them to fish with three customers. That was a big step in the guiding business. Lund and other boat companies moved toward producing bigger boats that had more space and allowed more horsepower.

"Bigger boats allowed us to start fishing the bigger lakes with our customers," recalled Glen. "Launches on Mille Lacs and Leech were very safe in rough weather, but in rough water, a sixteen-foot boat was not the best with customers. When I began guiding, I was probably more comfortable fishing for bass and Marv used me as a bass guide in my early years. The more I fished, the more comfortable I became fishing walleyes and other species. The first year I was in the league, we had twelve guys fishing. Harry was mostly interested in fishing walleyes. Now walleyes are my favorite fish to catch, too. I also love to fish for northern pike with a live-bait rig.

"There are more than four hundred lakes in the greater Brainerd/Nisswa area. It's amazing how the lakes turn on and turn off during the year. Some of the lakes turn on for fishing for seven to ten days and then the main bite is done for the year. Other lakes turn on and off during the whole year. Spending time on the water learning the lakes and observing when a lake produces and when it shuts down are key skills for a guide to learn. I think the lakes here still have great fish populations. The size is not what it once was because more anglers are better at catching fish and more of the big fish are harvested now, but the fishing is fantastic at certain times of the year. I am a huge supporter of stocking our lakes with young fish. Not every lake can support stocked fish, but those that can do really well when they are stocked on a regular basis. Another thing I have noticed over my twenty-five years or so of guiding is how the weeds change from year to year. How the weeds develop depends on rainfall amounts, snow, and other factors. Some years, the fish are in certain weedbeds and other years they are not. My favorite lakes to fish are Gull, North Long, and Whitefish. I really enjoy fishing the mine pits near Crosby—there are no houses and it is a peaceful area to fish.

On one special trip, a lady hired me for a half-day for $47. I took her, her husband, and her son. She was so happy to be fishing together that at the beginning of the trip she began to cry. We fished for the half-day, I cleaned their fish, she gave me a one-dollar tip, and began crying again! She was so happy that they were able to do that as a family because they didn't come from an area with any lakes. Those are the special trips that I will always remember as a guide.

"I fished with Senator Mark Dayton, singer Mac Davis, and baseball player Kirby Puckett. I fish with some of the customers I fished with more than twenty years ago. I think about safety every time I am on the water. I came close to hitting a boat at least twice in my career and that is really scary.

"I had a lot of help when I began guiding at the bait shop. Harry Van Doren helped me whenever I asked for advice and Royal Karels taught me a lot about the spots to fish on area lakes.

"Attitudes about fishing continue to change. We used to keep a lot more fish in the early days than we do now. Today, many customers are satisfied with the fishing experience, taking pictures of the fish, and releasing them. Fish are a limited resource and we need to take care of that resource to ensure that it will be here for our kids and grandkids."

Glen still teaches in the Brainerd school district. He loves guiding and probably enjoys fishing more now than he ever has. He plans to continue guiding as long as he is able to. He won't be hard to find during the fishing season. Just stop by Koep's Sport Shop and he won't be far away.

Chapter Thirty
Jim Minerich

J IM MINERICH WAS BORN on the Iron Range in the northeastern Minnesota town of Chisholm. Around 1972 or '73, I met Jim when he was a student teacher at the Model Elementary School in Staples, Minnesota. Jim was finishing his bachelor's degree at St. Cloud State University and the student-teaching assignment was his final quarter of college. After graduation, he began his teaching career in Pequot Lakes, a few miles north of Nisswa.

Jim, like many of the other guides, got his connection to the Nisswa Bait and Tackle store by stopping in on a regular basis to buy bait and tackle. He got to know Marv from being in the store often. One day, Marv mentioned that he could use a little extra help and he asked if Jim was interested in taking a few trips out of the store. Jim said he would be happy to help out and he took his first trip in 1978. He had been fishing with a little Crestliner with a thirty-five-horse motor. Since he had the opportunity to begin guiding, he figured he'd better upgrade, so he bought an Alumacraft with a fifty-horse motor.

He recalls one of the early trips out of the bait shop. He had a new boat, motor, and trailer, but he also had a little sixteen-foot Grumman sport boat that was lightweight and fit on top of his vehicle. The walleyes were biting in the river below the Cross Lake dam. The water was too shallow for a bigger boat, but the sports boat would slide into that area nicely. Jim had a little six-horse motor that he used on his sports boat. He told Marv he was going to give his customers the choice of fishing on a lake in his brand-new boat or squeezing into his lightweight sports boat. The customers took a chance on fishing out of the little sports boat and it paid off. They nailed the northern pike and walleyes on the trip. The average walleye was about two to three pounds and everyone at the bait shop was impressed with the catch.

When Jim began guiding, the lakes had a lot less pressure than they do now. "It was not uncommon in the late seventies or early eighties to catch a seven- to eight-pound walleye," recalled Jim. "The fall bite would be unbelievable. I think the fishing is just as good today as before, but we just don't see the sizes like we did then. The south end of Gull was a great spot for bass and northern pike. I don't think we have as many clambeds in the lakes as we used to. The clambeds were hard-bottom and they really attracted the walleyes." He also fished lakes that were hot. One week it might be Gull, the next week it might be North Long. Guides had to stay in touch with where the bite was or come back to the store with empty livewells.

Cully Swenson and Max Slocum were still fishing when Jim joined the league and he got advice from them as well as all the oldtimers that were still around. But he found that the only way he could be a truly successful guide was to go to the lakes and learn the structure. He spent many days on the water with a fish locator, learning the structure of the different lakes. He spent much of that time without even fishing—just learning where he could see fish on his locator.

Jim is a guide who likes fishing crappies and bass. He will fish anything, but has his preferences like all guides do. He also fishes lake trout with corn and marshmallows—not your average Minnesota bait.

Like Ron Kristofferson, Jim is also a great storyteller with a vivid recollection of many trips. He has fished a number of times when the static electricity was great enough to make the fishing lines go into the air eight to ten feet. (This condition occurs prior to a lightning strike. Some weather experts will say that this is God telling you to get your butts off the lake.). A serious medical emergency has never taken place in his boat while fishing, but he has had experience with hooks that had gotten stuck in a little boy. And Jim was once hit with a weight from a musky lure and required six stitches. He has also been trapped on islands a few times during storms that became much worse than they first appeared.

One memorable trip for Jim and his customers occurred while trolling crankbaits for walleyes on one of the mine pits in the Crosby area. They hooked a twenty-two-pound northern on four-pound test line. The hook caught the northern pike's lip just right and they were able to land the big brute.

He recalls another unbelievable trip that Hank Ebert had with two customers. For some reason, the two men got into a fight and one guy threw the other guy out of the boat. Jim doesn't know what caused the fight, but Hank was pretty excited about the whole trip.

Jim once fished for forty days without a break. That was his longest run one summer and he was pretty worn out. He even got heat stroke one day and became sicker than a dog. Jim has never fished a professional tournament, but he served as a volunteer guide at the Camp Confidence Fishing Tournament held each year on Gull Lake. He has guided players from the Minnesota Vikings, the Minnesota Twins, and Ray Schweigert of Schweigert Meats.

"I think customers used to fish more for the meat in the early years," said Jim. "Now people are content to go on the lake, enjoy the scenery, catch a few fish, and soak up memories. They also used to drink more in the old days, too. It got a little scary at times when people drank too much in a boat. That doesn't happen much anymore."

One day, when Jim was fishing with customers on Gull Lake, he saw a guy working on a fifty-horse motor. All of a sudden, the boat took off at full throttle, but there was no one in the boat. It started in a straight line, then began going in big circles. Jim saw a man fishing bass in the reeds a few hundred yards away and thought he had better tell the guy to get out of there. Jim pulled into the reeds by the fisherman and the man looked angry, as if he thought Jim was moving in on his spot. Jim shouted, telling him to get out of there. The guy just looked at him and said, 'Why?'

"'See that boat coming at you?' Jim yelled. 'There is no one in it!' The guy had an old Elgin motor and I thought he was going to have a heart attack trying to get it started. He got out of those reeds in the nick of time. Some other man picked up the owner of the empty boat. Eventually, the boat ran into the weeds and slowed down so we could catch up to it and the owner got his boat back. It was probably the last time he started it at full throttle."

Jim also witnessed a big speedboat that ran over a canoe. The man in the front of the canoe jumped out and the guy in the back was flipped into the lake. Miraculously, no one was seriously hurt.

"Here is a true story—one of the strangest things that ever happened while fishing. I was with a customer fishing for muskies and the customer caught about a twelve-pound musky. He started pulling toward the boat and I saw another fish coming in behind the hooked fish. I got pretty excited and told the customer to pull the fish alongside the boat and I would take a stab with my net at the other musky that was following his fish. It worked. He caught the musky on his line and I landed the second fish in the net! We let them both go, but that was worth the trip to see two fish caught on one line!"

Jim teaches elementary school in Pequot Lakes and he still guides at Koep's. He is an avid duck hunter, whitetail deer hunter, and spends a lot of time at his cabin on the Canadian side of Lake of the Woods.

Chapter Thirty-one
Tom Briggs

I N A WAY, Tom Briggs has been connected to the Nisswa guides since he
was a little boy growing up on the shores of Gull Lake. When he was only
four years old, he recalled fishing in one of his dad's fishing boats that was
tied up at the dock. He began fishing in the boat in the morning, ate dinner,
and fished again until suppertime. He never got tired of fishing!

Tom was born in Shakopee, Minnesota, and moved to Nisswa in 1970, when he
was about seven years old. His dad had purchased a marina at the north end of Gull
Lake and Tom began working at the marina at a young age. Tom's family lived on the
west shore at the south end of the lake. When Tom was only seven, his dad bought him
his first boat. Tom fished his way up and down the shoreline on his way to and from
work at the marina. He learned a lot about fishing the west side of the lake when he
was young.

As soon as he moved to Nisswa, Tom and fellow Nisswa guide Rick Boggs became
good friends. "Rick lived on the west side of the lake, too," recalled Tom. "We've been
friends since we were four or five years old and are good friends today. Dad sold bait
at the marina, so we usually got our bait there. When we got a little older, we went to
Nisswa Bait and Tackle to see the fish that were in the coolers and to watch the guides
bring in their fish.

"I got a job packing bait at Koep's when I was ten years old. I packed bulk packages of worms and leeches into smaller packages. I remember packing fifteen hundred
cartons of nightcrawlers before the fishing opener. I worked for a few years as a bait
boy and then worked in the "pit," where we could make pretty good money cleaning
fish for the guides. I worked on the floor in sales, I worked at the cash register when I
got older, and Marv let me guide when I was sixteen years old. Marv cosigned for me
and helped me get a guide boat—an Alumacraft Backtroller. I started out as a fill-in
guide for busy times and kept working in the store, too. The Koeps were like family to

me. My folks had gotten a divorce, so I practically lived with Marv and Judy—I called them Mom and Dad. Kevin Koep was one of my best friends. We were like brothers all through high school."

In 1978 or 1979, Tom was put on the chart as a full-time guide. At the time, Harry Van Doren guided a little, but his career was winding down. Joe Masik was a regular, hanging around the shop, and Cully Swenson was still working. Tom guided full time until 1983, when he began guiding in Alaska. He got the job with the help of Sam Karels, who had worked at Koep's for about three years and also had connections in Alaska. In Bristol Bay, Alaska, Tom guided anglers fishing for salmon. He also worked for Bob Curtis—the first Master Guide in Alaska—as a hunting guide for bear. (Bob's guide number was "1"—the first issued by the state. He also owned the first, real, sports-fishing resort in Alaska and logged thousands of hours as a bush pilot.)

Tom moved back to Nisswa in 1985, when he went into business with his father wholesaling Honda motors. He returned as a part-time Nisswa Guide—working on weekends and taking days off from the family business when Koep's needed help. He guided at Koep's until 1997, when he bought a resort on Lake of the Woods.

Since Tom was only seventeen years old in 1980 when he became a full-time Nisswa guide, he recalled that there was some controversy when his name came before the league for consideration, but the members voted him in that spring. Tim Collette was another of his friends who also became a Nisswa Guide, along with friends, Kevin Koep and Rich Boggs.

"Hank Ebert, Mark Lee, and Steve Collette helped me become a better guide. Hank was great with young guys like me. He went out of his way to show me how to do things and took me on hunting and fishing trips. I marveled at what he could do from a wheelchair. It never stopped him from doing anything and it still doesn't today.

"One of the memorable trips I had during that period was fishing with Richard Childress and Dale Earnhardt, the NASCAR driver. We fished until noon and when we went to Bar Harbor Supperclub for lunch, there was a NASCAR race on television. We watched the race until about 3 P.M., when someone came and picked up the guys after the race was over. I got $800, mostly for watching television. That was a pretty good day for a young kid.

"One of the great experiences I had as a guide was fishing in Alaska with the former football player and television star, Merlin Olson. He was on the television show, *Little House on the Prairie*. He also had his son with him. We camped and fished together for a whole week. He talked a lot about working on the set of the television series with Michael Landon and some of the other actors. He was a great guy.

"I'd rather forget one trip. I was bass fishing with customers and we were throwing plugs up into the weeds. I got my plug caught on weeds and I couldn't get it loose. It was probably about thirty feet away. I gave it one heck of a tug and it came back and stuck me in the leg and in my privates! I cut the hook off the leg, but I couldn't stand to touch the one in my crotch, so I pretended that I got all the hooks out and kept fishing. I was too embarrassed to say anything. Every time I moved, I saw stars. I made it through the trip and went to the emergency room as soon as I was done and they pulled the hook out. That was one long morning of fishing!

"On a blistering hot afternoon, I had three nurses fishing with me. One of them said it was too hot and they needed to cool down and go into the water, so I took them over by the rocks in Wilson Bay on Gull Lake. I didn't know what they were going to do, but they all stripped down to bare skin and went skinnydipping right in the middle of the afternoon. Wow, was I impressed! I think I was nineteen at the time.

"One day, I forgot to put the plug in my boat and when I got onto the lake, water started coming up through the floor of the boat. I had customers whose feet were getting wet and I couldn't figure out where the water was coming from. Finally, it dawned on me that the plug was out. Boy, was I embarrassed and wet!

"Being a member of the Nisswa Guides' League was a steppingstone. It was the most prestigious guide organization in Minnesota. It meant a lot to people in the industry to know that someone was a member of that organization. People know about the organization all over the country and I was really proud to be a part of the league.

"Marv and Judy Koep were wonderful to me—I owe them a debt of gratitude for almost everything I know regarding the fishing and tourism industry. I also owe a lot to Jim and Shirley Dullum, the owners of Martin's Sports in Nisswa. They helped me learn how to work with customers and learn how to run a business. All those experiences helped me become a better businessman.

"I have wonderful memories of working at Koep's and working with the Nisswa guides. Kevin Koep and I used to fish with Marv Koep a lot. We were always in the front of the boat and continually wanted to know the depth of the water we were fishing in. Marv finally put a sonar unit in the front of the boat so he wouldn't have to keep telling us how deep the water was.

"I learned how to fish most of the area lakes by fishing with Marv, Tim Collette, Rich Boggs, and Kevin Koep. When we weren't working, we were fishing. Kevin Koep is one of the best anglers I have ever fished with over the years. He could find fish in areas where no one else ever fished. He was good enough that he could have been a good tournament angler. I liked to fish Gull, North Long, Round, and Mille Lacs. I really enjoyed Mille Lacs and I enjoyed fishing the north end of Gull.

"I began fishing tournaments in the eighties and really enjoy the competition of tournament fishing. I sponsor a tournament every fall out of our resort on Lake of the Woods and I fish a few tournaments every year. I still guide and I love it. I now have a fishing boat and two charter boats on Lake of the Woods. I keep in touch with Gary Roach, the Lindners, and all my friends from Nisswa, even though I am about four hours away."

Tom Briggs ended a long career with Koep's and the Nisswa Guides' League in 1997. He packed bait, cleaned fish, served as a store clerk, and a guide for nearly thirty years. Tom and his wife purchased the Wigwam Resort on Wheeler's Point, located on Four Mile Bay on Lake of the Woods. Wigwam Resort has been a tradition on Lake of the Woods for more than seventy years. Tom guides, only now it is usually from a twenty-seven-foot Sportcraft boat with downriggers. He still loves to fish, loves working with customers, and thinks he has found heaven!

Chapter Thirty-two
Paul Coventry

PAUL COVENTRY GREW UP in the small town of Jessup, Iowa. His dad worked at a packing plant and had a small hobby farm where Paul, his four sisters, and one brother were raised. Paul graduated from high school in 1966 and got a job as a mechanic in nearby Independence, Iowa. He married his high-school sweetheart, Martha, and they moved to Orlando, Florida, where they lived for four-and-one-half years. In 1970, Martha's parents bought a resort in Park Rapids, Minnesota. Paul and Martha moved to Park Rapids to help Martha's folks with the resort—Paul got a job as a mechanic in the Park Rapids area. They had lived there for about two years, when Paul heard of a job opening at Tanner Motors in Brainerd. He got the job in Brainerd and Paul and Martha moved to the area in 1973.

As a young boy, Paul loved to fish—he was the only member of his family who liked it. There were no lakes nearby, so Paul fished in the river for bullheads and catfish. When he and Martha moved to Orlando, he began fishing for other kinds of fish. He always had a passion for the sport of fishing and that passion grew when he moved to Minnesota.

Paul came to know Joe Masik through the Lake Shore Rod and Gun Club. Joe was kind enough to take Paul fishing on the area lakes and he also introduced him to many of the local people who were associated with the fishing industry. In 1976 and 1977, Paul got his first taste of guiding when he worked as a part-time guide at Dave's Sportland Bait Shop in Nisswa.

Before coming to the Brainerd area, Paul had never heard of the Nisswa Guides' League. Joe Masik talked to Marv Koep about getting Paul into the league and in 1979, he began working as a Nisswa guide. He fished a lot in the late-seventies and early-eighties and even thinks he may have set the all-time record with more than 240 trips in one summer. That was a heavy load for being a father—he had a young family of three boys and the fourth one was born in 1982.

"I loved guiding from the first trip I ever took," recalled Paul. "I started at Dave's Sportland, took a few trips, and caught the bug. When I got the job at Koep's, I quit my job at Tanner Motors and went into guiding full time. I started a winter job of plowing snow and those are the two occupations I still have today—guiding and snowplowing. I spent every free minute learning the lakes and their structure. I owe a lot to Joe Masik for helping me get the job at Koep's, but also for helping me learn the area lakes. We spent a lot of time together. He helped a lot of guys learn area lakes, he was a special person.

"I had some great days fishing at Koep's—I worked there until 1991, when I started my own guide business, which I still operate today. I am fifty-five years old, so I don't take as many trips as I used to—I don't think I could do that anymore. I enjoy doing about eighty-five to ninety trips a year. That is a good number for me.

"I have many fond memories of the Nisswa Guides. We had some great times together. One time, Hank Ebert and I caught a seagull and took it into the store and told John Jensen, the store manager, that we wanted him to see our big fish. He opened the livewell and just about took that bird right in the head!

"Another day I had a morning trip and found some crappies on Gull Lake. Hank Ebert and Jim Minerich had no trips that afternoon and my afternoon trip was canceled, so I told them I would take them to a hot spot for crappies. We loaded Henry in my boat and drove to the north landing on Gull Lake with Henry riding in my boat. I took them to my spot and we caught our limit of forty-five crappies, but I only caught two of them. I never did hear the end of that story.

"Another trip had about five guides' boats fishing together with a company of about fifteen people. Hank had two guys in his boat who were drinking quite a bit and they got into an argument. All the boats were fishing on Gull Lake by the rock pile. We didn't know these guys were fighting, but all of a sudden they both fell into the lake. Someone went over and helped Henry get them back into the boat. He took them to the resort where they were staying and a couple of us helped them get to their cabins, because they were in no shape to make it on their own. They started fighting again at the resort. We took one guy into his cabin, we walked out, heard the screen door slam, and the guy stepped out of the cabin and landed face first on the sidewalk. He broke all the teeth in the front of his mouth. That was the end of that argument.

"There have been a number of stories about people falling out of boats. It has happened to me and I have a few stories about it happening to other guys, too. I had one guy, a huge man, sitting in the front of my boat. He reached down to get a snack out of his cooler and rolled right into the lake. I ran up to the front of the boat and waited for him to pop up. I grabbed him by the arms and I just barely got him back into the boat. He said he didn't move fast enough to catch his balance!

"Royal Karels was coming out through the no-wake markers on Booming-Out Bay on Gull Lake and he had an older couple with him. He and the wife were watching a boat that was coming in from the big lake and speeding toward the no-wake markers. The boat hardly slowed down. Royal watched the boat go by and all of a sudden, the lady yelled, 'Harold, Harold, where is Harold?!' Harold had been sitting in the front of the boat when a big wave from the passing boat hit and knocked him into the lake. Royal looked behind the boat and there was Harold waving his arms. He didn't get hurt, but it sure scared Royal.

"One other time, I was fishing with a guy I had picked up at the store who had just arrived in Brainerd on an airplane. I didn't know it at the time, but the guy had been drinking on the flight—perhaps drinking quite a bit. We were on the lake and the guy said he had to take a whiz. I got out my pee can, gave it to him, and turned around to get my trolling motor. All of a sudden, I heard a huge splash. The guy had fallen into the lake. He was another big guy that I could hardly pull back into the boat.

"My scariest time on the water happened about fifteen years ago on Mille Lacs Lake. I was fishing with two ladies and we had put in at the Garrison Creek Marina. I took them to the nine-mile flat to fish for walleyes. The distance was about eight or nine miles from the marina. I saw dark clouds moving in from the west and about the time I thought we should head in, one of the ladies got a bite. She landed a thirty-one-inch walleye and it was a great-looking fish. She wanted to take a picture of it and let it go. By the time we took pictures and released the fish, it started to rain. I waited too long. I headed to shore toward the casino. The wind came up and it rained so hard, I could hardly see three feet in front of the boat. I got about one hundred yards from land and followed the shore up the last four or five miles to the marina. Both ladies were lying in the bottom of my boat, dressed in raingear, and by the time I hit the marina, it started to hail the size of golf balls. We got into the marina and stayed under a roofed boat slip until it let up and we could get to the truck. I should have just gone to shore and beached the boat. I was really scared on that trip.

"One other interesting story about the guides was when a beer company came to town and hired a bunch of the Nisswa guides to go fishing to catch a ten-pound northern pike that was to be filmed in a beer commercial. One of the guides, I don't remember which one, caught the fish. The unusual part was that they had made a puppet of the fish head and they used that as an underwater shot, showing this big northern pike grabbing something beside the boat. They used the actual pike for some of the underwater shots, but the most realistic-looking shot was a fake. It sure looked real when it was on television.

"I caught my first ten-pound walleye on Gull Lake, fishing through the ice in a house that I shared with Joe Masik. I guess I have caught lots of walleyes that weighed more than ten pounds over the years. My biggest musky was fifty-two inches and weighed thirty-seven pounds. I always carry a camera in my boat—not many of my customers kill big fish anymore. Most people are happy to take a picture and let the big ones go back to the water. I think that is a neat trend that has developed in fishing today. I fish a lot of smaller lakes and I tell people that some of them are strictly catch-and-release, so if we catch big fish, they know we will take a photo and let it go back.

"I think two of my most memorable customers were Tommy Kramer, the former quarterback for the Minnesota Vikings, and his wife, Carrie. I fished with them for three days while they were on their honeymoon. Tom caught a nice seven-pound walleye that week. They were great people to take fishing."

Paul fishes the big lakes like Leech, Winnie, and Mille Lacs, and he fishes many smaller lakes in the Nisswa area, but his favorite lake chain is Whitefish. "I love the variety of lakes in the Whitefish Chain," said Paul. "I love the variety of fish, too.

"I think fishing in the area is still good. The variety is great and there are nice-sized fish and the quantity is very good. We don't catch as many big fish overall as we used to, but for people who know where to go, big fish can still be caught."

Paul lost his wife, Martha, to cancer in 2000. He lost his youngest son, Jeremy, to a car accident the same year. Paul has remarried and his new wife's name is Carol. Carol and Paul's remaining sons all love to fish.

"Guiding has been a great life for me and I plan to do this until I can no longer get into my boat. It is getting tougher for young people to guide because the competition is greater now and the equipment needed to guide is getting pretty expensive. I've lost a lot of customers over the years who have died off or aren't able to fish anymore, but I still have customers that I have been fishing with for more than twenty-five years. It's a great life and as long as I still have the passion for it, I plan to keep on fishing," concluded Paul, smiling from ear to ear.

Chapter Thirty-three
Kevin Koep

KEVIN KOEP GREW UP in the fishing and bait business. Being the only son of Marv and Judy Koep didn't mean he received any special privileges learning the trade. He worked his way into guiding the old-fashioned way—he earned it. His first real job at the store was cleaning fish in the pit, an area behind the shop set up to clean fish. Many young boys in the Nisswa area first worked at the bait shop by putting in time cleaning fish in the pit. For Kevin, it was his introduction to the business, the guides, and many famous customers who frequented the business.

His first real income came from cleaning fish—ten cents for each sunfish and crappie; twenty-five cents for each bass, walleye, or northern. That may not sound like much, but to a boy under ten years old that was pretty good money. He quickly learned who the best fisherman was by the amount of business he got from each of them. It was an honest promotion when he went from the pit to working with customers in the store.

Kevin recalled the time Rod Romine pulled him out of the bait tank. He was trying to get some big minnows to bite on a little hook and line that he had rigged up. As he leaned over the tank to entice the minnows to grab his hook, his sister gave him a little shove and he fell into the icy water of the tank. He thinks he could have gotten out on his own, but Rod grabbed him by the seat of the pants and pulled him out before he could react.

He took his first "professional" guide trip when he was only eleven years old. His dad fixed him up with a Lund boat—he thinks it might have been the 315 tri-hull model, with a six-horse motor. He picked up a customer on Nisswa Lake, about the only lake he knew how to fish at that age. The guy wanted to fish for bass and northern pike. Kevin enjoyed fishing for them, too. He didn't know much about fishing for walleyes at that stage of his fishing career. Kevin hooked on a couple of Bomber plugs and began trolling the lake. They had a good trip and landed some nice fish. Kevin's pay was a hunting knife.

Getting to know all the guides at the store, Kevin even went fishing with them, including Cully, Max, Royal, and the others. They were good to him, but he was too young to talk fishing with most of them. He recalled that Harry Van Doren always told him that he probably forgot more about fishing than most other fishermen.

He learned a lot about fishing from Royal Karels' son, Sam. Sam taught Kevin techniques and showed him where to fish on certain lakes. He also learned a great deal from the bass master himself, Royal Karels.

"Royal was a great teacher," said Kevin. "He didn't care if he was giving out secrets about certain lakes or techniques. He was very unselfish—he loved helping kids learn how to fish. One day, he asked me if I knew why he smoked a cigar. I told him I didn't. Royal said, 'Watch, I throw out the worm for the bass, take a puff of my cigar, and that gives that old bass time to look at the bait and think about it. Then I twitch the rod, take another puff, and if he is going to bite, he should be there.'"

Kevin tried this technique in the pond behind the store. There were always bass in the pond and some were nice sized. He took a plastic worm, threw it at the bass, then watched the bass look at the worm, and start to swim away. He twitched the worm a few times, and sure enough, the bass often returned and grabbed onto it. It taught Kevin a valuable lesson in patience while fishing bass, and later, other species of fish.

He learned a lot from other guides, but some weren't as willing to share information as others. Two young guides who fished together a lot and helped Kevin were Steve Collette and Mark Lee. Steve and Mark were both accomplished guides at a very young age. "Those guys saved the day for me so many times when I was having trouble finding fish," recalled Kevin. "Many days they showed me where to go and what to do and I really appreciated it. I was never much help to them, but they really helped me learn the lakes.

In 1980, Kevin began guiding consistently when he was sixteeen years old. He was the bottom guy on the guide chart, but business was good and he got to fish on a regular basis. He fished as a full-time guide until 1988, when he moved to the Twin Cities. In the beginning, he was mostly a bass and northern pike fisherman—he wasn't too comfortable fishing for walleyes. Walleye fishing on Gull Lake was very difficult in 1980. Kevin recalled most of the guides fishing on Mille Lacs and other lakes because the walleye bite was so tough on Gull and other area lakes.

Harry Van Doren told Kevin to keep a fishing log when he began guiding. He kept it up for a while, but he never took the time to keep it current. Kevin's early customers came from the resorts, but after a few years of guiding, he started building a good repeat business. Toward the end of his guiding career, most of his business came from repeat customers.

Sammy Karels taught Kevin the technique of hopping from lake to lake, until hitting a lake that had active fish biting. One day Kevin met Sammy on his thirteenth lake of the day. Kevin was practicing this technique the time he took off from the lake and forgot to put his motor up. He carved a strip down the tar road and wore off about four inches from the bottom of his motor. Kevin never did hear the end of that story!

While guiding, Kevin met and fished with many celebrities, including singer Mac Davis. He fished with Mac for about three years in a row and had some fun times in the boat with him. Mac had his own television show and when he got to Minnesota, he liked privacy. He loved to cast for bass and northern pike and preferred to fish away from other boats. Fishing new lakes was always interesting to Mac.

One day Kevin took Mac Davis to the iron ore pits by Crosby, not too far from Nisswa. The old mine pits had filled up with water after they were no longer being mined and they were home to bass, northern pike, trout, and other freshwater species of fish.

They fished the pits in the morning and decided to try a different lake in the afternoon. When they stopped at a drive-in restaurant in Brainerd for lunch, two carloads of young girls saw Mac Davis and began screaming. Mac told Kevin to get out of there as fast as he could, so Kevin took off north of Brainerd and headed for a small lake that he planned to fish that afternoon. The girls were in hot pursuit and Kevin couldn't get away from them. The lake had a small public landing with just enough parking for one or two cars. Kevin pulled up to the landing, backed his boat in the lake, and everyone jumped into the boat. He left his Jeep sitting in the water at the landing. The girls had driven up to the Jeep in two cars and parked at the landing for about two hours, waiting for the guys to come back and move the Jeep and the trailer. Kevin watched the girls from the lake. Finally, they gave up and left. Kevin and Mac kept on fishing. Luckily, no one else drove up to use the public landing that day. They left the Jeep in the water until they were through fishing and then put the boat on the trailer and went home.

One hot summer day, Kevin saw Mark Lee swimming in the water, pulling his customers in the boat with a long rope. He figured Mark must have had motor trouble, so he drove over to see if he could help. Mark wasn't in trouble—he was just cooling off in the hot water and acting like a trolling motor, pulling his customers along the weedlines. Kevin later tried that technique with customers he knew really well. It was a great way to cool off and his customers caught fish at the same time.

When he first began guiding, Kevin Koep was not a very good walleye guide. He became frustrated in the early stages of his career and went to his dad for advice. Marv told him he wouldn't give him advice—he had to learn how to fish on his own. That didn't work very well and Kevin was frustrated with his dad.

One day, Marv told Kevin to pay attention to the wind—the wind was an important element in finding walleyes. Watching the wind became Kevin's number one rule. It was not always a guarantee of finding fish, but it was good advice that helped him many times in his career. He also learned more about walleye fishing from spending time on the water and getting information from the guides who shared little tidbits with him. He was grateful to the guides who helped him out and he became more confident in his knowledge of the lakes and the techniques he had acquired.

Kevin learned an important lesson about the wind on a bass-fishing trip. His customers were willing to try a new lake and Kevin had found a small lake that looked like it would be a good bass lake. He fished around the entire lake and found some bays that were too shallow, with too few weeds to be good bass areas. He decided that he had made a bad choice and decided to try another lake. Heading toward the landing, his motor hit something. He stopped the boat and tilted up the motor, but he didn't see anything wrong. Going back to the area where he thought he had hit something, Kevin saw that he had driven over a small underwater island that topped out around eight feet in depth. He and his customers put on crankbaits and threw them over the hump—they caught twelve bass with twelve casts. It was an unbelievable experience. The wind was blowing out of the northwest and the bass were all around that little hump. Every bass was in the three-pound range. Kevin figured he had found a new "secret" lake for bass.

Two days later, Kevin got some customers who wanted to catch bass. He decided to take them to his new lake and give them a fun experience. It was a flat, calm day. They fished for half a day and never had a bite—not even a nibble. Kevin was upset and decided to analyze what had happened. "You knucklehead," he thought to himself. "Two days ago you caught fish on that hump with a northwest wind and today there was no wind. Try it again with a northwest wind."

A few weeks later, Kevin's dad asked him to take some Catholic priests fishing for bass. There was a northwest wind, so he decided to head to the secret lake for another try. None of the priests were accomplished anglers and none of them knew how to cast well, so Kevin went to the hump, put nightcrawlers on everyone's lines, and nailed the bass. He was so busy taking off fish and putting on bait, he didn't have time to fish. They caught more than thirty bass on that trip—ranging from two- to three-pounds each. It was one of the better bass trips he ever had and he never fished that lake again without a northwest wind.

Joe Masik was a retired friend of the Koeps who spent a great deal of his time at the store as a volunteer helper. He had a home on Gull Lake and loved to spend his time fishing, talking to the guides, and helping out around the bait shop. He cleaned bathrooms, swept the floor, and helped in any way he could. Richie Boggs and some of the younger kids got to know Joe because he was a kind and unselfish man who loved to take kids fishing. He hung around the store nearly as often as the regular guides and took Kevin fishing on a regular basis. He was almost like a grandfather to Kevin as well as a skilled angler who never missed the opportunity to fish.

Before Kevin became a guide, he and a friend went fishing on Gull Lake during the fishing opener. Joe also came along, but he fished out of his own boat. They fished all morning with no success. Joe had a spot he thought they should try in the after-noon, so Kevin and his friend went into the shallow water and Joe worked off the weed's edge in deeper water. Both boats found fish and they caught some very nice walleyes—by the end of the day, they all had a limit of walleyes. Joe told Kevin not to tell anyone where they fished. Joe knew there were lots of hungry anglers at the bait shop and many of them would not have had much luck.

Chuck Ross was a good customer of the Nisswa Bait Shop as well as a radio per-sonality from the Twin Cities. He had been fishing with Kevin's dad and they'd had a rough day, catching very few fish. Chuck saw Kevin's stringer of walleyes and wanted to know where he got the fish. Kevin had promised Joe he wouldn't tell anyone, but Chuck was so insistent that finally, Kevin, with tears in his eyes, told Chuck where they were caught. Kevin doesn't know if Chuck ever fished the spot, but he felt terrible that he had given up the secret and it bothered him for a long time.

One other Joe Masik trip turned out pretty scary. Kevin and a friend were walleye fishing on the north end of Gull Lake. Kevin had not had much luck so he decided to go right into the weeds to see if he could find some fish. He found walleyes in the weeds in an area that was less than eight feet deep. The nice-sized fish were in a feed-ing mood. Joe had pulled up next to Kevin's boat and he was getting nice-sized walleyes, too. They had five or six fish, when Kevin noticed a black cloud moving in from the west. Joe looked at the sky and said they better get off the lake, but just then,

Kevin and his friend both had a bite. They told Joe they needed to catch a couple more fish and then they would get off the lake. All of a sudden, the wind hit the lake. The storm had come out of nowhere and they were caught right in the middle of it because they didn't heed Joe's advice. Kevin and his friend both had a fish on, when their boat turned completely around and faced the opposite direction. The black cloud was on them. The wind howled and it rained so hard, they could hardly see the shoreline. They reeled in their lines and headed into the wind to get to the shoreline. Finally making it to shore, they worked their way to Joe's house. The wind blew so hard, they could hardly tie their boats to the dock. In addition to the storm's high winds, a few tornados even touched down in the area.

When Marv Koep heard about the approaching storm, he called Joe's house, but didn't get a response. He hurried over to the house to find everyone wet and scared, but safe. He read Kevin the riot act. Finally pausing in his lecture, Marv asked Kevin if he had learned a lesson from this night. Kevin said he had learned that walleyes will really bite just before a storm hits. That was the wrong thing to say to Marv that night. He didn't find any humor in the statement until many years later.

One other trip during a storm is also etched in Kevin Koep's memory. He was taking customers to fish on Gull Lake and he could see a storm coming across the north side of the lake. He decided that his best bet was to go to the landing on the south end of the lake. They drove to the south end of the lake, got out of the truck, and saw the storm moving in their direction. Another boat was coming off the water, so Kevin and his customers decided to help the guy land the boat and wait to see what the storm was going to do. They helped the guy get his boat onto the trailer and everyone was standing on the dock when lightning struck a tree a few yards from where they were standing. It happened so fast and it was so noisy that everyone froze on the dock. "My hat came off my head straight up in the air just like someone had tied a string to it," recalled Kevin. "That scared the crap out of all of us!"

Kevin had many experiences with static electricity in the boat, when fishing lines went straight up in the air and sparks snapped at the end of rods, but he prided himself in being a careful and cautious guide and always tried to make decisions that were safe for his customers.

One of the funniest trips Kevin ever had was fishing with a man who had just purchased a new outdoor coat. He was really proud of the coat. It had all kinds of pockets and zippers and special features. They were fishing on a spot that wasn't producing any fish, so Kevin suggested they try another spot. The guy was smoking an expensive cigar and didn't want to waste it, so he put out the cigar and stuck it in his pocket— planning to light it up again at the next spot. As they drove down the lake, Kevin smelled something burning. Suddenly, the guy jumped out of his seat and started pounding on his new coat. The cigar had started it on fire.

He began as a bass and northern fisherman, but he learned to really enjoy walleye fishing and became, by all accounts, a good multi-species angler. He is also an unselfish angler. I fished with Kevin a few times when he came home on weekends and took a few guide trips to help out at the store. He was always willing to help other guides to find fish if he knew where they were biting.

Kevin hated to quit guiding, but he got married and needed to develop a career that allowed him to work on a year-around basis. He moved to the Twin Cities area and now works as a representative for a sporting-goods company. The memories that Kevin has of the Nisswa Guides' League are the great people he worked with and the wonderful customers he met during his stay as a guide.

Chapter Thirty-four
Randy Hansen

T HERE ARE A LOT of funny characters in this book, but not many guys have more fun on the water than Randy Hansen. Born and raised in Brainerd, Randy's dad, Gene, was an elementary teacher and an avid fisherman. He initiated some Brainerd area fishing programs for children that are still going on today. So it is no surprise that Randy's dad got him started fishing—he began by the age of four or five. Randy can recall seeing a lot of Harry Van Doren on the lakes that he and his dad fished. He never got to know Harry, but he heard a lot about him as a guide.

Randy grew up knowing about the Nisswa Guides. He checked the local newspaper every week to see photos of who caught the most fish and he also had connections to some of the guides who were teachers. Royal Karels was not only a Nisswa Guide, he was also Gene Hansen's friend. He also knew Bert Lindberry and Lenny Hodgson.

Randy was a very good athlete, both in high school and college—athletics were a big part of his high school and college experiences.

When Randy was a sophomore in high school, there was a silver rush. Fortunately, he had quite a collection of silver coins. He cashed in the coins and had enough money to buy his first boat when he was in the tenth grade. All through high school, Randy fished a lot in the summer months. Married to Sheree during his sophomore year in college, he fished whenever he had time. He especially enjoyed fishing with his father—something they did together until his dad died.

Randy shopped at Koep's bait shop and he often fished the same lakes that Marv Koep fished. Randy graduated from college with a teaching degree and he got his first teaching job in Nisswa in 1979, where he became good friends with Lenny Hodgson, another Nisswa teacher and guide. In 1982, Marv Koep asked Randy if he would be interested in guiding on a part-time basis. Randy said yes.

His first trip was fishing with Marv Koep and the television fisherman, Virgil

Ward. Marv was going to take them to a secret lake and he made Randy promise not to tell anyone where the lake was. Randy had the camera crew in his vehicle and after they got to the lake, it rained so hard they went back to a restaurant and had an early-morning breakfast. "Virgil Ward was just like Marv!" recalled Randy. "He was great to be with and so kind, I decided right then that I wanted to be a guide.

"Marv helped me get my first program boat through the Alumacraft Boat Company. He did so many things for me over the years I guided that I will be forever grateful to him. Boy, I thought I was in heaven—I was guiding with a brand-new boat and motor. I think it was called the Northwood's Edition. It was a nice boat.

"I got a chance to guide full-time when Bobby Collette left the league. I was the low man on the totem pole, but I got lots of trips. John Jensen was the store manager and I remember I made more guiding in the summer than I did teaching during the school year! I remember getting $95 for a half-day trip and $110 for a full trip at one point in my guiding career.

"There was always a lot of discussion about who was in charge of the guides' league. Some of the guides thought they should be in charge and Marv thought he should be responsible, but we sure had fun and interesting discussions.

"My father had a passion for fishing. He and some of the other teachers in the Brainerd school district, such as Royal Karels, Bob Miller, and Merv Jensen, taught kids how to fish. They took the kids on fishing trips to Canada to practice their skills.

"The other guides at Koep's helped me learn the lakes. Hank Ebert, Lenny, Steve Collette, Mark Lee, and Mike Hager were all great. I knew some of the lakes pretty well, but not like Lenny, Bert, and the other guides.

"When I got my master's degree, my wife thought it would be cute to put the name, 'Master Baiter,' on the side of my boat. It took a while for me to convince her that was a bad idea!" said Randy, with a laugh.

Guiding became a full-time summer job for Randy and it was not unusual for him to guide seven days a week—averaging about 150 trips per year. "I never realized how intense I was during the guiding season," said Randy, "but when I look back at that era, I have to say that my family sacrificed a lot so I could be a guide.

"Harry Van Doren was no longer a guide when I began working at Koep's, but I remember him as a gruff old salt. I also recall his customers saying he was a fabulous guide.

"I knew Cully Swenson—he was a neat guy. He always wanted to talk about what I saw on the different lakes in terms of weed growth and fishing pressure. Many days when we got rained out, we went back to the store and listened to jokes from Cully.

"We used to make and hand out cards, like baseball cards, telling customers a little about us. The cards gave background about who we were and what species we liked to fish. The cards also had our phone numbers on them and this was one of the ways that we booked new customers.

"I was very proud to be a Nisswa Guide and I developed great relationships, both with people who worked at the store and customers. Many of those customers remained friends until death or are still friends today. In 1999, I quit guiding when I got a job as an administrator in our school district. My last year of guiding, I took all my regular customers on free fishing trips. I really appreciated all the friendships and the great experiences I had working at Koep's. If I had a specialty, I guess it was fishing with families that had kids. I really loved fishing with kids.

"I had one group of ladies, all widowers, who came up every summer to fish. They were all in their seventies when I began fishing with them and now there is only one of them left. She is in her nineties and she still stops to visit me every summer. These ladies had a little contest every year. They had a rule that if a fish was caught that was a certain size, every one of them would have a drink of something they called 'tiger's milk.' It was a mixture of three different kinds of booze. They all brought their own tin cups and if fishing was slow, the standards were lowered a bit. Sometimes they were drinking the tiger's milk after catching a tiny perch. I drove them home after every trip because they were in no shape to be driving," laughed Randy. "They were wonderful ladies and we had some great times on the water.

"I had a breathtaking experience on the water one summer! I was fishing North Long Lake with Miss Arizona and two lovely friends. It was a hot day, in the nineties and when they got in the boat, Miss Arizona, who shall go unnamed, asked if it was okay to strip down to their bathing suits if it got too hot. I thought about that—for about one second—and said that would be okay. Wow! We were fishing for a while and the fishing wasn't too good, but we were catching a few bass. Suddenly, Miss Arizona said they were going to get down to their swimming suits. I said okay. Then I got a bite on my fishing rod and I turned to give my rod to one of the girls, and there they all were—stark naked! I yelled and dropped the rod on the edge of the boat and it fell into the water, where it still lies today. Miss Arizona looked horrified and started to apologize. I said it's not your fault, I thought you had your bathing suits on under your clothes. I was just a little surprised. Boy, was I ever surprised.

"I had another crazy thing happen to me that about half the guides at the store witnessed. I had a morning trip and my afternoon trip had gotten canceled. I went home to clean my boat and the store called and said there were some other customers who stopped by and wanted to go fishing. I told them I would be there in twenty minutes. I jumped into my truck and drove to the Sportland gas station and restaurant to get gas for my boat. About six of the guides were in the restaurant eating lunch. I looked behind the truck and my boat was gone! I panicked. I thought, perhaps it came undone on my way to the store. Everyone in the store was watching me, so I filled up my truck and took off, forgetting to pay for the gas. I got home and there was my boat—I had forgotten to hook it back to my truck. It was a long time before the guys would let me forget about that day. It was the start of a summer of unhooking boats from trucks!"

Randy had one of his most uncomfortable fishing trips while fishing on Lake Winnibigoshish—about an hour and half north of Koep's. "We got to the lake and one of my customers, on his first cast, stuck a hook in my eyelid. It didn't hurt my eyeball, but it was buried in my eyelid. It was too far to drive all the way back to Nisswa to get the hook removed, so I cut the line and left the hook in my eyelid for the entire trip. It was like blinking with a rock on my eyelid. What was even funnier, my wife was waiting for me at the store and she thought I had gotten my eye pierced—it looked like some new kind of piercing job! I was lucky that it never hurt my eye, but boy, it was close.

"I fished the 1989 Governor's Fishing Opener with Sybil Smith—an outdoor writer who has written many books on fishing area lakes. She was a great boat partner," recalled Randy. "I heard there was a cold front moving in and I talked her into going out at midnight to beat the front. She had never done that before, so she thought that was a great idea. We began fishing right after midnight, as soon as the fishing was legal. She won the northern, walleye, and crappie divisions with the fish she caught that night. We came in early in the morning, took a short break, and went out again about 8 A.M. after the cold front hit. Sure enough, the fishing just shut down, but she had a great opener. Later that day, I went fishing with Governor Rudy Perpich. He later sent me a Les Kouba fishing print that showed the governor fishing in a boat and another boat depicted Harry Van Doren fishing in the background. I got the artist's proof of that picture and it still hangs in my office—I am really proud of that print. And I had a great time with Sybil!

"My favorite species to fish went from walleyes to bass. I really love to fish bass, because the fun is in the catching, and not so much the hunt. I always found walleye fishing to be less exciting because I love to cast. I learned to fish spots that had fish and then left and gave them a break. Otherwise, the fish usually spook and leave the area. I really like the catch-and-release ethic that has developed today. My favorite bass lake is North Long Lake and Gull Lake and Pelican Lake are my two favorite walleye lakes.

"I was very proud to be a Nisswa Guide—I had great experiences that I will never forget. I will always be indebted to Marv Koep, Lenny, Jim Minerich, Hank Ebert, and even Jim Wentworth, who rigged my first boat for free, to help me get started. All the guys at the store were incredible to work with and most of them will be lifelong friends. The number of famous people who have fished and continue to fish with the Nisswa Guides' League is incredible. We have fished with members of the Minnesota Vikings, the Twins, the Wild, and many other well-known organizations. It's a great group of guys. I fish with family and friends now. I lost my mom and dad—they died two years apart on the exact same day. Now I make sure I fish with my family and friends whenever I get the chance. We bought a home on North Long Lake, so fishing is just a few minutes away. I don't plan to ever guide again, but I plan to fish for the rest of my life. It is a part of me and my family."

Randy Hansen—one of the legacies of the Nisswa Guides and one great guy!

Chapter Thirty-five
Mike Hager

T HE BEST MEMORIES of fishing and the saddest chapter in this book are about Mike Hager. He was a good friend—one of my best friends. We hunted together, fished together, worked together, traveled together, and shared many of the same interests in life. It is because of Mike that I wrote this book. It was because of Mike that I got the chance to work at Koep's. I always talked about the concept of writing about the guides' league, but I didn't get serious about it until Mike's death.

Mike Hager grew up in Minneapolis and went to Roosevelt High School with a classmate who would later become a governor of Minnesota. That classmate was Jesse Ventura. He and Jesse were teammates on the swimming team. Mike had a wild streak that got him in trouble from time to time, but he had such a charming personality, he always found a way to get out of trouble in the nick of time. He joined the Marines shortly after high school and got himself into hot water while enlisted, but like some of his other skirmishes, he managed to slip out of the service in fairly good shape. He married after his enlistment was over and then got divorced after the marriage did not work out. He had one daughter, Rachael, from the marriage, and he remained close to her until his death. Mike had a strong interest in horticulture and he attended the University of Minnesota with the intention of getting a bachelor's degree in horticulture. While a student at the university, he met his future wife, Jackie, who was also working on a degree in horticulture.

In the spring of 1979, Mike did not yet have his bachelor's degree, when he saw an opening for a teaching position in horticulture at Brainerd Technical College. Jackie had completed her degree and Mike was nearly finished with his, so he applied for the position. He was hired to fill the position for five years while an instructor took a five-year leave of absence. Jackie and Mike were married on a Saturday and Mike reported to work the following Monday. It was a whirlwind time. They did not have a place to live, had no money, and owned a dog. They found a place to rent for one month on

Bertha Lake, which is part of the Whitefish Chain. A month later, they found a small cabin to rent on Roy Lake, part of the Gull Lake Chain.

He was attracted to the Brainerd area because he wanted to be a guide. His long-term goal was to get to an area that had a variety of lakes. He would have been happy in three or four areas of the state, but Brainerd was a dream-come-true with its lakes, rivers, and hundreds of places to hunt for gamebirds and deer.

Mike spent many of his summers working on his grandfather's farm in Silver Lake, Minnesota. His grandfather and his father were avid anglers and Mike spent much of his youth fishing the Mississippi River. He speared catfish and suckers out of the Mississippi and still had pictures of a monster catfish he had speared that was featured in the local newspaper.

When he first moved to the Brainerd area, Mike was unfamiliar with the lakes. He and Jackie borrowed some money and invested in a new boat. To learn where to fish on area lakes, Mike fished whenever he got a chance. On many nights, Jackie fished with him and many times he fished alone. He didn't know any of the area guides, so he concentrated on spending time on the water to learn the lakes. He fished the Whitefish Chain, Pelican Lake, Gull Lake, Hubert, and many of the other small lakes in the area. He did this for about two years—logging an incredible amount of time on the water.

Developing a relationship with Dave Erlandson, owner of Sportland Bait and Tackle in Nisswa, Mike eventually began guiding for Dave. Mike guided for Dave until Dave decided to get out of the guiding business to focus on bait sales and renting recreational equipment. Mike began spending time at Marv Koep's and developed a friendship with Marv. In 1983, Marv asked Mike if he was interested in guiding out of the shop. It was a dream-come-true for Mike and he guided at Koep's until his death.

Mike and Jackie had two sons, Shawn and Matt. Both sons developed a keen interest in fishing from an early age, due in part, to Mike's passion for the sport. The boys had the opportunity to fish with their dad for fun, and eventually, in tournaments. Both sons have continued Mike's legacy of having a passion for fishing.

Mike Hager was a good fisherman, a superb guide with clients, and a great storyteller. As with all guides, it was sometimes a challenge to separate fact from fiction. When he found fish, he always said, "Look at this, there must be a million fish under my boat!" Mike loved being on the water and when he had spare time he loved to explore new water and try new fishing techniques.

On a trip to Lake of the Woods in Canada, we were fishing an area that I had fished a number of times, when Mike took off to an area never known for walleyes. I lost track of him for about an hour. I finally tracked him down behind a huge rock that I had never seen anyone fishing near. He and the three people with him had a stringer of beautiful walleyes. He looked at the structure between the rock and the shore and figured it was a spot that should be holding fish and he was right.

One year, Mike and his youngest son, twelve-year-old Shawn, were fishing a tournament that I was also fishing on Leech Lake, in northern Minnesota. Mike had gotten a rough start in the tournament. The day before the tournament, his motor quit. He drove to Grand Rapids and got a smaller boat from his father and used that in the tournament. Then the first morning of the tournament, Mike and Shawn had been skunked. I saw them early in the afternoon, and again, no fish.

When I saw them again, around 2 P.M., Shawn was in tears. My partner, Rick Otteson, and I were concerned and asked what had happened. Exploring, as he usually did, Mike had been searching deep water for big fish. Shawn hooked and lost by the boat, not one, but two walleyes, estimated to be in the nine- to ten-pound class. They were both just sick about their run of bad luck. They never did place in the tournament, but I was really impressed by Mike's ability to find water that was hardly ever fished and find some really nice fish.

One true measure of a good guide is the amount of repeat business that the guide develops over time. Mike Hager developed an impressive list of repeat customers in the sixteen years that he guided at Koep's. He was proud to be a guide and really proud to be a member of the Nisswa Guides' League. It was not uncommon to see Mike wearing his guide jacket on a day when the temperature was in the upper eighties or low nineties. He loved being a part of the organization.

Mike found a spot on Gull Lake that he loved to fish when the wind was out of the north. He showed many of us that spot and we all started calling it Hager's island, or Hager's hump, or Hager's reef. He caught some nice stringers of fish from that spot. Of all the places Mike and I have fished together over the years, that place is sacred ground to me. I seldom go by that spot without fond memories of Mike and all the good times we had together on the water, in the woods, or at work. Mike died Easter Sunday, 1999. He had just bought a brand-new Lund boat and was going to enter the Professional Walleye Trail as a professional tournament fisherman. He picked up the beautiful new boat on Friday. Sunday morning he was dead of a heart attack. He was not yet fifty years old. His funeral was huge and many of the folks in the church were customers from all over Minnesota. Some left memorials to help his kids—others came to say goodbye to one heck of a nice guy who really knew how to fish.

Mike was buried under a huge pine tree in a Nisswa cemetery, about one-and-one-half miles away from the old Koep's store. He would have liked that.

Chapter Thirty-six
Bob Hanson (Minnesota's Fishing Ambassador)

BOB HANSON IS a professional tournament angler who spent a number of years guiding for the Nisswa Guides' League before "retiring" temporarily. He needed to devote more time to tournament fishing as well as promoting fishing for the Minnesota Office of Tourism as Minnesota's Fishing Ambassador—a title he was given during the tenure of Governor Jessie Ventura. He hopes to come back to the league when his other fishing activities slow down a little.

Bob Hanson grew up in New Brighton, Minnesota, and except for a brief stint in North Dakota, he has lived his entire life in Minnesota. Bob's interest in fishing developed through his parents—the family spent a great deal of time fishing together. His dad took him fishing for northerns on the Long Lake Bridge, crappie fishing for slab crappies on Lake Osakis in western Minnesota, and bluegill fishing in the Alexandria area. They also vacationed in the Nisswa area each summer and stayed at a resort on Nisswa Lake. He and his dad also spent time on the old train trestle on Rice Creek, fishing for big, yellow-belly bullheads, and they hunted the wily pheasant in Pipestone, Minnesota. Bob's dad was not only an avid fisherman, he was also a very good pheasant hunter who taught Bob the value of patience and persistence. His dad was not too excited about fishing on big lakes so most of Bob's earlier fishing experiences occurred on smaller lakes and rivers.

After Bob graduated from college, he and a friend started a trucking company in the Twin Cities area. He never stopped fishing, however, for a few years at least, fishing took a back seat to his business.

In 1980, Bob purchased a summer cabin in the Brainerd area and began spending as much time in the lakes area as he could. Eventually, he decided that was the place he wanted to raise his family, so he sold his business and moved to Brainerd in 1984. Fishing became a priority after moving to the area and Bob spent a lot of time at Koep's Bait Shop. As he watched the guides go by his lake place every morning and every afternoon, he began to think that guiding would be a neat job. He got to know Marv Koep and in 1987, Marv hired Bob to guide overflow trips.

His first guide boat was sixteen-feet long with a twenty-horse motor. The next year he invested in a new Crestliner boat with a thirty-horse Yamaha motor. After that, he went to a Yarcraft boat with a forty-horse-power, rear-tiller handle. Like many of the other guides, Bob recalls going to a bigger boat, a Ranger with a fifty-horse-power motor. Marv Koep told him he thought it was too big—it would scare the customers.

Bob knew some of the area lakes when he began guiding, but there were many more that he didn't know—ones he needed to learn to fish in order to be a good guide. Mike Hager showed Bob where to fish on the main lakes. Mike also gave Bob a lot of trips when Mike worked for a landscaping company one summer. Marv Koep was also very helpful in teaching Bob some of the guides' spots on the lakes. But like everyone who guides, Bob really learned the lakes by spending time on the water whenever he got the opportunity to fish. Tom Whitehead, an area bass pro who also worked for a while at Koep's, was another good mentor for where to catch bass.

He was a full-time guide for the summers of 1989 and 1990 and he plowed snow during the winter. In 1989, he began fishing tournaments on a part-time basis. He loved the competition aspect of tournament fishing. He even got lucky and won his first tournament, the World Series of Bass, while fishing with Tom Whitehead. That win, and his love of competitive fishing, moved him in the direction of fishing more tournaments. Bob was on the guide chart at Koep's until 1994 when he started fishing as an overflow guide and began devoting time to tournaments.

When Bob met Ron Lindner in 1990, they became good friends and often fished together. Bob fished bass tournaments for a few years with Ron in the southern part of the United States. Ron taught Bob a lot about fishing tournaments and he also created lasting memories that Bob will never forget, such as the time they were bass fishing in Florida.

"Ron was making a cast and he hooked something in the boat," recalled Bob. "When he threw the bait, he threw the rod and reel into the water, lost his balance, and fell in, too. I saw where the rod went—it was a rather expensive piece of equipment— and I told Ron to hang onto the boat and I would take him to the spot. Before I even finished my sentence, Ron grabbed the side of the boat and jumped back in the boat.

"Ron said, 'Forget the equipment, I have others.' We didn't go ten yards and two alligators, as long as our boat, slid into the weed cover. 'Why do you think I got back into the boat so fast?' Ron said. Ron was tough and durable. We would prefish tournaments from sunrise until sunset and all we took to eat were a few sandwiches."

In 1990, Bob was named executive director of Ski Gull, an area ski business, and held that job until a few years ago. He began working at the local community and technical college on a part-time basis in 1991. Today, Bob is the full-time customized training representative for Central Lakes College. He coordinates training for business and industry customers through the college. He also continues to be a tournament fisherman and part-time Fishing Ambassador for the Minnesota Department of Tourism.

Bob loved guiding at Koep's. He enjoyed meeting new people and never got tired of fishing. He just had too many other things going on to be able to continue as a full-time guide. He teamed up with the Lindners in 1992 and was given an entry into the PWT (Professional Walleye Trail) tournament on Lake Erie in Michigan. He talked Ron Lindner into prefishing the tournament with him and his life has been focused on tournaments ever since.

He recalls a terrifying trip to Gull Lake with a boat full of customers. The fish were biting and they were in an area where they couldn't see the western sky very well. Suddenly, the sky grew dark. Bob told the customers they had better head to the landing, in case a storm was coming. One of the customers wanted to wait a few more minutes because the fish were biting so well. Moments later, a screaming wind was upon them. Bob headed for shore before anyone had time to reel in their lines. He ran his boat into a sandy beach and everyone crawled under a boatlift for protection. They looked across the lake and saw boatlifts and docks flying everywhere. Bob still doesn't know whether it was a small tornado or a waterspout, but it was destructive and scary. The customer who had insisted on staying, apologized all the way back to the bait shop. They were lucky no one was hurt and no equipment was damaged.

Bob fished with many celebrities during his fishing career, including Hank Parker, a well-known fishing television personality; and Mae Schunk, the Lieutenant Governor of Minnesota. He also recalled a fishing trip with Joe Fellegy, the Mille Lacs Lake guide and author. "I call Joe the human GPS [global positioning system]," said Bob. "It's unbelievable how much he knows about Mille Lacs Lake without modern electronics. It was a great experience fishing with Joe."

His favorite lakes include Gull, the Whitefish Chain, and North Long. Bob remembers fishing on Gull Lake in the early nineties, when fishing the lake was really tough. He believes that the stocking programs implemented by the Department of Natural Resources really help area lakes.

Bob still has an unofficial position as Minnesota's fishing ambassador—promoting the sport through shows and special events. He has been featured a number of times on the *In-Fisherman* television series as well as many other radio and television shows. His website, "Minnesota Bob," is a link to the Minnesota Office of Tourism.

As a tournament angler, Bob has enjoyed success with four wins; two second-place finishes; three third-place finishes, many top-ten finishes; the PWT Sharp Angler Award; and numerous big fish awards.

Through all his success stories, his biggest thrill of all is fishing with his boys. Bob Hanson is another of the fishing legacies to come from the Nisswa Guides' League.

Chapter Thirty-seven
Richard Boggs

RICK BOGGS IS ONE of the younger guides at the league, but his connection to the league goes back to his days as a young boy, growing up on the east side of Gull Lake. Now he is also a full-time tournament angler who travels the country during the fishing tournament season and guides when he has breaks between fishing contests.

Rick's stepfather was a good friend of Rod Romine and Rick used to hang out at Koep's Bait Shop when he was barely old enough to buy bait. Kevin Koep and Tom Briggs were boyhood friends and after school and on summer weekends, Rick and Tom fished Gull Lake together. Through Rick's friendship with Tom, Rick got to know Kevin Koep and he was introduced to some of the legends that worked at Koep's. He met the crappie-fishing guru, Gene Shapinski, who taught him how to fish with the Quiver Jig for crappies. He also met oldtimers, Harry Van Doren and Cully Swenson. He was too young to know the guides on a personal level, but he knew who they were and he saw them on the lake from time to time.

He fished a lot as a young boy. His parents had a small boat that was always in the water on Gull Lake, so Rick spent countless hours fishing the lake and trapping during the trapping season. He was just a regular kid doing what many kids his age did living in north-central Minnesota.

One summer, while working as a dock boy at Bar Harbor, Rick got to know Red Frey, a salesman who spent a lot of time on Gull Lake. Red took a liking to Rick. Red loved to fish bass and so did guide Royal Karels, so when Red hired Royal to guide for him, Red often brought Rick. Royal taught Rick how to fish bass and the two became good friends, despite their thirty-year age difference. The two even fished some bass tournaments together over the years, and to this day, Rick credits Royal with teaching him how to be a bass fisherman.

Rick loved to fish and he spent a lot of time fishing, but he never gave much thought to guiding when he was growing up. He didn't know much about the guiding business and mostly enjoyed fishing for fun.

After graduating from high school, Rick moved to Arizona and worked in the sheetrock business. His stepfather died when Rick was twenty-five years old, so he decided to return home to Minnesota to help his mother. In 1989, Rick began guiding almost by accident—just helping out when Marv Koep needed some backup help. Most of his trips were out of larger resorts, such as Madden's, Cragun's, and Grand View. Rick had a lot of help from the guides he worked with in learning the area lakes. He helped out for about two years and then became a full-time guide in 1991. In 2000, Rick became serious about tournament fishing and today he fishes the Professional Walleye Trail tournament circuit. Tournament fishing has become his part-time business, requiring marketing and promotional skills as well as a significant time on the road away from his family.

Rick's first guide boat was a Tuffy with a fifty-horse Yamaha. A few years later, he upgraded to a seventy-horse power motor. He recalls that Marv told him that a seventy-horse motor was too big and people wouldn't want to fish in a boat with a motor that large. (An interesting fact is that now Marv fishes with a ninety-horse motor.)

Like many of the other guides, Rick likes to fish for whatever is biting. He is somewhat partial to walleye fishing and really enjoys fishing for walleyes with a live bait rig. He has guided many pro football players, some coaches from the major leagues, and many corporate dignitaries.

On one of his favorite lakes, he has a favorite dock close to a public landing where he bets customers five dollars that he can catch a bass under the dock. Someone always takes him up on the bet and he has always caught a bass under the dock, even though some of them haven't been too big.

His favorite lakes to fish are Gull, Hubert, and the Whitefish Chain. His scariest experience on the water happened in Green Bay, Wisconsin, while fishing on Lake Michigan. Global positioning systems had recently become available for small craft and Rick had just installed a system in his boat, but he was not very confident in the new technology. He was out on the big lake, a few miles from shore, when a thick, dark fog set in, which made nearly impossible to go in any direction. Rick and his fishing partner found a channel marker and tied up to it—hoping to wait out the fog. They had been sitting for quite a while when a small fishing boat came by at a slow speed. Rick decided to try to reach shore, so he looked at his GPS system and headed back toward the shore. Just then, he heard a ship blow its whistle. Traveling about twenty-five yards, he looked up to see the black side of a ship about two stories high. It was moving right at him, making waves almost large enough to swamp his boat. He missed the ship, but was almost run over. It was an experience that he hopes he won't repeat!

Rick thinks that water quality on area lakes has greatly improved and believes there is a reduction in the size of area weedbeds. According to his experience, he has found that the numbers of fish to be found in area lakes are about the same as twenty-five to thirty years ago, but he agrees with other guides who feel the quality has suffered due to fishing pressure. He also believes that guides take unfair criticism because they do not get credit for the catch-and-release ethic that is currently being practiced.

"I think many people in our area still think guides kill everything we catch," said Rick, "the way the business was practiced thirty years ago. That is just not the case. We practice catch-and-release with all species of fish now. We keep fish for customers, too, but we really encourage folks to keep trophies only if they want them for their walls."

He sees icefishing as being a big factor in the demise of larger fish. Anglers now get map coordinates of the "honey holes," sit on them all season, and keep taking the big fish. "That is a big factor in keeping fish sizes down, in my opinion."

Rick has the passion for the sport possessed by so many of the good guides. When he is not fishing tournaments or guiding, he can probably be found on the water, fishing with his two daughters. He guides a lot, loves to fish, and sees himself doing what he is now doing as long as he is healthy and able to continue. About 80 percent of his business are repeat customers and that says a lot about the kind of guide Rick is—fun, funny, and always ready for a new experience on the water. Rick has a distinctive voice that carries a long way on the lake and the sound one usually hears from his boat is that of laughter.

Chapter Thirty-eight
Don Karlgaard

DON KARLGAARD GREW UP on a farm near Fergus Falls, Minnesota. His father was a farmer who also liked to fish, especially panfish such as crappies and sunfish. His father was not an exceptional fisherman, but he enjoyed the sport enough that he took Don to area lakes to fish and swim, which few farm kids got to do on a regular basis. Don's family fished some of the lakes around Fergus Falls and the nearby community of Pelican Rapids. He loved to fish, but his fishing skills were centered around panfish until he got to college, where his roommates taught him how and where to catch other fish such as bass, northern pike, and walleyes.

Don graduated from college with a teaching degree and found his first teaching job in Pipestone, Minnesota. After Don got married, he and his wife, Cheryl, decided to move to an area that had more lakes, so they moved to Brainerd in 1980. Their first home was on Hartley Lake, north of town. They had three boys, so Don always had someone to take fishing—he fished twelve months a year.

Before moving to Brainerd, Don had never heard of the Nisswa Guides' League or Koep's Bait and Tackle Shop. His connections to the league and the store came from his teaching teammate, Glen Belgum. Glen Belgum became a fishing mentor to Don—showing him fishing techniques, such as how to read a flasher, lake maps, and how to focus on productive areas of lakes while fishing for different species of fish. Glen became a central figure in helping Don become a good angler. Don also honed his skills by fishing with his family in Canada.

Don started shopping at Koep's Bait and Tackle Shop and became acquainted with Marv Koep, Steve Collette, Mark Lee, and other guides. Don loved to fish, but he recognized that his fishing had become more of a passion than a hobby. In 1989, he asked Marv Koep if he could guide when extra help was needed. To his surprise, Marv replied, "Yes, I would love to have you guide for us." He has been working with the Nisswa Guides' League ever since.

He took thirty trips his first year and decided that he would try to use guiding as a way to upgrade his fishing gear, boat, and motor. That was more than sixteen years ago and Don continues to guide today. The most trips he took in one year were fifty, in 1991. In 1996, he began working as a math consultant to Minnesota teachers for the Minnesota State Department of Education. He has learned to balance the duties of his job with guiding and family. It is not a hard choice for Don. His family comes first, teaching and consulting are his second priority, and guiding comes in third. He figures that will change over time, but for now he has his priorities in place.

In addition to being a math teacher and math consultant, Don has also been a basketball coach at the K-12 level and the community-college level.

Teaching is an aspect of guiding that Don really enjoys. He is especially happy to guide kids and show them how to fish. "Teaching kids is usually more rewarding than teaching older men," said Don. "Kids will try to do what they are taught, but the older guys like to do it the way they always have, even if that way doesn't work."

Don learned a lot about fishing from Glen Belgum, but like most of the other guides, he learned about area lakes by putting in time on the water. He received help from the other guides, but there is no substitute for learning the features of a lake like spending time on it—getting to know how the lake performs under different conditions and at different times of the year.

If Don had to fish one species and one lake it would be walleyes on Gull Lake. That would be his passion, but like all of the guides, he has developed into a multi-species angler with one exception—he never developed a desire to be a musky fisherman. His favorite lakes to fish are Gull, Whitefish, North Long, and Round.

One of his most memorable fishing trips was to a small area lake with Jim Wacker, who at the time was head coach of the University of Minnesota football team. Wacker had a number of his staff along for the fishing trip, including Jim Zorn who was the quarterback coach and a former NFL quarterback. The department decided to have a little fishing tournament and placed wagers on who would catch the most fish. Don thought Wacker had no chance at winning because when they started fishing, Wacker's rod was upside down and he reeled backwards. He was not an avid angler, but he was competitive and he won the contest. It was a great day and Don enjoyed his experience with the entire staff.

Another memorable trip involved another retired NFL player who met Don at the dock wearing clothes that had his name on everything—hat, shirt, shorts, and shoes. He was out for a good time and kept the heat on Don to move around to find fish.

The player was a stitch and when they boated in for lunch, the ladies at the resort recognized the player and gathered around him as if he were a rock star! It was a crazy day that Don won't soon forget.

Perhaps his most unusual trip involved a Hmong family who hired Don for a half-day trip. Don took the father and his boys to a small lake to see if they could get some action, fishing for anything that would bite. Don spent the first twenty minutes showing the family how the rods and reels were used and then headed onto the water to see if they could catch fish. Well, they did catch fish and they kept every fish they caught, whether small bass, small sunnies, or small pike. The size or species of fish didn't matter—they kept them all. Don realized that folks in the Hmong culture use nearly all fish parts, including the brains, so he let them keep the fish they caught. They had quite a bag of fish when the morning was done, including a large number of rock bass, a species that most area anglers will not keep. Everyone was happy and Don wished them luck at the end of the trip and sent them home with their fish.

Later that evening, Don got a call from the bait shop, saying that he had a party who wanted to fish with him the next day. The clerk at the store wouldn't say who the party was because they wanted it to be a surprise. Well it was a surprise because it was the Hmong family again. They went fishing on the same lake with the same results and again had a great time. They went home with another huge bag of fish. That was about eight years ago and Don never saw them again.

Don has fished with a television personality and her family, and over the years, has developed repeat customers from states such as Nebraska and Iowa. He still fishes regularly with his father and mother and his immediate family. Don's annual fishing highlight is taking his three sons on their fishing trip to Canada. Don is one of the newer guides in the Nisswa Guides' League and he has more than sixteen years of experience with the organization.

Every guide has his or her own personality and the first impression is the lasting impression when meeting Don. He is a stately gentleman with a kind disposition and kind manners. He is a teacher who has patience and loves to instruct—he receives great joy from watching others learn to be successful.

Chapter Thirty-nine
Mike Zauhar

MIKE ZAUHAR, OR "Z" as he is known by most of his friends, grew up in Crosby-Ironton—a small mining community about fourteen miles east of Brainerd. His dad worked in the iron ore pits in the Crosby-Ironton area for forty-two years. His dad's job was seasonal—based on demand for the iron ore. He usually worked from fall to spring and took off the summer months. The Zauhar family was one of ordinary means, not poor but not wealthy, either, and fishing was a family summer pastime. The family fished for fun as well as to put food on the table. They didn't own a boat so most of the fishing on area lakes was done from shore. Local lakes, such as June, Serpent, and Black Hoof were the ones the Zauhar family usually fished. Mike recalls that his dad kept nearly every fish they caught and used it for food.

Mike was active in athletics and the time he spent fishing revolved around sports activities such as baseball, basketball, and football. Mike graduated from high school in 1969 and went to St. John's University near St. Cloud, where he graduated in 1973. He had a difficult time getting to hunt and fish as much as he wanted to in high school, but he spent more time doing those things in college as a way to escape from the pressures of school and sports. During his last few years in college, he spent more time with classmates who hunted and fished and his time outdoors almost became a religious experience.

His first teaching job was in Apple Valley, Minnesota, but he began spending more and more time hunting and fishing in central Minnesota. His second teaching job was in his hometown of Crosby-Ironton, which brought him close to the lakes and woods he knew as a kid. During his tenure as a Crosby-Ironton teacher, he started hearing stories of the Nisswa Guides' League and some of its members. Fellow teachers heard of guides such as Glen Belgum, Royal Karels, and Bert Lindberry, and referred to seeing many photos of the guides in the local newspaper every week.

Two years later, Mike took a teaching position in Nisswa, where he got to know some of the guides firsthand, such as Lenny Hodgson, Bert Lindberry, and Glen Belgum. His first introduction to the Koep family came from Wendy Koep—Marv and Judy's youngest daughter. Mike had Wendy as a student in class and through that connection became acquainted with Marv and Judy. About two years into the job, another teacher was hired at the Nisswa School who became one of Mike's best friends and his very best fishing and hunting partner—Randy Hansen. Mike and Randy fished almost every day during the fishing season. They had a lot in common. They were both married, without children, and shared a passion for the outdoors. Randy was a Brainerd native who knew the area lakes pretty well, and he had a boat, so most of the time Mike was the passenger in Randy's boat. Randy's father, Gene, was also a frequent companion and through his relationship with the Hansen's, Mike became a pretty good angler.

Mike lost his best fishing partner in the early eighties, when Randy was hired as a Nisswa Guide. Mike was disappointed about losing his fishing and hunting partner. While they still spent a lot of time together, it would never be quite the same again. And once they began having children, their time together became even more limited. They are still good friends and they spend some time together around busy schedules.

"When Randy joined the Nisswa Guides' League, it forced me to learn to do more things on my own," said Mike. "I always went with Randy, in his boat, and on his spots. Randy took me fishing when he was a guide, but we didn't go as often as we once did. I bought my first boat—a seventeen-foot Alumacraft with a fifty-horse Mercury—and I started to learn how to fish on my own. I became good friends with other guides, such as Lenny and Mike Hager, and they helped me learn the lakes better. I remember fishing with Mike Hager in the middle eighties and seeing him throw back some big fish. He asked me if I minded if we returned some of the bigger fish we caught. I didn't want to throw them back because I was raised to keep and eat everything, but I went along with him. Boy, did we throw back some nice fish. Mike Hager was the first person who got me thinking about catch-and-release. He thought about fishing for future years and stressed letting big fish go back into the water.

"After being lobbied by Mike Hager, Randy Hansen, and Lenny Hodgson, Marv Koep called me about helping out with overflow trips. Those guys helped me get into guiding and into the Nisswa Guides' League and I will always be grateful to them for that. My first trip was with our area representative to the legislature, Kris Hasskamp. I also fished the Governor's Fishing Opener that year and was very involved in fishing the national crappie-fishing tournament. I was fishing with Bing Brodzinski, who is a fabulous fisherman. We also fished northern pike tournaments together.

"I started at Koep's on the bottom of the chart in about 1989. I was never interested in fishing every day because I had two children at home and I liked to spend part of the summers with my wife and kids. I also coached during the summer months. I stayed on the chart until 1998, when Marv sold the store and Mike Blanch became the new owner. I told Mike that I would help him out if he was ever in a bind, but I decided to start guiding a little on my own and try to build a small business that I could manage during the summer months. My wife and I purchased a small cabin on Round Lake and we began booking out the cabin to my fishing customers—that has turned into a nice little business. I guide at some of the local resorts when they need help as well as at Koep's. I try to take twenty-five to thirty trips a year. That works well for me." His favorite lakes to fish are Round, Hubert, North Long, and Gull.

Guiding was a good summer job for Mike—it complemented his teaching and coaching activities. His most-famous customer is Glen Frey, a musician with the nationally known rock band, The Eagles.

"Glen has been a customer for five or six years and we've had some great fishing trips," he recalled. "I've also guided Joe Sensor, the former tight-end of the Minnesota Vikings. He's a great guy to fish with and he has invited me down to his place for a social get-together. I've met members of the Detroit Pistons basketball team as well as Hank Parker, who has his own television fishing shows. I've had great experiences guiding, along with some days that I would rather not remember. I have had a few people in the boat who have had too much to drink and have fallen down, but no one has ever been hurt. I've been out when storms are moving in and the static electricity makes the fishing lines go straight up into the air. That's when I go home.

"The worst thing that ever happened to me in the boat was when I was fishing about eight miles from shore on Mille Lacs Lake one afternoon. I left the key on in my boat motor for about three hours while we trolled with my electric trolling motor. When I went to start it, it was stone dead. I was trying to figure out how I would get off the water with no power. Luckily, I had enough juice left in the trolling motor to jump-start the big motor. There were no other boats around, so I don't know how I would have ever gotten back otherwise.

"Being a member of the Nisswa Guides' League was a great experience. I learned so much about fishing and working with customers. I will be grateful forever to the guides who helped me as well as Marv and Judy Koep for giving me the chance to work for the most famous and prestigious guide organization in our state," said Mike.

Mike regrets that he doesn't get to fish more with his son, Mike, and his daughter, Molly. They are both very involved in school, so finding time to fish with the family has become challenging. He is a teacher, a coach, and a fishing guide—and he still has the passion for fishing.

Chapter Forty
Jon Stolski

JON STOLSKI WAS FIVE years old and living in Princeton, Minnesota, when John, his devoted grandfather, made it a practice to take him fishing on weekends during the summer months. Grandfather Stolski taught Jon how to fish and how to practice good fishing ethics. Sometimes his grandfather felt the ire of the other grandchildren and their parents because Jon was the grandchild he had chosen to be his fishing buddy. But that was just the way it was for his grandfather.

They stopped for breakfast at the same restaurant every morning on the way to the lake. Jon's grandfather told him if he got tired while fishing, to lie down in the boat and take a nap. He taught Jon to eat what they caught and only take what they needed for a meal as well as how to be patient in the boat and have fun fishing. At the end of every trip, they stopped at the same pizza shop in Princeton and had pizza for supper. This was the routine for Jon until he was nine years old and his family moved to Brooklyn Park, Minnesota. That made it more difficult to fish with his grandfather, but they were still able to fish from time to time.

In 1974, Jon's dad, Ron, got a job in the Brainerd school district. The family moved to Brainerd, where his dad also became head football coach. His father bought his first fishing boat—a Lund 315—from Royal Karels. Jon and his dad often fished area waters, such as the Mississippi River, Gilbert Lake, and other smaller bodies of water. Jon developed a good relationship with a number of buddies who also liked to fish and he spent much of his youth on the lakes and rivers in the Brainerd area.

Jon heard about the Nisswa Guides when his family moved to Brainerd. He recalls waiting for the fishing report in the newspaper, to see how big the fish were.

Lee Johnson became one of Jon's best friends when he first moved to Brainerd and they have been inseparable since the fourth grade. They also considered themselves pretty lucky because their elementary teacher—Bert Lindberry—was also a Nisswa guide. He was, without a doubt, their favorite teacher. Bert knew both boys loved to fish, so he spent a little extra time showing them new knots, different fishing techniques, and new baits. The year Jon and Lee spent in Bert's class was very helpful in teaching them many new things about fishing.

Jon spent many days fishing with Lee Johnson and his dad, Marv, and sadly, fished with Lee and his dad on the last fishing trip Lee's dad was able to take. He had been ill for some time and died shortly after making the trip with the two boys.

Marv Koep used to sponsor workshops for kids at the bait shop. Jon still has certificates for winning a casting contest when he was an elementary student. He and Lee spent many hours hanging around Koep's bait shop and other bait shops as kids— always trying to find out the latest news about fishing.

Royal Karels also had a big influence on Jon's life. Royal was Ron Stolski's friend, so Jon had many chances to be around Royal and listen to him talk about fishing.

Jon participated in a summer fishing class that was taught by Royal Karels and Gene Hanson. The students learned about lake structure, fishing techniques, lures, and knot tying, and then they went to different lakes to practice what they had learned. It was a great experience that taught Jon good fundamentals of fishing. "Royal Karels was a fantastic teacher with kids," said Jon. "He had so much patience and he really made the classes fun." On one memorable trip to Mille Lacs Lake, the class fished on a launch with the legendary guide, Joe Fellegy.

Royal showed the Stolskis where and how to fish the king salmon on Lake Michigan. Jon landed a thirty-two-pound salmon on his first trip to the great lake.

When Jon was in college, he visited a large sports show in the Twin Cities. He was attracted to a booth promoting fishing in Alaska. He was so amazed at the size of the fish and how nice the people in the booth were that he came back to visit the booth every day. Finally, he decided to go to Alaska and get a job. He told the people at the booth that he would come and work for them for free. They said they didn't have any job openings, but they eventually decided to make room for Jon and paid his airfare.

The year was 1988—Jon worked the first year as a dock boy and fish cleaner, along with other odd jobs around the resort. He had the same job a second summer and by the third year, Jon had gotten his guiding license and United States Coast Guard certification and became a full-time guide on the Kenai River in Alaska. It was a job he held for eight years. He loved the work, loved fishing the Kenai, and had fabulous experiences during his stay in Alaska. He fished the Kenai during the salmon runs and returned to Minnesota after the season was over. Jon met his wife-to-be, Kim, and continued to work in Alaska for a few years after getting married.

Jon and Kim spent parts of some summers together in Alaska, but guiding was a job that didn't allow much social time. After their first child was born, they decided that fishing in Alaska was too demanding and Jon began checking into guiding in the Brainerd-Nisswa area.

In 1991, Duke and Terri Fischer were the owners of Koep's. Jon stopped by the store to tell the Fischers that he was an experienced guide and he would be available if they needed extra help. The Fischers gave Jon a few trips and that was the beginning of Jon working his way into the Nisswa Guides' League.

For a few years, Jon guided in Alaska during the salmon run and then returned to Minnesota and fished in the Nisswa area later in the summer. He also got a teaching job in the Brainerd school district. He taught during the school year, guided in Alaska until late-July, and then guided at Koep's later in the summer. He kept up that hectic schedule until around 1994, when he stopped guiding in Alaska and began working full-time as a Nisswa guide during the summer months.

Jon had learned some of the area lakes while growing up in the area and he had a grandfather who owned a cabin on Mille Lacs Lake, so he knew the east side of the lake quite well. He learned new spots on other lakes by working with guides and spending many hours on his own learning to fish the lakes he didn't know very well.

Walleye fishing is Jon's first love, but he considers himself a multi-species angler. He had heard of the legends of the Nisswa Guides' League, but he was too young to know any of the early guides except Marv Koep. Marv helped Jon get into the Nisswa Guides' League by promoting him to Duke and Terri Fischer.

One of Jon's celebrity customers was the rocker Stevie Ray Vaughn, a rock guitar player who was killed in a plane crash only two weeks after fishing with Jon in Alaska. Jon has also fished with a few Minnesota television celebrities and he has one customer who fishes about thirty trips a year with Jon.

One of his most memorable and scary fishing experiences involved a group of gentlemen that Jon had fished with for about six years—all three men were getting up in years. They were fishing Leech Lake and the wind was blowing, but it wasn't too bad. The fishing was tough and Jon decided to try running bottom bouncers across a rock reef to see if he could find stray walleyes.

The wind picked up and waves began coming into the back of Jon's boat, and then, of course, they found fish. The walleyes they caught were really nice, but Jon was concerned about the size of the waves and the well-being of his customers. Two of the guys were catching fish and the other one wasn't having much luck. Jon suggested going in because he was concerned about landing his boat at the narrow harbor at the resort. The gentleman who didn't have a fish asked if he could wait a little longer to see if he could catch one. Jon fished until the wind was so strong that he got scared. He put life jackets on all three men and headed to the resort—barely able to get into the harbor through the big waves. The gentleman who didn't catch anything thanked Jon for staying out longer so he could try to catch a fish, saying, "You never know if you are going to get another chance to fish again." The man died about four months later. Jon said it was eerie because the man seemed to know that would be his last fishing trip. They caught some nice fish, but Jon was really happy to get everyone back to the resort safe and sound.

Jon loves to take kids fishing, he really loves to fish, and he never gets tired of guiding. He has been a guide for around sixteen years and he has demonstrated the rare passion that it takes to be a good guide. Most of his clients are repeat customers and when he is not fishing with customers, he usually fishes with members of his own family. Like many of the Old-School guides, Jon just never seems to get enough time on the water.

Chapter Forty-one
Lee Johnson

LEE JOHNSON BEGAN WORKING with the Nisswa Guides' League in 1994. He remembers his first trip very well because he couldn't sleep the night before. He was so excited, he felt as if he were going on his first deer-hunting trip. Someone at Koep's asked him if he was willing to help out with extra trips, and before long, he was in the guiding business. It was something that he had always dreamed about.

Lee, too, had a connection to the Nisswa Guides' League long before he was old enough to think about guiding. His father was a highway patrolman and also a good friend of Rod Romine, the Brainerd dispatcher for the highway patrol. Lee fished with his father and Rod many times as a young boy. His dad was an avid fisherman and spent many hours fishing the Pine River near the Whitefish Chain as well as the Mississippi River. Rod Romine was an expert on the Whitefish Chain and he often took the Johnsons fishing on his favorite lake. Lee learned a lot about fishing from his father and Rod.

He grew up on White Sand Lake in Baxter, just outside of Brainerd. Much of his early fishing was off his family's dock. His family loved the outdoors and they spent many summers fishing. Lee and one of his best friends, Jon Stolski, another Nisswa guide, became good friends in the fourth grade. They spent a lot of time together as friends, fishing buddies, and teammates on sports teams. As a boy, Lee recalls waiting for the newspaper's fishing edition, when the photos from Koep's and other area guides were published. He couldn't wait to see the fish photos and read about how the guides caught their fish. Most of Lee's early fishing experiences were in a canoe. Later, he moved up to fishing out of a fourteen-foot Alumacraft boat.

Lee graduated from high school in 1984 and started college at St. John's, west of St. Cloud, Minnesota. He later transferred to Bemidji State University. Both colleges were near lakes, so Lee never stopped fishing. As many often do when pursuing a college degree, he never took time off from fishing.

Duke and Terry Fischer owned Koep's Pro Shop when Lee began guiding. He felt a tremendous amount of pressure to produce when he began. It took a long time to realize that it was impossible to catch fish on every trip—customers were usually happy just knowing that he was giving his best effort.

He worked as a full-time bartender at Kelly's on the west side of Gull Lake. As he began getting more trips, soon he was working at Kelly's until 2 A.M., grabbing about four hours of sleep, and hitting the lakes as a guide by 7 A.M. It was a grueling schedule, but he never got tired of fishing. On days when his trip was cancelled, he even went fishing on his own.

Like all the Nisswa guides, Lee was a good fisherman, but he didn't know all the area lakes he needed to learn in order to be a complete guide. Mike Hager pointed out some of the spots Lee had never fished before. Other guides also showed Lee spots, but Mike Hager was a big help and an influence on helping Lee learn the area lakes. The rest of his learning was accomplished by spending time on the water, studying the lakes, and learning where to fish.

Lee's busiest summer occurred when he still worked full time at Kelly's—he took 132 trips, but he never got tired of fishing. One lesson he learned, however, is that being a full-time guide is hard on a young family. He goes out of his way to make sure he takes his wife and two daughters fishing and does other activities with them on a regular basis.

Although Lee loves fishing and guiding, he tells people that guiding is hard work. It is especially tough when it is cold and windy, or hot and humid, and when the fish won't bite. But he loves to take families fishing and he takes guiding very seriously.

Lee currently guides part time, along with working full time in a local sports shop. He fishes some tournaments and will continue to guide and fish tournaments on a selective basis. At one point in his life, he dreamed of being a full-time tournament angler, but at this stage of his life that isn't very realistic.

Some of the interesting people Lee has fished with include Irwin Jacobs and his family. The Jacobs own Genmar Industries, which manufactures many of the major fishing boats produced in America. He also fished with Don, "The Bear," Haskins, who had compiled one of best basketball records in Division 1A. Another customer, one who Lee found to be absolutely delightful, was reportedly one of the richest men in Texas.

Lee spends some of his fishing time on smaller lakes in the Brainerd/Nisswa area. He likes to fish for walleyes, musky, and bass and loves catching anything that bites—

priding himself on being a multi-species angler. Lee still uses an early-model flasher fish locator for finding spots to fish.

He has had a couple of memorable experiences on the water. More than once, he has witnessed his customers' fishing lines rise in the air from static electricity before an approaching storm hit. He also experienced true, nine-foot waves on Lake of the Woods. On that occasion, he didn't think he would make it off the lake. "I always hear people talk about four- to five-foot waves," he recalled, "but when you are in eight- to nine-foot waves, you have all you can do to keep the boat from going into and under the waves. It is terrifying!"

Since Lee began guiding, he has noticed a change in the tourism patterns. More people seem to play golf or take in area attractions and not as many people go fishing. If they fish, they spend less time doing it than they used to.

Lee has a passion for fishing—he looks forward to the next day of fishing just as much as he did the day before. He enjoys 98 percent of his customers and absolutely loves to take kids fishing. "I love to see the looks on kids' faces when they catch fish, there is just nothing else like it for me."

Chapter Forty-two
Robert Rasinski

ROBERT RASINSKI, BEST KNOWN as Robbie, is one of four Nisswa guides who was raised on the shores of Gull Lake. Born in 1978, long after the Nisswa Guides' League was founded, Robbie had ties to many of the guides who were members of the league. His dad, Ray, was a classmate of both Steve Collette and Mark Lee, and Robbie's uncle was Tom Briggs. All three of these classmates were members of the league. Robbie grew up learning to fish with his dad and his grandfather on his dad's side of the family. His dad is a contractor and loves to fish and many of the family trips involved fishing with Grandpa Rasinski. His father and grandfather were both lifelong Gull Lake residents, so naturally, Robbie fished Gull Lake a lot.

Robbie didn't grow up dreaming of being a guide—he doesn't even remember when he found out there were guides in the area. He liked to fish, but he is also athletic and enjoyed playing in sports. In 1990, when he was eleven years old, Robbie interviewed for a job at Koep's Nisswa Bait and Tackle. He got the part-time job packing bait, nightcrawlers, and leeches, and worked about four days per week. At the time, there were eighteen guides on the chart at Koep's. Robbie recalls being impressed with the number of fish that came in at the end of a shift. He began thinking that the guides really knew how to catch fish.

His parents got him his first boat when he was twelve years old and he moored it at their home on the lake. He fished whenever he had free time and he spent many hours learning to fish the south end of Gull Lake. By the time he was thirteen years old, he pretended to be a guide and took people out in his boat to see if he could find and catch fish. At this age, guiding was not something he seriously thought about making into a career. He developed into a very good high school athlete—excelling in football and other sports. But he spent his summers working at Koep's.

In 1993, Robbie took his first, guided fishing trip to Gull Lake. Mark Lee was unable to take a trip and when he discovered that all the other guides were booked for the day, he asked Robbie, who was working in the store, if he could pick up some customers at the Gull Lake Resort. Robbie had a boat and said he would give it a try. He doesn't remember whether or not they caught fish, but he does recall being nervous about finding fish. He wanted them to at least have some action. When the other guides were booked, he began getting a few trips. He did not have a car license yet, so the only trips he took were to Gull Lake.

Robbie graduated from high school and decided he didn't want to go away to college—he wanted to go to college in Brainerd. His dad told him he could work for him in the off season. The next year, 1996, Robbie told the guides he was interested in getting on the chart and taking overflow trips, so he took about twenty-five or thirty trips that summer. The next winter, the guides voted to put Robbie on the chart and made him a full-time guide. Robbie guided fulltime for six years, making him the youngest guide on the chart at the time. In 2003, he "retired" from guiding, when he felt he needed to make a career change and focus more time on his extended family and a new lady in his life. He also realized that a guiding career didn't offer some of the essentials in life, such as health and disability insurance.

An outstanding person, he also emerged as a superb angler. It was not uncommon to see other boats following him around the lakes, which is the ultimate compliment to a guide, but sometimes, also, the ultimate curse.

Robbie learned other area lakes by spending time with the guides and Marv Koep. "Marv took the time to show me key spots whenever I fished lakes with him that I didn't know," recalled Robbie. "He got me started in areas and then checked on the radio to see how I was doing. Other guides were also great at helping me get started."

During his last few years of guiding, Robbie fished six to seven days a week. He really got the feel for the kind of work involved in being a full-time guide. "A lot of people think guiding is a great job if you like to fish, and it is, but it is also hard work and very demanding—especially during the cold fishing months. There is always the pressure you put on yourself to catch fish. If you catch fish, you feel great, if you get skunked you feel pretty bad."

His first guide boat was a sixteen-foot Lund Rebel. He later went to an eighteen-foot Lund, then a 2025 Pro V, which is just six inches short of twenty-one feet long. That boat could handle four people very nicely.

"I have a couple of funny stories that happened when I was guiding," said Robbie. "One day I picked up two ladies from Grand View Resort on Gull Lake and we were fishing on the north side of the lake. I had gotten a bite and told the lady at the front of the boat to set her rod down and come back and I would let her land the fish. I forgot to tell her to reel in her line first. She came back and took my rod and I looked up at the front of the boat just has her rod and reel were being pulled over the side of the boat. The outfit was gone in a flash. It was probably a northern pike that hit the line and pulled everything into the lake. The lady felt terrible, even though I told her that it was completely my fault. She wanted to know how much the rod and reel was worth. I said don't worry about it, but of course, it was a G-Loomis with a high-end reel worth about $300. She asked if there was any way we could get back the equipment. I said, no, it was probably a northern pike and was two miles across the lake by now. We worked across that spot once more, because we had gotten a few fish from the area. Wouldn't you know—I hooked the reel we lost! I pulled it out of the lake and it must have been a northern pike that bit the line because the hook was gone. Everything else was the same as it was when we lost it fifteen minutes earlier. I was pretty lucky."

"Some other customers that I fish with quite often have a son, Casey. Casey loves to have fun. He is fifteen or sixteen years old and is a great kid. We were fishing late into the fall and it was so cold I couldn't wait to get off the water. The fish were biting, but it was so cold, I could hardly pick a minnow out of the livewell. Casey's dad thought they had enough fish and it was time to go home. I was glad to hear it, because I could not warm up. Casey wanted to stay, but his dad said it was time to go. Casey decided to protest with a little demonstration when we were about four miles from the landing. He took off his coat, shirt, and shoes, and spread out at the front of the boat, like the guy in the movie, *Titanic*. He sat in the wind the whole way back without freezing to death. I couldn't believe it!

"The next year, Casey got me even better. It was a hot day and we were fishing and I got a call on my cell phone. I turned away from the front of the boat to hear better and all of a sudden I got a tremendous bite on my line. I started reeling and the fish is almost pulling the rod out of my hand. I stood up to loosen the drag on my reel and out of the water popped Casey! He had jumped into the lake, swam under the boat, and pulled on my line! He was a great, funny guy.

"On another memorable trip, I was fishing with Joe Schmidt from the ABC television station in the Twin Cities. Joe and his crew were fishing with Chip Lohmiller, a kicker for an NFL football team—I think the Washington Redskins. I fished with Joe and Chip and got some nice crappies. They wanted to fish the next day with a camera crew, to show how the crappies were biting and put it on the local news. I took the crappies home to clean them.

That night, a storm with a big cold front came through, so I never cleaned the fish. I left them in the livewell. The next day, I picked up the guys and the camera crew and went crappie fishing again. We fished for a couple of hours and couldn't catch a fish. It was cold and everyone was cold. The cameraman went over to the livewell, looked inside, and saw the crappies swimming around—practically jumping out of the boat. He said, 'What are we doing freezing to death, when we have a livewell full of fish?' I knew the fish were there, I just never remembered to say anything, not thinking that they could be used to shoot a fishing scene. We put some of the fish on hooks, threw them out into the lake, reeled them in, and put the whole scene on camera. I thought that would look like a real fake job, but it turned out great on TV the next day."

Robbie's favorite lake is Gull. He likes fishing many area lakes, but Gull is the one he considers home. Although he is a multi-species angler, his favorite fish is the wall-eye—he really enjoys the hunt of finding and catching walleyes.

I think it is fair to say that all who still guide at Koep's hated to see Robbie quit the league. He was a great ambassador for the league as well as for the fishing indus-try—a good fisherman and a great person. We also recognize that guiding is a tough way for a young man to make a living and Robbie has enough talent to go on to big-ger and better things in his young life. Working at the store and as a guide for a total of fifteen years, he especially enjoyed working with the other guides and meeting many new people. Robbie now spends his fishing time with family and friends. He is not on the water as much, but he enjoys fishing and is happy for the great experiences he had working at Koep's and with the Nisswa guides. And the door is still open for Robbie to come back the league!

Chapter Forty-three
Ray Gildow's Stories
from the Water!

I HAVE SEEN SOME FUNNY THINGS during my years of guiding and it seems that strange things always happened when I didn't have a camera.

One day, while fishing on the south end of Leech Lake on a hot July afternoon, the sky began turning black to the west. Leech Lake is the third-largest Minnesota lake—not one to be on when a storm is approaching—so I told my customers we needed to head to shore because it looked like a storm was coming.

I worked my way around the south end of Pelican Island, a large island about five miles north of the south shore, when I noticed a boat or something about a mile away with odd colors or something that was visible, but not recognizable. I told my customers I was going to head toward the object to see what it was because it was sitting out in the open water. As we approached the object, it became clear that it was a boat, about twenty-five feet long, with clothes strung up around the entire boat. Waving and hollering, was a man dressed only in his undershorts. The man was probably in his mid- to late-fifties and was truly frightened beyond behaving normally. In a complete panic, he was just one pair of Fruit of the Looms away from being stark naked. He had his shirt, pants, coat, and towels hanging on fishing line from one end of the boat to the other. He had been sitting on the water for about an hour with a dead motor, trying to get the attention of another boater to help him. A number of other boats had gone by, saw him waving, and just waved back. When he saw the storm coming, he thought this would be his place to die. He was absolutely shaking when he got into our boat. We towed his boat to the closest resort, put him ashore, and got off the water before the storm hit. That was a story with a happy ending.

The Nisswa Guides have often guided racing crews, drivers, and racing sponsors from Brainerd International Raceway. The race track attracts drivers from all over the world as well as corporate sponsors. One summer we had about eighteen guide boats taking crews and sponsors for an afternoon fishing trip. It was a hot, blistering afternoon with temperatures in the mid-nineties. I picked up three gentlemen at the public landing on the north end of Gull Lake. One of guys had two huge tackle boxes—I was really impressed. We often provide all tackle and equipment so I thought this guy was really going to be a challenge with lots of weird tackle.

All eighteen boats left the landing at the same time and headed through the narrows in single file to the big lake. All the boats have to pass Bar Harbor—one of the historic nightclubs on Gull Lake—to get to Booming Out Bay, which is the first big bay on the north end of the lake. Bar Harbor has a huge patio along the shore so everyone on the water can see everyone on the patio and vice versa. It is quite an impressive sight to see eighteen boats full of customers heading out to the big lake.

My boat was almost in front of the patio when the customer with the big tackle boxes opened one of them. To my amazement, they were full of booze. He grabbed a bottle of something and took a drink. Then he turned his back to the patio and dropped his shorts—sticking his bare butt in the direction of the people on the patio. I couldn't believe it and I didn't have time or the sense to do anything. I just looked ahead and kept going, hoping no one recognized me. The guy doing the mooning was more than fifty years old and well on his way to having a good time. It was a long and "entertaining" afternoon.

The next day, I arrived at Koep's to pick up some customers, along with some of my fellow guides. We were met at the door by Marv Koep who had a combination scared-and-angry look on his face.

"Fellas," he said, "we have a big problem with the county sheriff's office. Someone went by Bar Harbor yesterday in one of our guide boats and mooned the customers on the patio. There were some ladies there who were really upset."

"Marv," I said, "that was my boat." (Staples Sports is a boat dealership where I get my boats and I serve as a member of their pro staff, so they have "Staples Sports" printed on both sides of my boat, which makes it easy to identify the boat that was involved in the incident). Marv stared at me for a second and started to laugh.

"How did it feel?" Marv asked. "That guy did the same thing in my boat last year, so when I saw him get into your boat, I knew you were in for an interesting day." The joke was on me. Luckily, no one had called to complain and I was not in trouble. I don't think I ever got even with Marv for that one.

One Sunday summer afternoon, I picked up three customers in Brainerd and took them to the south end of Gull Lake. It was a beautiful, hot afternoon and as I approached the public landing on Government Point, I told the guys to be prepared because one often sees weird things at the public landings on Sundays. Just as I finished saying it, I drove over a small hill and steered toward the edge of the water. Right before our eyes was a pickup truck, underwater, with the motor running and a boat drifting off the trailer into the lake. True story! The landing was packed with boats and people and the owner of the truck was in the water in a complete state of panic with bubbles coming up from his truck's running engine. My customers couldn't believe that I had just said to watch for weird things and there was a truck in the lake. I couldn't believe it either. I think the guy's truck was a total loss.

The funniest thing I ever saw on the lake also happened on Gull Lake. It was a beautiful, autumn day in October. Three customers and I were walleye fishing on a little hump in front of Quarterdeck Resort. We heard the sound of an outboard motor, but couldn't see a boat. We kept fishing and the sound got closer, but we still didn't see a boat. Suddenly, I saw a sixteen-foot fishing boat coming along the shoreline, heading toward the resort. I told my customers to look at the boat—it didn't appear to have anyone in it. As it got closer we could see that it was empty.

The boat had a twenty-five-horse motor and it appeared to be going wide open. One of my customers saw a man about eight hundred yards down the shore, running after the boat. He had fallen out of the boat. The boat was about three hundred yards between us and the resort, heading right toward the resort docks, when it turned away from shore and began going in a large circle on the lake in front of the resort. Another boat with two men in it saw the empty boat about the same time we did and drove over when the boat began going in circles. Luckily, it was far enough away from shore that it wasn't heading towards the docks or the boats at the resort. The boat was really flying! The guys in the other boat drove in a large circle until they were able to get next to the runaway boat, when one of them jumped into the empty boat and shut down the motor.

It was quite a scene, seeing an empty boat motoring along, with a man running on the shore behind it, but it was even more amazing to see two men get into position to jump into and stop the empty boat—especially at the speed it was going. No one was hurt and both boats were unscathed. I didn't go over to find out how the boat owner fell out of his boat, but he had an animated discussion with the guys that saved his boat. My customers thought it was worth the price of a guide trip to see that event.

Chapter Forty-four
History of the Nisswa Bait and
Tackle Shop and Its Owners

1961: Marv and Judy Koep bought the Nisswa Bait and Tackle business from Pete Link.

1992: Duke and Terry Fischer purchased the store and operated it with sons, David and Ryan.

1997: Duke Fischer passed away. The store is now operated by Terry Fischer and sons, David and Ryan.

1998: The Fischers sold the store to Mike and Lynne Blanch. They completely remodeled the store and expanded its business to include more marine products.

2004: Mike Blanch sold the business to Bill and Maria Erickson. He sold the original Nisswa Bait and Tackle property to a marine dealer and Bill and Maria relocated the business to a new location about six hundred feet south of the original store. The business is now called "Koep's Sport Shop."

The Fischers

Duke and Terry Fischer bought Koep's on April 1, 1992. Duke and Terry had owned three resorts on Lake Carlos near Alexandria, Minnesota, before moving to Omaha. Duke missed being around the lakes, so after spending six years in Omaha, the Fischers bought the store from Marv and Judy. Duke's long-term goal was to run the store for about ten years and then turn the business over to his sons, David and Ryan. David got a job working with the Crow Wing County Sheriff's department and Ryan stayed and worked in the store with Terry. The Fischers were wonderful people to work with and Duke loved being in the bait-and-tackle business. Duke died of cancer after only a few years in the business. He had a bad cough for a few months and couldn't figure out what was wrong. The doctors finally diagnosed him with lung cancer. He put up a brave battle with the disease, but lost. After Duke's death, Terry, David, and Ryan continued to operate the store. In 1998, they made the decision to sell the business to Mike and Lynn Blanch.

The Blanches

Mike and Lynne Blanch bought the store from the Fischers in 1998. They tore down a major part of the old store and completely rebuilt the majority of the building. They also remodeled the home that once housed the Koep and Fischer families. The Blanches operated the business until 2004, when they sold the building to Marv Zimmerman of Nisswa and sold the business to Bill and Maria Erickson.

Bill and Maria Erickson—Koep's New Owners

Bill and Maria Erickson became the new owners of Koep's Sport Shop during the spring of 2004. They have a slightly new name to their business as well as a new location, approximately one-quarter mile south of the original store.

Bill Erickson grew up in Minneapolis and took yearly fishing trips with his parents to northern Minnesota's International Falls area. Bill graduated from high school in 1977. His father worked for a paper mill for many years and got tired of life in the Twin Cities, so he decided to buy Point Narrows, a resort on Upper Gull Lake. While working for his father at the resort, Bill became very familiar with the resort industry as well as Koep's and the fishing industry.

He had made plans to go to North Dakota State University, but then his dad had a heart attack. Bill decided to stay at the resort and help run it until his dad recovered to good health. He worked at the resort until his father was well enough to run the resort again, and then he got a job with the Holiday Company, where he worked at a Holiday gas station for two years.

Bill enrolled at Central Lakes College in Brainerd and also held a part-time job working in the new K-Mart store. He finished his associate of arts degree in 1991 and was promoted to the store manager's program at K-Mart the same spring. He moved to Hibbing, Minnesota, where he managed two departments. A short time later, he was promoted again and was moved to the Grand Rapids, Minnesota, store. After another promotion, he became the store manager at the store in International Falls, Minnesota.

The Ericksons were married in 1989. Bill left the K-Mart store and took a part-time job at a sports store in International Falls and eventually became the manager of the full-line sports shop that contained about six thousand square feet of sporting goods. Bill worked at the store for twelve years, until coming to Koep's in 2002, to manage the store for Mike Blanch.

Maria was a local person—originally from Emily, Minnesota, northeast of Nisswa. Maria is a trained, medical-records technician and currently works at St. Joseph's Medical Center in Brainerd. The Erickson's have two children, Bill and Cassy, and a dog, Lindy.

"When I decided to come back to Nisswa it was because of the love of the area and we had a lot of friends here. Business had gotten tough in International Falls with the paper mill laying off lots of workers so we decided to come back to this area. I didn't come to work at Koep's with the idea of buying it, I just had so many great memories of the store and the guides' league that I wanted to be a part of that. When Mike Blanch said he was going to sell the business, he wanted me to buy it and one thing led to another and we did end up purchasing the business," said Bill.

"I have always loved to fish and our whole family loves to fish and I have a number of goals for the store now that we own it. Koep's always had a tradition of promoting fishing for kids and we plan to continue and enhance that tradition. We are going to promote "catch and release" and we are going to promote activities for kids somewhat like Marv Koep used to do. We are smaller now, about the size of the store when Marv and Judy first bought the business. We are going to promote good and friendly customer service. We are always going to have coffee and donuts on hand and we want our store to be a fun place to come to visit," he said.

"The Nisswa Guides' League is a league known all over the upper Midwest. We plan to keep that name and that tradition going at our new store."

Chapter Forty-five
Let's Reel Them in
and Go Home!

WELL, THERE IT IS—my attempt to capture some of the history of the people who were and are the Nisswa Guides. I wanted to record this valuable information before it became lost in time. I must admit that writing the book turned out to be a much bigger project than I ever dreamed it would be and it was much more fascinating than I ever imagined. Thanks to all the people who contributed to this book through the sharing of information, photos, and encouragement.

I have been a member of the Nisswa Guides since the middle nineties, but I worked with the league since 1989 and I still marvel at the impact the league has had on freshwater fishing. Harry Van Doren developed his own rubber set of splash guards and fined-tuned the art of trolling backwards long before anyone had ever seen or heard of such a thing. Guides began using flashers and other new items of equipment that companies donated to the league to get exposure in the marketplace. And finally, there was the impact that guides had on motor and boat design, fishing rods, plugs, the Lindy Rig, flashers, and other electronics—the list goes on.

The guides influenced and fished with outdoor writers, sports and television personalities, movie stars, and not mentioned in the book, members of the Underground. They have served as guides through many fishing openers with the governors of Minnesota and Wisconsin and have volunteered hundreds of hours fishing for fundraisers for worthy causes.

The history of the Nisswa Guides' League is a history of the people who were members of the league, but it is also a history of the evolution of fishing, recreation, and the resort business in the upper Midwest. Fishing has changed since the sixties and so has the recreation industry. Resorts are declining in the area and private cabin ownership is increasing as more and more resorts are sold as individual lots. Golfing and golf courses have greatly increased and more people than ever are spending time on the water in personal watercraft and other recreational watercraft without picking up fishing poles.

Technology and education are the two primary reasons fishing today is so different from thirty years ago. Pioneers like Bill Binkelman, the Lindners and others paved the way for today's anglers to help them catch more and bigger fish. The sonar, mapping technology, and underwater camera innovations have forever changed the way anglers see and fish. Selective harvest and catch-and-release are two fishing ethics that have also changed the way anglers fish.

The Brainerd-Nisswa area has changed a great deal over the past forty years, too. Marv Koep was right when he said forty-three years ago that the area must be going to grow if they put in a four-lane highway. The area has grown immensely during those years and the projections are for about another twenty thousand new people to move to the area in the next fifteen to twenty years. That growth will require some careful planning if the lakes area is to remain attractive to tourists in the future.

Five men who were members of the Nisswa Guides' League are now members of the Minnesota Fishing Hall of Fame. That is verification of the impact the league has had on freshwater fishing.

I hope that I have illuminated the passion that the fishing guides have for the sport of fishing. None of the members started fishing to be in the Hall of Fame. Such a place did not exist. They fished because they loved it. Those still alive still fish because they love it. Marv Koep stands alone as one of the first members of the league still guiding. He is following in the footprints of Harry Van Doren and some of the other early guides who fished until they were no longer able to get in the boat. I have seen him on the water in pouring rain, cold northwest winds, and yes, snow storms. I have seen Al Lindner fishing on the water in late November when the only way to get on the lake was to break through the ice. They are not alone. Royal Karels is sixty-six years old and can't wait to wrap up the fall fishing so he can get his fish house on frozen ice. Ron "Crash" Kristofferson and Ron Lindner still fish together every winter in the south. It is that passion and commitment that makes these people so unique and such characters. That passion and commitment is there with the younger guys, too, such as Glen Belgum, Steve Collette, Mark Lee, Lenny Hodgson, Henry Ebert, Jim Minerich, and others. They are all still guiding, still experimenting, and still having fun.

Almost every person featured in this book had a grandfather, grandmother, mom, or dad who took the time to take them fishing when they were kids. Fishing is a tradition that all of us in this book want to pass on to the kids of today.

One of the missions of the Minnesota Fishing Hall of Fame is to promote fishing to kids. That is something that Marv Koep and the Nisswa Guides' League have been promoting for almost forty-five years. The Hall of Fame is now located at the new Reeds Sport Shop in Baxter, which is located between Brainerd and Nisswa. There is a pond behind the store with a massive fishing dock for kids. Stop by and take a young boy or girl on a short fishing trip. It will be a good investment—for them and for you!

The next time you go fishing, remember the Nisswa Guides' League. Recognized as Minnesota's oldest, organized league it has passed on legacies and legends for today's kids and tomorrow's anglers. See you on the water!